Extras the school
did not need.

BEING HEALTHY

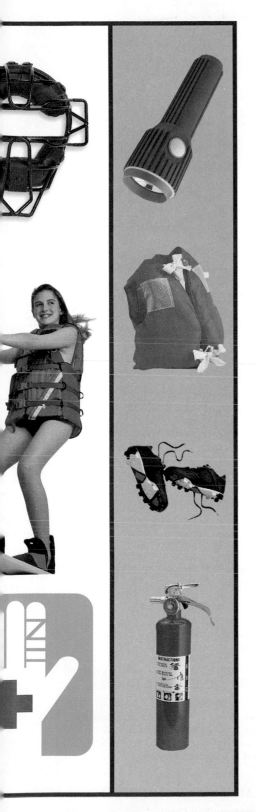

BEING HEALTHY

Larry K. Olsen
Professor of Health Education
The Pennsylvania State University
University Park, Pennsylvania

Richard W. St. Pierre
Professor and Head
Department of Health Education
The Pennsylvania State University
University Park, Pennsylvania

Jan M. Ozias, Ph.D., R.N.
Coordinator of Health Services
Austin Independent School District
Austin, Texas

SENIOR EDITORIAL ADVISORS

Ernest D. Buck, M.D.
Pediatrician
Corpus Christi, Texas

Barbara A. Galpin
Teacher of Health and Physical Education
Islip Public Schools
Islip, New York

Howard L. Taras, M.D., F.R.C.P.C.
Assistant Professor of Pediatrics
University of California, San Diego
  and District Medical Consultant
San Diego Unified School District
San Diego, California

HARCOURT BRACE & COMPANY

Orlando   Atlanta   Austin   Boston   San Francisco   Chicago   Dallas   New York
Toronto   London

ACKNOWLEDGMENTS

CONTENT ADVISORY BOARD

MENTAL HEALTH

Sharon Smith Brady, Ph.D.
Licensed Psychologist
Lawton, Oklahoma

Charlotte P. Ross
President and Executive Director
Youth Suicide National Center
Burlingame, California

HUMAN GROWTH AND DEVELOPMENT, DISEASES AND DISORDERS, AND PUBLIC HEALTH

Thomas Blevins, M.D.
American Diabetes Association, Texas Affiliate, Inc.
Austin, Texas

Ernest D. Buck, M.D.
Pediatrician
Corpus Christi, Texas

Linda A. Fisher, M.D.
Chief Medical Officer
St. Louis County Department of Health
St. Louis, Missouri

Howard L. Taras, M.D., F.R.C.P.C.
Assistant Professor of Pediatrics
University of California, San Diego and District Medical Consultant
San Diego Unified School District
San Diego, California

CONSUMER HEALTH PRACTICES

Robert C. Arffa, M.D.
Adjunct Professor of Ophthalmology
Medical College of Pennsylvania
Allegheny General Hospital
Pittsburgh, Pennsylvania

Bertram V. Dannheisser, Jr., D.D.S.
Florida Dental Association
Pensacola, Florida

John D. Durrant, Ph.D.
Professor of Otolaryngology and Communication and Director of Audiology
University of Pittsburgh Medical Center
Pittsburgh, Pennsylvania

NUTRITION

Janet L. Durrwachter, M.N.S., R.D.
Nutrition Consultant
Cogan Station, Pennsylvania

Maryfrances L. Marecic, M.S., R.D.
Consultant
Montville, New Jersey
(Former Instructor in Nutrition, The Pennsylvania State University)

Linda Fox Simmons, M.S.H.P., R.D./L.D.
Registered Dietician
Austin, Texas

EXERCISE AND FITNESS

Steven N. Blair, P.E.D.
Director, Epidemiology
Cooper Institute for Aerobics Research
Dallas, Texas

Deborah Waters, M.D.
Colorado Springs, Colorado
(Former Team Physician, The Pennsylvania State University)

MEDICINE

Donna Hubbard McCree, M.P.H., R.Ph.
Assistant Professor
Pharmacy Administration
Howard University
College of Pharmacy
Washington, D.C.

Judith Ann Shinogle, R.Ph.
M.S. Candidate
Harvard School of Public Health
Boston, Massachusetts

SUBSTANCE ABUSE

Robert N. Holsaple
Supervisor of Prevention Programs
The School Board of Broward County
Fort Lauderdale, Florida

SAFETY AND FIRST AID

American Red Cross
Washington, D.C.

CONTRIBUTORS AND REVIEWERS

Danny J. Ballard, Ed.D., C.H.E.S.
Associate Professor of Health
Health and Kinesiology
  Department
Texas A&M University
College Station, Texas

Linda Barnes
Teacher
Wahl-Coates School
Greenville, North Carolina

Robert C. Barnes, Ed.D., M.P.H.
Associate Professor and
  Coordinator
Health Education
East Carolina University
Greenville, North Carolina

David L. Bever, Ph.D.
Coordinator of Health
  Education
Department of Human Services
George Mason University
Fairfax, Virginia

James M. Eddy, D.Ed.
Professor and Chair
Health Studies
The University of Alabama
Tuscaloosa, Alabama

Sue Ann Eddy
Teacher
Stillman Heights Elementary
Tuscaloosa, Alabama

Ruth C. Engs, Ed.D., R.N.
Professor
Applied Health Science
Indiana University
Bloomington, Indiana

Tina Fields, Ph.D.
Associate Professor
Health Education
Texas Tech University
Lubbock, Texas

Patricia Barthalow Koch, Ph.D.
Associate Professor
Health Education
College of Health and Human
  Development
The Pennsylvania State University
University Park, Pennsylvania

Patricia Langner, P.H.N., B.S.N., M.P.H.
Health Educator and Nurse
San Ramon Valley Unified
  School District
Danville, California

Samuel W. Monismith, D.Ed.
Assistant Professor
Health Education
The Pennsylvania State University
Capital College
Middletown, Pennsylvania

Marcia Newey, P.H.N., M.P.H.
Health Educator
San Ramon Valley Unified
  School District
San Ramon, California

Brenda North
Chair of Health and Physical
  Education
Lanier Middle School
Houston, Texas

Florence R. Oaks, Ph.D.
Psychologist
San Ramon Valley Unified
  School District
Danville, California

Bea Orr
Past President of the
  American Alliance for
  Health, Physical Education,
  Recreation and Dance
Health and Physical Education
  Supervisor
Logan County Schools
Logan, West Virginia

Nancy Piña
Teacher
Braeburn Elementary School
Houston, Texas

Kerry John Redican, Ph.D., M.P.H.
Associate Professor
Health Education
Virginia Polytechnic Institute
  and State University
Blacksburg, Virginia

David Sommerfeld
Instructional Supervisor
Ysleta Independent
  School District
El Paso, Texas

William J. Stone, Ed.D.
Professor
Exercise and Wellness
Arizona State University
Tempe, Arizona

Patrick Tow, Ph.D.
Associate Professor
Department of Health,
  Physical Education,
  and Recreation
Old Dominion University
Norfolk, Virginia

Donna Videto, Ph.D., C.H.E.S.
Adjunct Professor
Health Department
SUNY College at Cortland
Cortland, New York

Molly S. Wantz, M.S., Ed.S.
Associate Professor
Department of Physiology
  and Health Science
Ball State University
Muncie, Indiana

Dianne Whisnant
Health Education Coordinator
Cleveland County Schools
Shelby, North Carolina

READING/LANGUAGE ADVISOR

Patricia S. Bowers, Ph.D.
Associate Director
Center for Mathematics and
  Science Education
University of North Carolina
  at Chapel Hill
Chapel Hill, North Carolina

Contents

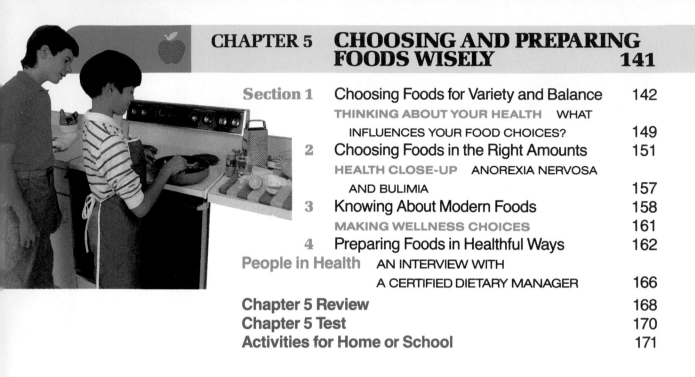

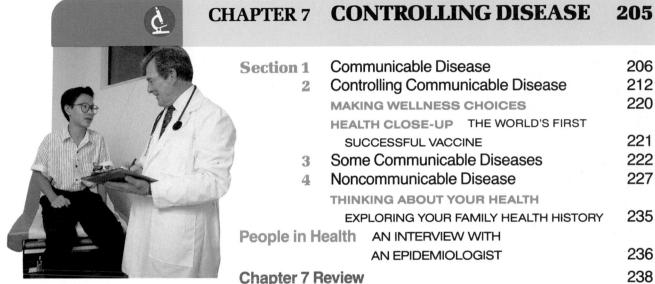

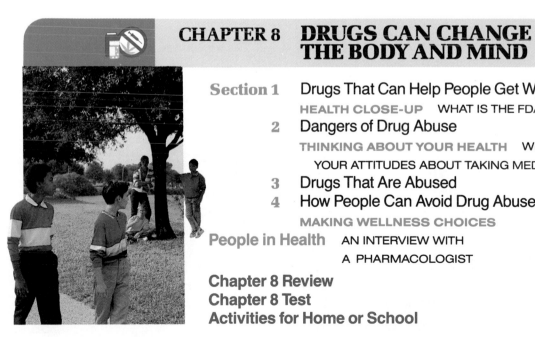

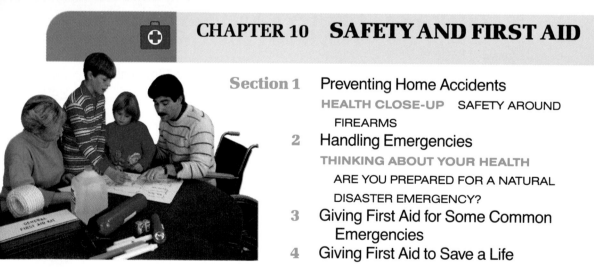

FOR YOUR REFERENCE   **389**

THINKING ABOUT YOUR HEALTH

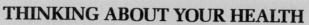

REAL-LIFE SKILLS

HEALTH CLOSE-UPS

PEOPLE IN HEALTH

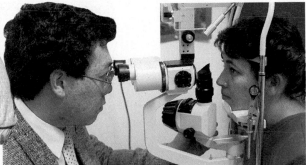

You are at your best when you are healthy. When you feel good, you are able to enjoy life to its fullest. However, staying healthy can be a challenge. To handle this challenge, you will need knowledge—not only about health issues, but about yourself and your environment. With the right information and thoughtful preparation, you will find the challenge of being healthy both exciting and enjoyable.

As you read *Being Healthy,* you will learn about many health habits that can help keep you feeling your best. Some of these habits require special knowledge. With up-to-date health information and good health habits, you can meet the challenge of being healthy. By taking responsibility for your health now, you are preparing for a healthy future.

You probably think that good health requires exercise and a healthful diet. You are right; it does. However, these are not the only things that contribute to good health. To be healthy, you must also satisfy mental, emotional, and social needs. In other words, your mind, feelings, family, friends, and community are also important to your health. Just about everything you do during a day can affect your health.

Practicing good health habits can help you avoid many kinds of diseases. Also, the healthier you become, the better you will feel about yourself. You will increase your self-esteem. When you refuse to use dangerous drugs, you will increase your self-esteem even more. In refusing harmful substances, you are protecting not only your own health, but also the health of others in your community.

Being healthy does not just happen. You must choose to live in a healthful way. You must take responsibility for your well-being and develop habits that will help keep you healthy. This responsi-bility will require you to make some important and sometimes difficult decisions. By reading *Being Healthy* you will help your-self prepare for these decisions. You will then be ready to make the wise choices for being safe and being healthy.

KNOWING YOURSELF AND SETTING GOALS

You make many decisions every day. Some are simple decisions. You choose which clothes to wear or which homework assignment to do first. Other decisions are more difficult. They may affect how you use your time. You may have to choose between an activity you enjoy and one that helps you meet a responsibility.

Your needs, interests, and goals affect the decisions you make. How do your family, teachers, counselors, and friends help you make decisions? How do you set goals and use them to plan your time and activities? Finding out about yourself and your goals will help you form decisions that make you feel good about your efforts and achievements.

GETTING READY TO LEARN

Key Questions

- Why is it important to learn about yourself?
- Why is it important to know how you feel about yourself?
- How can you learn to set goals that you can meet?
- How can meeting goals help you feel good about yourself?

Main Chapter Sections

1 Discovering Yourself
2 Setting Goals in Healthful Ways
3 Help in Meeting Goals

1 Discovering Yourself

Young people your age often feel "between." They are between being children and being teenagers. They are between doing only what adults tell them to do and needing to make their own choices.

Even though all young people have the same basic needs, each young person is different in many ways. The activities you like to do, the skills you learn, and the things you care about will make your choices unique to you. Knowing what you like to do, what you do well, and what you care about will help you understand why you make certain decisions. Knowing about yourself helps you form a good self-concept. **Self-concept** is the way you think about yourself.

self-concept (sehlf KAHN sehpt), the way you think about yourself.

What Do You Like to Do?

Steve collects stamps. He is always looking for more stamps to add to his collection. He spends a lot of his free time working on his stamp albums.

Jan has a dog, two cats, and some tropical fish. She is responsible for the daily care of her pets. She enjoys visiting zoos and reading about all kinds of animals.

■ *Different people have different interests. Jan likes to care for animals. Steve likes to collect stamps.*

An activity that you enjoy a lot is an **interest.** Interests can help you explore possible careers. Steve's interest in stamp collecting has helped him set a goal of becoming a stamp expert. Jan's interest in animals has helped her with one of her goals, too. She is thinking of becoming a veterinarian.

Think about your interests. Many of these are first formed in your family. Parents and other family members teach children the skills connected with their own interests. Fishing, playing board games, and working at crafts are activities often shared in families for many years.

Most people's interests do not stay the same. Your interests may change as you meet new people in your neighborhood and school. You may find new interests through schoolwork, jobs, or helping others.

Kay did not know anything about weaving until she became friends with Joanna. Joanna owns a loom, and she has woven many scarves and rugs. She taught Kay how to weave on her loom. Kay discovered that she enjoyed weaving. She added weaving to her other interests.

John loves to swim. One summer he taught young children how to be safe in the water. He learned that he likes working with children. Now John is exploring his new interest. He helps take care of younger children in his neighborhood when their parents are working.

interest (IHN truhst), an activity you enjoy doing.

REAL-LIFE
SKILL

Interviewing an Older Person

Talk to an older person. Find out how the person formed interests related to a job or hobby.

■ *John likes helping children. He has been helping to care for children whose parents are working.*

What Do You Do Well?

aptitude (AP tuh tood), a
special ability you have.

A certain skill may come easily to you because of an
aptitude, or special ability, you have. There are three main
kinds of aptitudes. If you have *physical aptitudes,* you work
well with your body. Dancing and swimming well are
examples of physical aptitude. If you have *intellectual
aptitudes,* such as being good at solving puzzles, you work
well with your mind. If you have *social aptitudes,* such as
being a good listener when friends have problems, you
work well with other people.

Like your interests, your aptitudes help determine how
you choose to spend your free time. Beverly has an
aptitude for writing. She wants to work on a school
newspaper. Mark has an aptitude for music. He practices
the guitar each afternoon because he wants to play in a
band someday.

■ *Some people have
physical aptitudes, such
as dancing ability.
Others may have an
intellectual aptitude for
chess or a social
aptitude for making
friends.*

People have different aptitudes. Even people who have aptitudes for several things do not have an aptitude for everything. Rick has an aptitude for mathematics. But he does not have an aptitude for making repairs. When his bicycle breaks, he asks Rita to repair it. Rita has an aptitude for repairing bicycles. She understands how bicycles work and knows how to repair them when they break.

Think about your aptitudes. You were born with some of them. Other aptitudes formed as you grew older or as you learned and practiced new skills. You probably know about some of your aptitudes. But it is likely that you have some that you do not yet know about. Trying new things can help you discover your aptitudes. School counselors have some simple tests to help young people discover their aptitudes.

What Do You Care About?

The way you think and feel about something is your **attitude.** Some people have a *positive attitude* about trying new things. They think that learning is exciting. They look forward to new experiences. Other people have a *negative attitude* about trying new things. They worry about not doing well at something new, so they do not want to try.

attitude (AT uh tood), the way you think and feel about something.

Lynda has a positive attitude about her surroundings. Having a clean neighborhood is important to her. She picks up trash that she sees on the sidewalk. She encourages her friends to put any litter they see into trash cans.

Think of what you care about. You probably care about many of the same things your family cares about. The things you care about help determine many of your goals.

Because Lynda is concerned about her surroundings, she may want to become a park ranger or a scientist. Someone who cares about helping others may want to become a nurse, a teacher, or a police officer.

An important thing for people to care about is health. People need to care about their health to gain wellness. **Wellness** is a high level of health. It needs to be one of your main goals in life. Wellness can be gained by having a positive attitude about your health. You may show your attitude by practicing good health habits. You can take responsibility for your own wellness by practicing good health habits, avoiding harm, and taking action if a health problem starts.

Wellness includes self-esteem. **Self-esteem** is liking and respecting yourself. Self-esteem is part of a good self-concept. When you feel good about yourself, you can believe in yourself. When you believe in yourself, you can be in control of your life. You can work toward meeting goals that you set for yourself. Self-esteem is built on feeling good about your interests and aptitudes.

wellness, a high level of health.

self-esteem (sehlf uh STEEM), liking and respecting yourself.

■ *Having high self-esteem can help you in many ways. It helps you work toward being healthy.*

REMEMBER?

1. How are aptitudes and interests different?
2. What are the three main kinds of aptitudes?
3. What is a positive attitude?

THINK!

4. How might your positive attitude about health have an effect on other people?
5. How might a family member's positive attitude about health have an effect on you?

Thinking About Your Health

Knowing Your Attitudes

How do you know what your attitudes are? Here is a way of noticing your attitudes and deciding how to act according to those attitudes.

You and your friend George are leaving his house. George yells angry words at his mother because she will not let George spend the night at his cousin's house. George keeps walking.

■ Identify your feelings. Do you feel that something is not right? Is everything okay?

■ Consider why you feel the way you do. Do you feel that George should not have yelled at his parent? Does it bother you that he walked away? Do you care one way or the other?

■ Think about how you feel about the people involved. Do you lose or gain respect for George? Do you like or dislike what he did? Do you like the way you are feeling?

■ Decide what you should do. Maybe you feel you should tell George how you and your mother work out disagreements. Maybe you feel you should not say anything to George. Do you have an opinion about how young people should talk with adults?

If you are aware of your attitudes, you can make choices about them. You can form positive attitudes about things. You can form negative attitudes. You might also not form any attitudes at all.

7

2 Setting Goals in Healthful Ways

goals (GOHLZ), things you want to achieve.

Every day, you make decisions about how to spend your time. You may not have enough time for everything you want to do. You need to decide which things are most important to you. Then you can plan how you want to spend the rest of your time.

The first step in deciding how to spend your time is to set goals for yourself. Your **goals** are the things you want to achieve. You may set a goal of finishing your homework in time to play with your friends. Or your goal may be to improve your backstroke by practicing swimming every day. Your goals should be realistic enough for you to be able to achieve them. Then you can decide how to organize your time so that you can reach your goals.

What Kinds of Goals Are There?

Elaine wants to be able to run with friends in a Fun Run. Andrew wants to go on a weekend camping trip with a church group. Patrick's goal is to help his father, who is a rescue worker in town. These goals are *long-term goals*.

■ *Keeping your goals organized can help you achieve them.*

■ *Playing the piano well is a long-term goal that takes many hours of practice to achieve.*

8

A long-term goal is something a person wants to do or to be in the future. Some long-term goals may take months or years to reach.

To make a long-term goal seem more realistic, each of these students has set *short-term goals*. Short-term goals are goals you wish to reach in the near future. For Elaine, a short-term goal may be to run a little farther each day until she reaches the distance of the Fun Run. Andrew's short-term goal may be to learn how to prepare balanced meals on camping trips. Patrick may ask his father to teach him a rescue skill, such as rescue breathing, as a short-term goal.

Reaching a short-term goal shows you that you are making progress toward your long-term goal. Seeing progress can encourage a person to keep working toward his or her long-term goals. Each time you reach a short-term goal, you may decide to make a new goal that will lead you closer to your final long-term goal. Setting short-term goals divides the journey toward a long-term goal into manageable steps. At each step, you gain new skills, new experiences, and more confidence. Most long-term goals are reached by accomplishing many short-term goals.

■ *Reaching a long-term goal, such as being a good ice skater, requires learning new skills along the way.*

■ *Careful planning can help you reach certain goals. If your goal is to improve your study habits, maintaining a regular study time in a quiet area would be a good short-term goal.*

How Can Planning Help You Reach Your Goals?

Many things you do are important in some way. Some of your activities are important for your health. Some are important because they help you relax and enjoy yourself. And some are important for your education. Good planning can help you make sure you have time to do everything that is important to you. It helps you find the time to reach your goals.

Alicia's long-term goal was to improve her grades by the end of the first half of the school year. Alicia set a goal and made plans in order to reach that goal. Her goal of improving her grades was important enough for her to give up some other activities.

Making time to study can be hard. Applying these tips will help you plan your study time:

- Find a comfortable place to sit while you study. Try to pick a place where you will not be distracted by a radio or television or by other people.
- Set aside a regular time each day to study. Talk with a parent to choose a time that is best. You may want to do some of your studying after school and the rest after dinner.

- While you study, do not do anything else, such as eating or watching television. Take short breaks once in a while to stretch, relax, have a healthful snack, or rest your eyes.
- Make time to review your work in the morning. This will help you remember what you studied the evening before.

Why Do Some Goals Require You to Make Choices?

As you grow older, you may find that more of your goals require you to make choices. Reaching some goals can take much time and work. You may have to give up some activities you enjoy in order to reach a goal. Like Alicia, you may decide that your goal is important enough for you to give up other activities. Or you may decide that the goal is not realistic or not worth giving up other activities you enjoy.

Kimberly wants to dance with a major ballet company someday. She is a very talented dancer, so her goal is realistic. Kimberly knows that reaching her goal will take a lot of time and hard work. She must plan her activities carefully to leave enough time for ballet lessons and practice. She discussed her plan with her parents. She quit the chorus and her bowling club. Because her goal to be a dancer is important to her, Kimberly has chosen to give up other activities in order to work toward it.

MYTH
AND
FACT

Myth: You should only set goals for very important things.

Fact: Setting goals for even small tasks or projects is a good way to organize your work and have positive feelings about yourself.

11

■ *After deciding to become a ballet dancer, Kim needs to choose activities that will help her reach that goal.*

Kimberly followed some steps in choosing activities to meet her goal:

1. She saw she had choices to make. When Kimberly set her goal, she needed to do something about meeting it. She had to make choices.
2. She thought about possible choices. Kimberly could choose any number of activities. Or she could choose those that would best help her reach her goal.
3. She thought about the **consequences,** or results, of her possible choices. She knew she had to take responsibility for the consequences of her choices if she wanted to meet her goal.
4. She chose what she thought was the best plan for meeting her goal. She chose not to be active in the chorus and bowling club so she could have more time for ballet lessons and practice.
5. She acted in a way that would make her feel good about herself. She started to carry out her plan.
6. She looked back and saw what happened as a result of her choice. She is becoming a better dancer and has begun to meet her short-term goal.

consequences (KAHN suh kwehn suhz), results of your actions.

Think about some of your goals. Are they important enough to you to be worth the choices and effort they may require? To use time in ways that help your well-being, you must think carefully about what is important to you. You need to set realistic short-term goals. Then you can plan your activities so that you can reach those goals. Setting goals and planning to reach them will help you learn to set and meet your goals as a teenager and later as an adult.

STOP REVIEW SECTION 2

REMEMBER?

1. What do you need to think about when you set goals?
2. How can planning help you reach your goals?
3. What are four tips to help you plan your study time?

THINK!

4. How might setting short-term goals that are too easy or too hard keep you from meeting your long-term goals?
5. How might having several interests have an effect on choosing a realistic goal?

Making Wellness Choices

Eleven-year-old Roger is a better-than-average runner in his age group. Roger has placed in the top three in every race he has run in the last year. Roger's goal is to do just as well in a race for twelve-year-olds. The race will be held in three weeks. Instead of practicing in the weeks before the race, however, Roger decides to save his strength until the day of the race.

? How realistic is Roger's goal of placing in the top three in a race for twelve-year-olds? Did he plan the activities that would help him reach his goal? Explain your wellness choice.

13

Health Close-up

Learning to Handle Stress

Stress is a part of daily life. However, too much stress can be harmful to your health. There are three ways you can reduce stress. First, learn what things cause stress in your life. Second, learn to remove or avoid some of those things. Third, learn to handle stress better.

Stress can be either physical or emotional. Physical stress can be caused by such things as getting to bed too late, missing breakfast, or being in a noisy environment. Emotional stress can be caused by any positive or negative situation that makes you feel tense. Taking a test, playing a sport, going through a change in the family, and quarreling with a parent or friend can all cause emotional stress. Emotional stress often leads to worry or to an uneasy feeling. Both physical and emotional stress can cause illness if they are not handled well.

There are several things you can do to reduce physical stress. Good daily habits, such as eating balanced meals and getting enough rest, sleep, and exercise, can help you handle changes in your life.

You can also reduce the tension from emotional stress by learning better ways to handle it. For example, you can do the following:

- Admit you feel stress. There is nothing wrong with having this feeling.
- Talk with someone you trust about your feelings during stressful times. This is a good way to release tension.
- Exercise vigorously, such as by pedaling your bicycle hard. It relaxes your mind, lessening tension.
- Do a kind deed for someone. You will feel better about yourself.

■ *Sometimes learning new skills, such as tying a tie, can cause stress.*

Thinking Beyond

1. How might talking about a stressful situation help you feel calmer?
2. What might a person do to handle the emotional stress before giving a speech in front of the class?

14

3 Help in Meeting Goals

Some athletes, such as ice skaters and high jumpers, perform by themselves. Others, such as members of a hockey or basketball team, work as a group. But they all **compete,** or test their abilities against those of other people, to meet the same goal.

People compete in areas other than sports. They may compete against each other in other kinds of games, in schoolwork, or in their jobs. Competing against other people can be a healthful experience. Competing in a healthful way means doing your best and trying hard. Sometimes it means winning a prize or recognition. It also means being prepared to lose, because no one can win all the time. Competing in a healthful way can help you develop your abilities. It can also teach you how to work well with other people.

KEY WORDS

compete
cooperate

compete (kuhm PEET), to test one's abilities against those of other people.

■ Competing is one way to try new skills. It can help you learn what you need to do to develop your skills further.

What Does It Mean to Compete?

Charles and Sandra share a goal. They both want to win first prize at the science fair. In working for the same prize, Charles and Sandra are competing against each other as individuals.

When you compete as an individual, you learn to depend on yourself. You try to gain the skills and knowledge needed for the task. You must work as well as you can. You are responsible for reaching your goal.

You are also responsible for competing in an honest manner. If Charles told lies about Sandra in order to win, he would not be competing fairly. He probably would not feel good about himself.

What Does It Mean to Compete Against Yourself?

When Luis entered a new school, he discovered that students in his new science class had learned more than he had. He felt he could not do as well as the other students. So Luis decided to compete against himself instead of against them. He did not worry about getting the best grade in the class. He asked the teacher about things he did not understand in the lesson. On each test he tried to get a higher grade than he had received on the test before. Before long, Luis caught up with the other students.

■ There may be times when you need to ask others to help you compete against yourself.

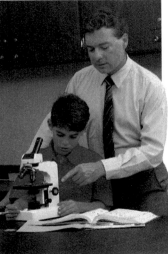

16

When your goal is to improve yourself in some way, you do not have to compete against others. You can compete against yourself. Competing against yourself can help you learn about your abilities and develop them. Then you can set goals that are right for you.

What Does It Mean to Cooperate?

Maria and Pamela are excellent tennis players. One day the girls decided to play as a team in a tennis match. They did not play well together. Each of them played as if she were playing on her own. They ended up in each other's way much of the time.

■ Sometimes Maria and Pamela compete against each other in tennis. At other times they cooperate as a team to play well together.

After the match, Maria and Pamela talked about what had happened. They saw that they could not play well as a team when each girl was playing for herself. They decided that they needed to work together, or **cooperate,** to play as a good team. So the girls began to practice playing together. They found ways to help each other. They were more successful in their next match because they had learned to compete as a team instead of as individuals.

cooperate (koh AHP uh rayt), to work together.

17

Sometimes people in groups share goals other than winning. Each member of a group must cooperate with the other members to reach the group's common goal. When people cooperate, they achieve more than any one person can achieve alone. If any person in the group is competing as an individual, the group may not be able to achieve its common goal.

■ *A large number of people may cooperate to reach the same goal.*

Some of the students in Mr. Williams's class wanted to decorate the hallway outside their classroom. Becky, Eric, Bob, and Kuni decided to work as a group to paint a mural. Mr. Williams helped them organize the task. They listed the activities they had to do and the materials they needed. Eric and Kuni took charge of finding paint and brushes. Becky and Bob planned the mural and drew it on a large piece of paper. Then the whole group painted the mural together. They were able to do a good job and clean up quickly because they cooperated.

18

■ *Sharing a goal often leads to cooperation on a project.*

You, too, most likely cooperate with others to complete tasks that could not easily be done alone. Your family needs your cooperation to keep your home clean, safe, and pleasant. You may need other people to help you reach some of the goals that you have set for yourself. When you cooperate with others, you are showing that you are becoming a responsible person.

STOP — **REVIEW SECTION 3**

REMEMBER?

1. What are some ways in which people compete with each other?
2. What are some ways in which people can cooperate to reach a goal?

THINK!

3. How might competing against yourself help you reach a goal?
4. Why might it be difficult for people to cooperate on a project if their goals are different?

People in Health

An Interview with a School Guidance Counselor

Joyce Terry helps students solve problems. She is a guidance counselor at a middle school in Orlando, Florida.

What does a middle school guidance counselor do?

A guidance counselor in any school helps young people solve personal problems and problems they have in school. A guidance counselor works with students, parents, and teachers.

What are some of the problems a young person in middle school might have?

Going from elementary to middle school is a big change for students. Many are unsure about themselves and

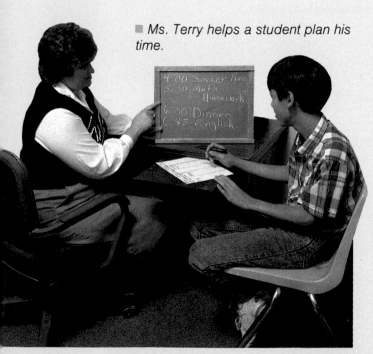

■ *Ms. Terry helps a student plan his time.*

their new responsibilities. In middle school, they have to change classrooms for different subjects. They also have different teachers. The uncertain feelings students sometimes have may cause mixed-up behavior. This behavior can cause a student to do poorly in school.

How do you help students solve these school problems?

The student and I first set some short-term goals. For example, if a student has not been doing his or her homework, we might set a goal of completing all homework assignments for the next two weeks. Part of setting goals involves managing time successfully.

Why should young people have to learn about managing time?

You would be surprised how busy many of the students are. Some do a lot of things outside of school. They take dance classes, music lessons, or are on sports teams. When I help a student learn how to manage time, I begin by having him or her keep a daily homework sheet. On this form, the student writes down all daily assignments. I also suggest the use of a weekly progress report. On this report, the student's teachers note grades, assignments not handed in, and tests to be made up. I review the progress reports with the student. Together we set new goals to solve the student's problem.

MIDDLE SCHOOL IN AMERICA
WESTRIDGE

■ *New students are assigned "buddies" to help them learn their way around the school.*

What other school problems might a young person have?

Every year new families move to our area. Many new students are angry about having to leave old friends. They also might be worried about going to a school where they have no friends.

What do you do to help new students in your school?

I meet with new students, answer their questions, and try to make them feel better. Our school also has a buddy system for new students. On the first day of school, a new student is assigned a buddy who shows him or her around the school. This gives the new student a chance to meet teachers and other students. The more we do to help a new student build self-esteem, the more comfortable that student will feel about exploring new interests and activities.

How do you help students form positive attitudes about themselves?

Our middle school has many programs that help students form a good self-concept. Every week the teachers choose a "student of the week." The student might be a boy or girl who once had a behavior problem but is now cooperating in class. Also, the school guidance counselors have set up an honor roll. Students who achieve a certain grade point average find special ribbons attached to their report cards. Programs such as these recognize individual students' efforts and achievements. These programs also show that the school cares about students and how they learn.

Learn more about people who work as guidance counselors. Interview a guidance counselor. Or write for information to American School Counselor Association, 5999 Stevenson Avenue, Alexandria, VA 22304.

Main Ideas

- Caring about your health should be one of your main goals in life.
- Self-esteem is built on feeling good about your interests, aptitudes, and attitudes.
- To make decisions about how to spend your time, you need to decide which things are most important.
- Reaching a short-term goal shows that progress is being made toward a long-term goal.
- Competing in a healthful way means doing your best and trying hard.
- When people cooperate, they are able to achieve more than one person is able to achieve alone.

Key Words

Write the numbers 1 to 10 in your health notebook or on a separate sheet of paper. After each number, write the letter of the definition that best matches the term. Page numbers in ( ) tell you where to look in the chapter if you need help.

1. self-concept (2)
2. interest (3)
3. aptitude (4)
4. attitude (5)
5. wellness (6)
6. self-esteem (6)
7. goals (8)
8. consequences (12)
9. compete (15)
10. cooperate (17)

a. natural ability in a certain area

b. things you want to achieve

c. to test one's abilities against those of other people

d. an activity you enjoy a lot

e. to work together

f. the way you think or feel about something

g. liking and respecting yourself

h. high level of health you can achieve

i. the results of a possible choice

j. the way you think about yourself

Remembering What You Learned

Page numbers in ( ) tell you where to look in the chapter if you need help.

1. Where do you first learn your interests? (3)

2. Name the three kinds of aptitudes with which you may be born. (4)

3. How are interests and aptitudes similar? (4)

4. Why is stamp collecting considered an interest rather than an aptitude? (3–4)

5. Give an example of both a positive attitude and a negative attitude. (5)

6. How can you gain wellness? (6)

7. What is a long-term goal? (8–9)

8. What is a short-term goal? (9)

9. What does reaching a short-term goal show? (9)

10. What activities do people compete in besides sports? (15)

11. What are two results of competing in a healthful way? (16)

12. What are two things you might learn

about yourself when you compete against yourself? (17)

13. What is a benefit of cooperating with others on a project? (17–19)

Thinking About What You Learned

1. Why do most people's interests change over time?

2. How might people's aptitudes be related to some of their goals?

3. Why is it important to learn how to lose when competing against others?

4. What are some of the benefits of cooperating with others to achieve a goal?

5. Suppose you have a realistic long-term goal. How might having some setbacks, or failures, in reaching your goal have an effect on your attitude?

Writing About What You Learned

1. Think about one of your interests. Describe in one or two paragraphs the answers to these questions: What type of aptitude do you have for this interest? What is your attitude toward the interest? What goals have you set that involve this interest? How can working toward these goals affect your self-esteem and wellness?

2. Imagine that you are a news reporter. Your assignment is to report on someone who has achieved a long-term goal. Write two or three paragraphs describing the person you meet and the long-term and short-term goals he or she had set. Ask what his or her plan was and how the plan changed to reach the goal. Summarize your report by telling what the results were and how you think the person's attitudes and self-esteem were affected by the outcome.

Applying What You Learned

PHYSICAL EDUCATION

Think of a sport or physical activity that you like to do. How does your ability in this sport or activity compare to that of others your age? Why do you keep doing this activity? How do you feel about yourself when you do well or when you do poorly during this activity?

Modified True or False

Write the numbers 1 to 15 in your health notebook or on a separate sheet of paper. After each number, write *true* or *false* to describe the sentence. If the sentence is false, also write a term that replaces the underlined term and makes the sentence true.

1. A <u>goal</u> is something you want to achieve.

2. Collecting butterflies is an <u>aptitude</u>.

3. Interests can help you explore possible <u>careers</u>.

4. Not trying a new activity because you are afraid of failing shows a <u>negative</u> attitude.

5. Meeting short-term goals can increase your <u>wellness</u>.

6. Deciding to increase the distance you run each day is setting a <u>goal</u>.

7. Doing your homework at <u>a different</u> time each day will make it easier to study.

8. A <u>consequence</u> of exercising every day is improved wellness.

9. Emotional <u>stress</u> can cause illness if not handled well.

10. <u>Cooperation</u> is testing your abilities against those of other people.

11. Your <u>self-esteem</u> is the way you think and feel about something.

12. Your <u>interests</u> will probably change as you get older.

13. People have <u>the same</u> aptitudes.

14. Self-esteem means <u>liking</u> and respecting yourself.

15. Set goals that are <u>unrealistic</u>.

Short Answer

Write the numbers 16 to 23 on your paper. Write a complete sentence to answer each question.

16. What is the benefit of setting short-term goals?

17. What are three tips that can help you plan your study time?

18. What are some questions you should ask yourself about your goals?

19. How can you work toward increasing your self-esteem?

20. What is the difference between aptitude and attitude?

21. When would you compete against yourself?

22. What is an advantage of cooperating with people on a project?

23. How do interests affect aptitudes?

Essay

Write the numbers 24 and 25 on your paper. Write paragraphs with complete sentences to answer each question.

24. Describe how wellness is a combination of interest, aptitude, attitude, and self-esteem.

25. Explain how sports like volleyball show how people can compete and cooperate to meet goals.

ACTIVITIES FOR HOME OR SCHOOL

Projects to Do

1. Interview at least two adults you know. Ask each person about his or her aptitudes and interests. Then ask each person to describe his or her job or hobby. How do you think each person's aptitudes and interests affect a choice of job or hobby?

■ *Talking with someone about a special interest, such as woodworking, is a good way to learn about aptitudes.*

2. What information about yourself helps you form a good self-concept? Who can help you by telling you what they like about you? Ask one adult and one person whom you consider to be a friend.

3. Choose an important activity you would like to do in the next week or two. What plans can you make ahead of time to accomplish your goal? Do you need to change your schedule or give up any regular activities? Make a schedule that includes the plans and the choices you will need to make. Check your schedule each day to be sure that you are following it.

Information to Find

1. What are aptitude tests? What kinds of things do they test? Your school counselor can help you answer these questions.

2. What kinds of decisions do young people have to make before they start high school? Ask your school counselor or check your library for books on early adolescence to help you find the information.

3. Find out about a competition called the Special Olympics. Look in your library for magazine and newspaper articles about this annual event.

Books to Read

Here are some books you can look for in your school library or the public library. They will help you learn more about yourself and about setting goals.

Cleary, Beverly. *Dear Mr. Henshaw*. Dell.

Daniels, Kim. *Your Changing Emotions*. Pinnacle.

Rodowsky, Colby. *What About Me?* Franklin Watts.

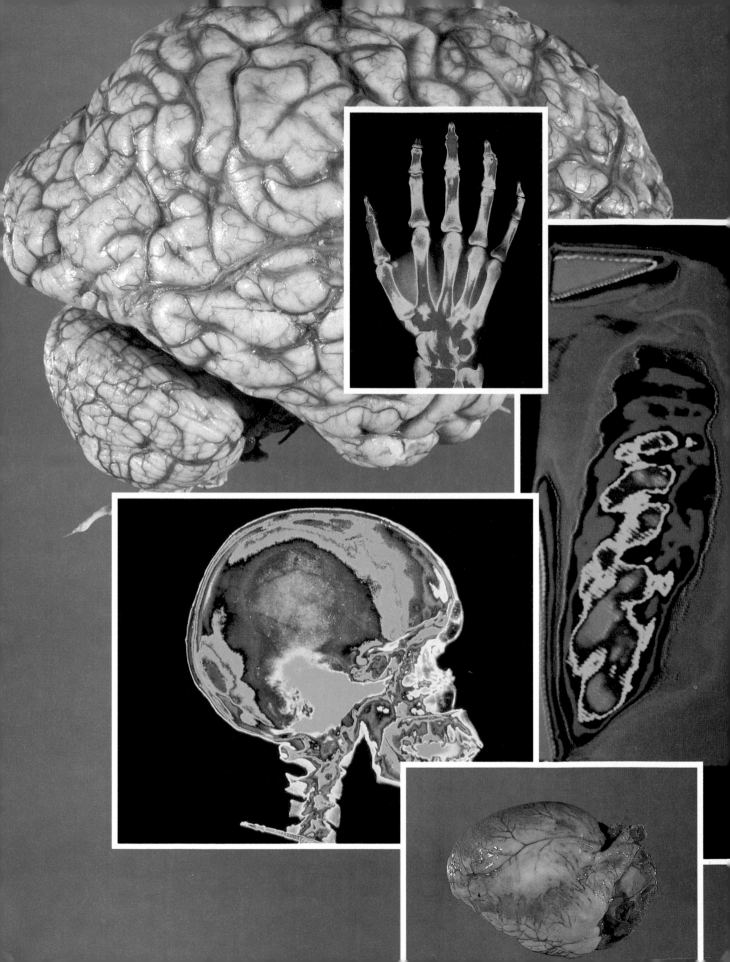

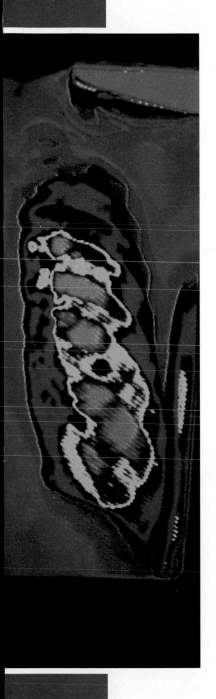

BODY SYSTEMS AT WORK

Your brain is more complex than an advanced computer. Your heart works longer and harder than a mechanical pump. All the parts of your body working together can do more than any machine that was ever built.

What makes your body still more remarkable is the way it is organized. It is made up of many parts that work together. At this moment, your bones, muscles, eyes, and brain are all working together to help you read this book. Knowing how your body works can help you understand the need to keep your body working as it should.

GETTING READY TO LEARN

Key Questions

- What are the parts of your body, and what do they do?
- Why is it important to learn how your body works?
- How does knowing about body systems help you understand how you can take care of them?

Main Chapter Sections

1 The Parts That Make Up Your Body
2 Your Circulatory System
3 Your Respiratory System
4 Your Digestive System
5 Your Excretory System
6 Your Skeletal and Muscular Systems
7 Your Nervous System

SECTION
1

The Parts That Make Up Your Body

Look at your hand. See the skin that covers it. Feel the hard bones inside. Both your skin and your bones are made up of parts too small to see without a microscope. It takes millions of these tiny parts to make up your whole body. These very small parts are called *cells.*

What Are Your Cells?

Cells are the smallest parts of your body. There are many different kinds of cells. Your skin is made of skin cells. Your bones are made of bone cells. The different kinds of cells in your body have different shapes and do different jobs. But almost all cells have the same three basic parts.

All cells have a thin outer covering called the **cell membrane.** The cell membrane holds the cell together. It lets in water and everything else the cell needs. The cell membrane also keeps out most things that could harm the cell.

Almost every cell has a small center called the **nucleus.** It stores information and directs all the activities of the cell.

KEY WORDS

cell membrane
nucleus
cytoplasm
tissue
organ
body system
nutrients
oxygen

cell membrane (SEHL · MEHM brayn), the thin outer covering of a cell; holds the cell together.

nucleus (NOO klee uhs), the small central core in almost every cell; stores information and directs all the activities of the cell.

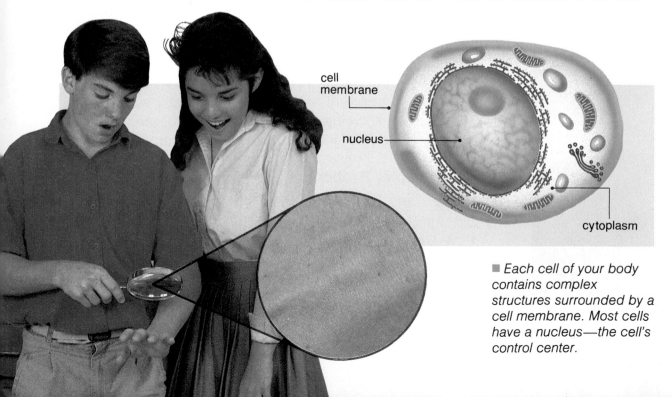

cell membrane

nucleus

cytoplasm

■ Each cell of your body contains complex structures surrounded by a cell membrane. Most cells have a nucleus—the cell's control center.

The nucleus sends out messages telling the cell what to do, how to do it, and when to do it.

Between the nucleus and the cell membrane is cytoplasm. **Cytoplasm** is a material made up of many parts that help the cell work. Some parts take energy from food. Others digest or change things that enter a cell. Cytoplasm is important to the life of a cell.

What Are Your Tissues?

All the work of your body is done by your cells. Groups of cells that are alike work together to do the same job. A group of like cells forms a **tissue.**

Muscle, blood, skin, hair, and bone are some of the kinds of tissues in your body. Each of these kinds of tissues does a different job. Bone tissue helps give your body its size and shape. Muscle tissue gives your body firmness. Skin tissue covers and protects your other body tissues.

The cells that make up tissues are specially formed for the work they do. Bone cells have hard shells that cannot bend. They make your bone tissue stiff and strong. Skin cells are flat and thin, and they fit tightly together at the edges. Their shape makes your skin tissue flat and thin.

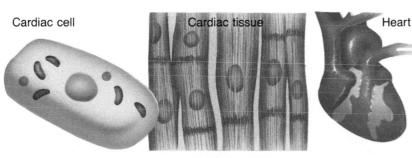

Cardiac cell   Cardiac tissue   Heart

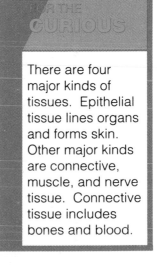

■ *The heart is an organ made of special cells and tissues.*

What Are Your Organs?

Like your cells, your tissues work together in groups to do certain jobs. Groups of tissues working together make up an **organ.** Your body has many organs. Each organ does a certain job that helps you stay alive and healthy. For example, your heart is an organ that pumps your blood. Your eyes are organs that let you see the world around you.

DIGESTIVE SYSTEM

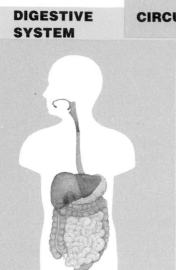

CIRCULATORY SYSTEM

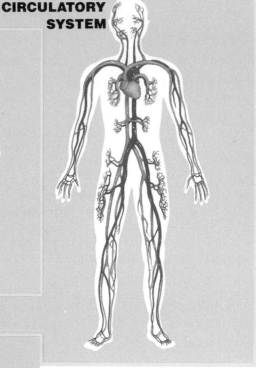

URINARY SYSTEM

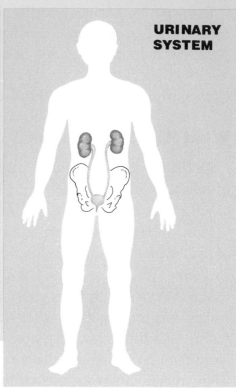

RESPIRATORY SYSTEM

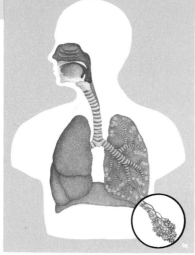

body system (BAHD ee · SIHS tuhm), a group of organs that work together to do a certain job.

nutrients (NOO tree uhnts), the parts of food the body needs for energy, growth, and good health.

oxygen (AHK sih juhn), a gas in the air your cells need to live.

What Are Your Body Systems?

When you eat, your mouth helps you by chewing your food and breaking it up. Your esophagus is an organ that helps move the food you swallow from your mouth into your stomach. Your stomach and small intestine are organs that continue the work of breaking up the food. All four organs work on the same job. They help turn the food you eat into a form your cells can use.

Organs that work together to do a certain job make up a **body system.** Each body system takes care of a different need. Your mouth, esophagus, stomach, and small intestine, for example, belong to your digestive system. This system changes the food you eat into **nutrients,** the parts of food your body needs for energy, growth, and good health. **Oxygen,** a gas your body takes from the air, is taken in by another body system. Yet another system rids your body of wastes. Body wastes are substances your cells make that cannot be used and must be removed from the body.

30

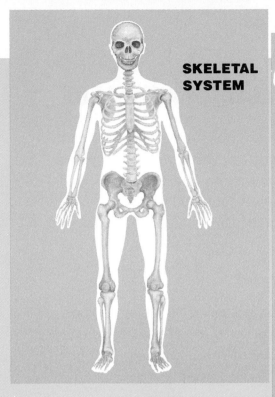

SKELETAL SYSTEM

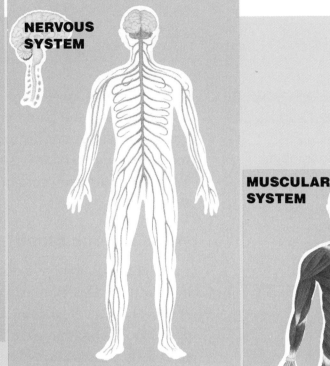

NERVOUS SYSTEM

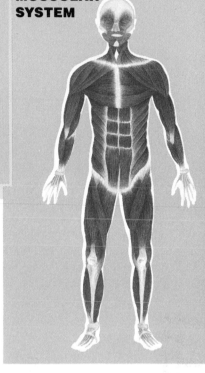

MUSCULAR SYSTEM

While each system has a certain job that no other system can do, some organs are part of more than one system. For example, the liver does important work for several systems. It is part of the digestive, excretory, and circulatory systems.

All of your body systems work together as a whole. This whole is your body. All its parts work together to keep you alive and healthy.

 **REVIEW SECTION 1**

■ *Keeping your body systems healthy is your responsibility.*

REMEMBER?

1. What are the three main parts of a cell?
2. What are the three jobs of a cell membrane?
3. Why are skin, hair, and bone considered tissues?

THINK!

4. How are your brain and the nucleus of a cell alike?
5. How might the breakdown of one body system have an effect on the rest of your body?

31

2 Your Circulatory System

Your circulatory system has three main parts: the heart, the blood, and the blood vessels. The heart pumps blood, which carries substances to and from the cells. The blood moves through a dense network of blood vessels. Sometimes the term *cardiovascular* is used to describe this system.

What Is Your Blood?

People your age have about 1 gallon (4 liters) of blood in their bodies. This blood circulates through your body over and over. It never stops moving. Your body cells take from your blood what they need to stay healthy. Your cells also send their wastes into your blood to be taken away.

The blood you see from a cut is a red liquid. But most of this blood is made up of a clear, light-yellow liquid called **plasma.** Certain cells that float in the plasma give your blood its red color. In addition to plasma, your blood contains red blood cells, white blood cells, and platelets.

KEY WORDS

plasma
hemoglobin
carbon dioxide
antibodies
platelets
atrium
ventricle
lymph

plasma (PLAZ muh), the clear, light-yellow liquid that makes up most of your blood.

■ *The blood in these tubes has been separated. Plasma is floating on top of various kinds of blood cells.*

Red Blood Cells. Your red blood cells have a substance called hemoglobin. **Hemoglobin** is what makes these cells red. Hemoglobin picks up oxygen in your lungs. It carries oxygen to your body cells. Each body cell takes the oxygen it needs. When a cell takes oxygen, it releases carbon dioxide. **Carbon dioxide** is one of the wastes made by your cells. The hemoglobin picks up the carbon dioxide and carries it away from your cells.

Your blood has more red blood cells than any other kind. About 60,000 of them would fit in the dot of an *i*. A red blood cell looks like a doughnut with the hole filled in. It has thick edges and a thinner middle.

hemoglobin (HEE muh gloh buhn), a substance in red blood cells that picks up and carries oxygen.

carbon dioxide (KAHR buhn • dy AHK syd), a gas that is one of the wastes made by your cells.

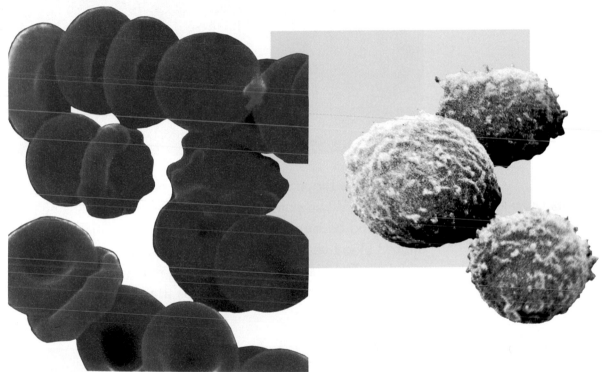

■ *Red blood cells, left, carry hemoglobin and oxygen to all the cells. White blood cells, right, can destroy microbes.*

White Blood Cells. Your largest blood cells are called white blood cells, although they really do not have any color. White blood cells help fight disease. They destroy the germs that cause infections and illnesses. This part of the circulatory system is also part of the *immune system.*

There are several kinds of white blood cells. Each kind defends the body in different ways. Some destroy disease-causing microbes. Others form substances called **antibodies.**

antibodies (ANT ih bahd eez), substances in blood that attack and destroy microbes.

33

Antibodies attack and destroy disease-causing microbes. This way the microbes cannot make you ill. When you have microbes in your blood, your body makes extra white blood cells. The extra white blood cells then make more antibodies to fight the microbes.

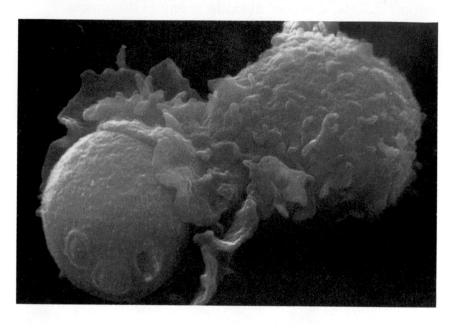

■ *This white blood cell, right, is attacking a microbe.*

platelets (PLAYT luhts), tiny parts of cells in your blood that help the blood thicken, or clot, when you have a cut or wound.

Platelets. Blood also contains tiny parts of cells called **platelets.** When you have a cut or wound, platelets help your blood become thick. Platelets stick to the walls of injured blood vessels. Other cells in plasma are trapped by platelets. The platelets and other cells make a clot that closes the torn vessel. The clot stops the bleeding. A dried clot is called a *scab.*

■ *Platelets form a clot to close a torn blood vessel.*

34

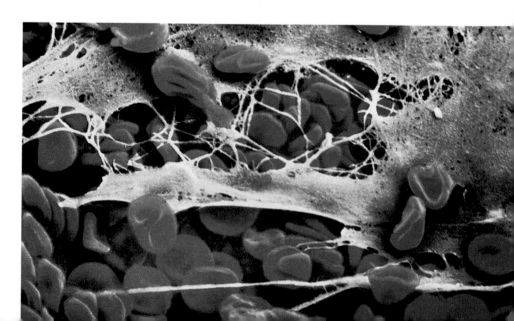

What Is Your Heart?

Your heart is a hollow, muscular organ about the size of your fist. It is near the center of your chest, where you can feel it beating hard if you run very fast. During your lifetime, your heart will beat more than 2½ billion times. During 1 minute, almost 1 gallon (4 liters) of blood moves through your heart.

Inside your heart, a wall divides the right side from the left side. Each side has an upper and a lower part. The four parts of the heart are called chambers. Each upper chamber is called an **atrium.** Each lower chamber is called a **ventricle.**

atrium (AY tree uhm), an upper chamber in your heart.

ventricle (VEHN trih kuhl), a lower chamber in your heart.

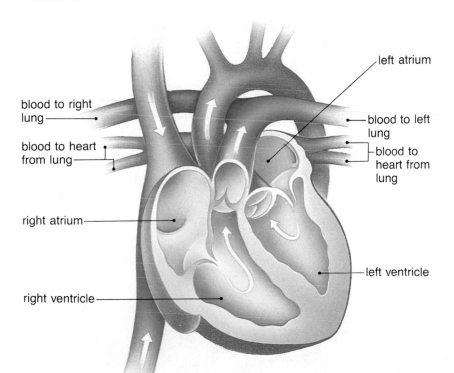

blood to right lung

blood to heart from lung

right atrium

right ventricle

left atrium

blood to left lung

blood to heart from lung

left ventricle

■ *The heart pumps blood through your lungs, where the blood picks up oxygen to be carried to every cell in your body.*

The ventricle on the right side of your heart pumps blood to your lungs. In your lungs, your blood gives off the carbon dioxide it contains and picks up more oxygen. The blood then goes from your lungs back to your heart. It enters the atrium on the left side and moves to the ventricle below. The left ventricle pumps the oxygen-rich blood to the rest of your body, where cells take oxygen from the blood.

Your blood flows back to the atrium on the right side of your heart. From there it moves down to the right ventricle and begins the same path again.

The beating of your heart helps keep you alive. By pumping blood through your body, your heart helps your cells get what they need to live and to be healthy.

What Are Your Blood Vessels?

Blood moves to every cell in your body through three kinds of blood vessels. *Arteries* carry blood away from your heart. Arteries have thick, flexible muscle walls. They can stand the pressure of blood being pumped out of the heart.

Veins carry blood toward your heart. Veins have thinner walls than arteries because the pressure of blood is lower in veins. Small flaps in the veins keep the blood flowing in only one direction.

Capillaries are tiny blood vessels that connect arteries to veins. Capillaries have very thin walls. Every tissue in your body has capillaries next to it. Nutrients, oxygen, and wastes pass in and out of your blood through the capillary walls.

The blood vessels that you see just below your skin are veins. Arteries are deeper in the body than veins and are protected by muscle and fat tissue.

■ *Capillaries are very narrow. Red blood cells can only move single file through them.*

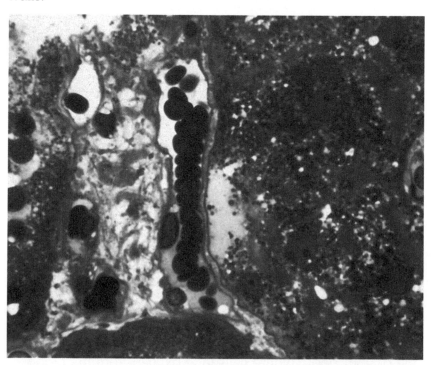

CIRCULATORY SYSTEM

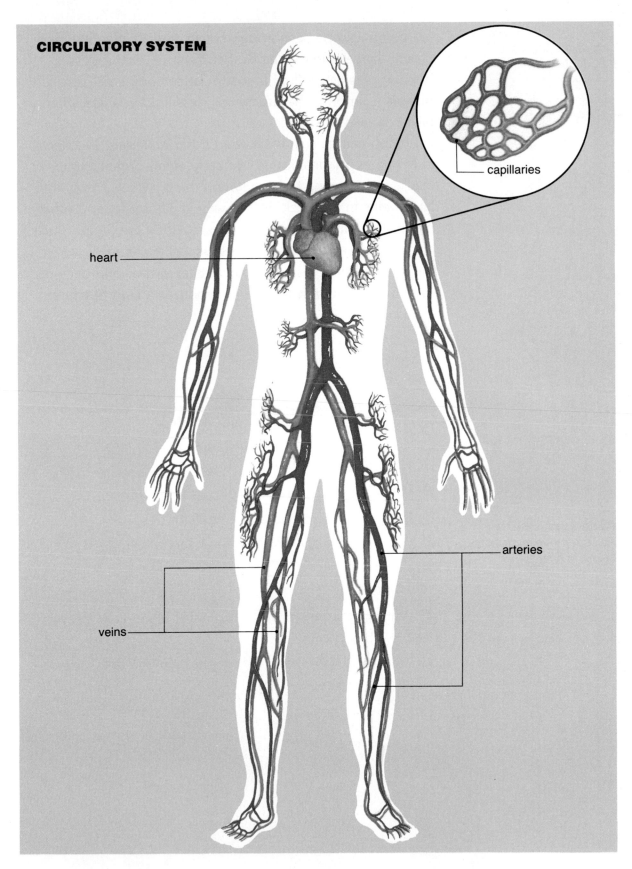

capillaries

heart

arteries

veins

lymph (LIHMF), a mixture of plasma and tissue fluid that collects cell wastes.

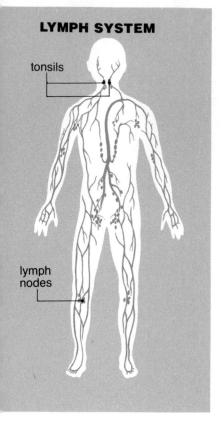

LYMPH SYSTEM

tonsils

lymph nodes

■ *The lymph system helps remove microbes from the blood.*

Plasma also passes through capillary walls. Slightly more plasma leaves the capillaries than returns. This excess plasma, plus tissue fluid that surrounds body cells, is called **lymph.** Lymph is the nearly colorless fluid you see when a blister breaks open.

Lymph carries cell wastes and other materials. It collects in lymph capillaries, found in nearly every organ. Lymph capillaries combine to form lymph ducts, which empty into large veins in the neck. In this way, fluid, waste, and other materials return to the bloodstream. Along the lymph ducts are lymph nodes. These organs, as well as lymph tissue in the tonsils, adenoids, and spleen, filter viruses and bacteria from lymph. Lymph tissue also produces a kind of white blood cell.

STOP **REVIEW SECTION 2**

REMEMBER?

1. What are two main kinds of cells in blood?
2. How do white blood cells help fight disease?
3. What are the chambers of the heart called?

THINK!

4. Why does a person need more red blood cells than white blood cells?
5. What is a health habit that might help you take care of your circulatory system?

3 Your Respiratory System

Allison takes a deep breath and dives into the pool. She swims underwater to the other end. Then she comes up to the surface for more air. She cannot hold her breath any longer. Most people cannot go much longer than a minute without breathing. Breathing brings oxygen into your body. Your cells need the oxygen in order to stay alive.

KEY WORDS

trachea
bronchial tubes
alveoli

■ *You must breathe to take in the oxygen that your cells need.*

The organs that help you breathe make up your respiratory system. This system draws air into your lungs and takes oxygen from the air for your body to use. It also helps remove carbon dioxide from your body.

How Does Air Travel to Your Lungs?

When you breathe in, air comes into your body through your nose or mouth. The air then enters a tube in your throat called the **trachea,** or windpipe. The trachea divides at the bottom into two branches called **bronchial tubes.** The air moves into your lungs through these tubes, which branch into smaller tubes. The lungs are two large, spongelike organs in your chest.

trachea (TRAY kee uh), the tube through which air moves from your throat to your chest; the windpipe.

bronchial tubes (BRAHNG kee uhl • TOOBZ), two branches of the trachea, which go into the lungs.

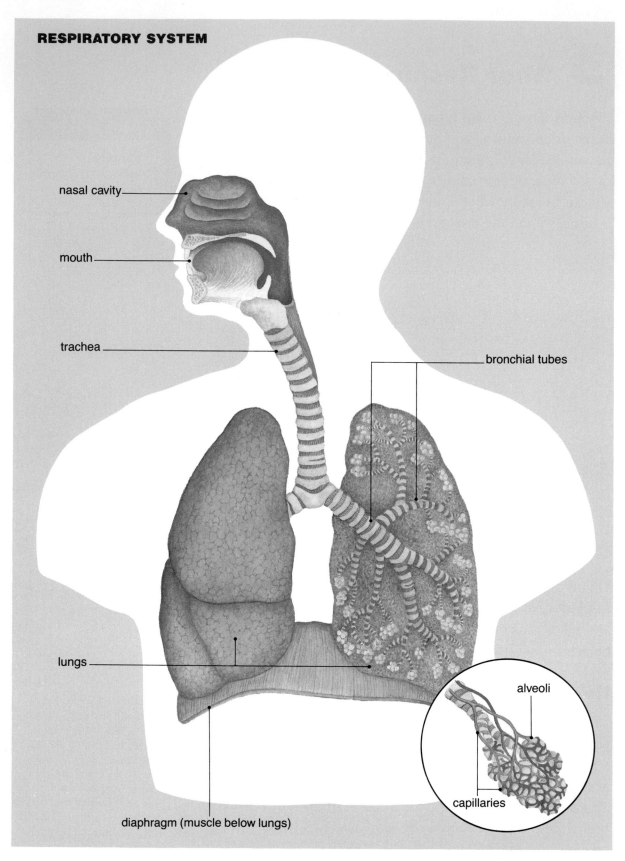

RESPIRATORY SYSTEM

nasal cavity

mouth

trachea

bronchial tubes

lungs

alveoli

capillaries

diaphragm (muscle below lungs)

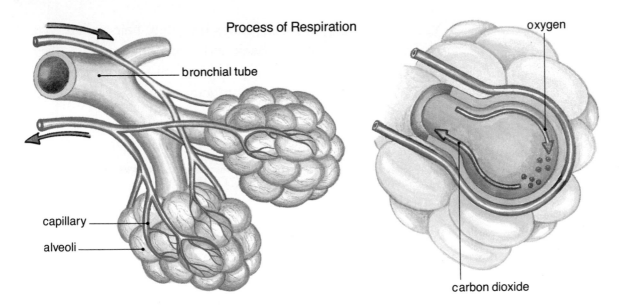

Process of Respiration

oxygen

bronchial tube

capillary

alveoli

carbon dioxide

Inside your lungs are many small, hollow air sacs at the ends of the smaller tubes. These air sacs are called **alveoli.** Each of the alveoli has capillaries around it. The air you breathe in fills up the alveoli. Oxygen passes from the alveoli into the capillaries. Red blood cells in the capillaries pick up the oxygen. Then your blood takes the oxygen to the rest of your cells.

As the blood delivers oxygen, it picks up carbon dioxide given off by your cells. The carbon dioxide moves through the body to the capillaries in the alveoli and into the lungs. Then it leaves your body when you breathe out. This exchange of oxygen and carbon dioxide is called *respiration*.

■ *The alveoli are the structures at which respiration occurs in the lungs.*

alveoli (al VEE uh ly), small, hollow air sacs inside your lungs.

How Does Your Body Clean the Air You Breathe?

The air you breathe may have dust or other harmful matter in it. But certain parts of your respiratory organs clean the air as it moves to your lungs. These parts also make the air warm and moist.

Hairs in your nose begin the cleaning. They screen out some of the particles in the air. A sticky substance called *mucus* traps more. Mucus lines your nasal passages and the walls of your trachea and bronchial tubes. Mucus may trap microbes and other harmful matter, as well.

Your trachea and bronchial tubes have tiny hairs called *cilia*. The cilia wave quickly back and forth. They push mucus that has trapped dirt and dust up toward your throat. When you swallow, much of the mucus passes into the digestive system.

REVIEW
SECTION 3

REMEMBER?

1. What does your respiratory system do?
2. What is the job of the alveoli?
3. How is the air you breathe cleaned by the respiratory system?

THINK!

4. What can you do to protect your respiratory system while you are in a dusty or smoke-filled room?
5. What is a health habit that helps you take care of your respiratory system?

Making Wellness Choices

Arturo and his parents have been shopping in the city. Their city has a very busy downtown area with many new buildings. Arturo and his parents are walking from a store to their bus stop. To get to the bus stop, they must pass a busy construction site. They can hear the machines and see a lot of smoke and dust in the air ahead of them as they walk. Arturo and his parents need to go past the construction site to get to their bus stop. They also need to be careful not to breathe the smoke and dust that might harm their lungs.

 What could Arturo and his parents do? Explain your wellness choice.

42

4 Your Digestive System

Kevin has not eaten for hours. Now his cells need nutrients from food in order to do their work. Kevin feels hungry. He decides to eat an apple.

The apple is much bigger than any of Kevin's cells. But Kevin does not have to worry about that. His body has a system for breaking down and changing the food he eats into material his cells can use. This system is the digestive system.

Your digestive system is made up of several organs, each connected to the next. This system crushes, grinds, mashes, dissolves, and changes food. It breaks food into pieces even smaller than your cells in a process called *digestion*.

What Happens in Your Mouth?

Digestion of food begins in your mouth. When you chew food, your teeth chop and grind the food into small pieces. These pieces mix with saliva in your mouth. **Saliva** is a liquid that starts to break down food. The liquids in your digestive system that help break down food are called *digestive juices*.

Your mouth always has a little saliva in it. It makes more when you eat. Saliva makes it easy for you to swallow food.

■ Digestion begins when the food that you chew mixes with digestive juices in saliva.

KEY WORDS

saliva
peristalsis
pancreas
bile
gallbladder

saliva (suh LY vuh), a liquid in your mouth that starts to break down the food you eat.

DIGESTIVE SYSTEM

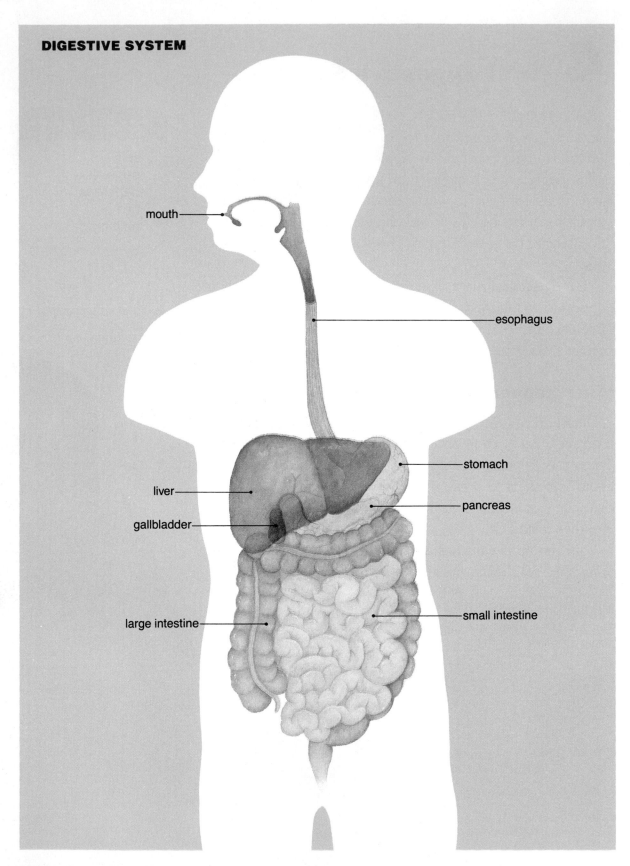

mouth

esophagus

stomach

liver

pancreas

gallbladder

large intestine

small intestine

What Happens in Your Esophagus and Stomach?

When you swallow, food passes into the esophagus. Food is moved through this long tube by a wavelike, squeezing action, something like squeezing toothpaste out of a tube. This action is called **peristalsis.** It moves food all the way through your digestive system.

The food you eat passes through your esophagus into your stomach. Your stomach is a hollow, muscular organ that helps break down food. Your stomach walls contain glands that make acid and other digestive juices. These walls squeeze the food to break it up and mix it with the juices. The squeezing and mixing turn the food into a thick liquid.

peristalsis (pehr uh STAWL suhs), the squeezing action of organs that moves food all the way through the digestive system.

What Happens in Your Small and Large Intestines?

When food leaves your stomach, it enters your small intestine. This is a long, narrow tube where most of the work of digestion takes place. The small intestine is about 20 feet (6 meters) long. Your small intestine fits inside your body because it is folded back and forth many times.

Digestive juices from several organs in your digestive system help your small intestine break down food. The **pancreas** is a digestive organ that makes *pancreatic juices.* These juices help break down starches, proteins, and fats in the food you eat. Certain cells in the pancreas also make a hormone called *insulin.* Insulin helps your body use sugar.

pancreas (PANG kree uhs), the digestive organ that makes pancreatic juices, which help break down starches, proteins, and fats.

■ *The pancreas and gallbladder make digestive juices that flow into the small intestine.*

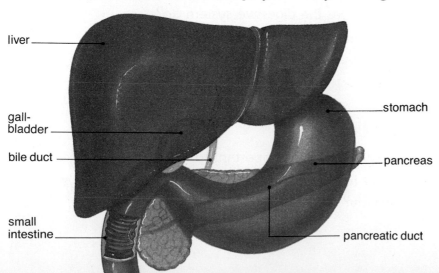

liver

gall-
bladder

bile duct

small
intestine

stomach

pancreas

pancreatic duct

MYTH
AND
FACT

Myth: The skin turns yellow when the liver is not working properly.

Fact: The skin and eyes become slightly yellow when there is too much bile in the bloodstream. Too much bile may be caused by eating too much fat.

The liver is another of your digestive organs. The liver makes a digestive fluid called **bile,** which flows into the gallbladder. The **gallbladder** is a digestive organ that stores bile. The gallbladder does not make any digestive juices of its own. It squirts out bile when fats from food enter the small intestine. Bile is used in the small intestine to help digest the fats.

In your small intestine, food is broken down into nutrients small enough to enter your blood. The nutrients enter your blood through capillaries that line the inside wall of your small intestine. Then your blood carries the nutrients to all the cells of your body.

Your body cannot digest all parts of the food you eat. The parts that are left pass into your large intestine. Your large intestine is wider and shorter than your small intestine. It is about 3 feet (1 meter) long. Your large intestine takes most of the remaining water out of the food. The water passes through the wall of the large intestine. Then it goes into your blood. Your large intestine stores the wastes that are left. These parts leave your body as solid waste when you have a bowel movement. The food you eat should include plenty of water and indigestible material, such as that found in fresh fruits and vegetables. They help the large intestine to empty regularly without working too hard.

REVIEW

SECTION 4

REMEMBER?

1. What does the digestive system do?
2. What happens to food in the stomach?
3. How do the materials in food get to the cells of your body?

THINK!

4. Why is peristalsis important to the process of digestion?
5. What habits can help you keep your digestive system healthy?

Health Close-up

Blood Groups

Did you know that different people have different blood groups? There are four blood groups. These groups are determined by whether or not antigens are present. *Antigens* are substances found on the surface of red blood cells. There are two kinds: antigen A and antigen B. Blood that has only antigen A is group A blood. Blood with only antigen B is group B blood. If blood has neither antigen, it is group O blood. If it has both, it is group AB blood.

When a person loses a lot of blood, a blood transfusion may be necessary. In a *transfusion,* blood that has been donated by a healthy person is given to an ill or injured person. Every person, however, cannot give blood to and receive blood from every other person. There are limits because of the way

BLOOD TRANSFUSION CHART		
Blood Group	Can Donate To	Can Receive From
O	all blood groups	O
A	A, AB	A, O
B	B, AB	B, O
AB	AB	all blood groups

antigens work. Antigens in some groups of blood do not match those in other groups. When the wrong blood groups are mixed, the red blood cells clump together. The clumps are made by antibodies trying to protect the body. These clumps can block the blood vessels and stop the blood from moving through the body.

When a person gives blood or needs to receive blood, his or her blood is tested to determine its group. Physicians and certain other health workers know which blood groups can be safely mixed.

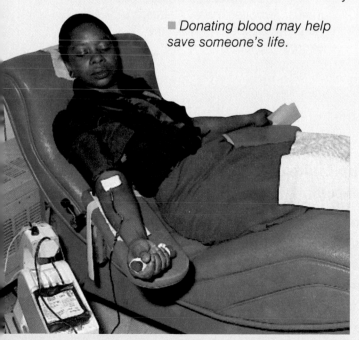

■ *Donating blood may help save someone's life.*

Thinking Beyond

1. Which blood group would it be best to have a large supply of at a blood bank? Why?
2. Dr. Moser has delayed Mr. Chin's operation. Mr. Chin has group B blood. The only blood available is group A blood. Why is the delay necessary?

5 Your Excretory System

Carla takes out the garbage often. She must do this job to keep garbage from piling up in the house. Your cells must keep wastes from piling up, too. They must get rid of the wastes they make as they use up food. Your cells push their wastes and extra water into your blood. Certain organs gather the wastes and the extra water. They move them out of your body. These organs make up your excretory system, the waste-removal system.

One set of organs, called the urinary system, handles the removal of one kind of waste. Other body systems also help remove wastes. They are the digestive system, the respiratory system, and the skin.

■ *Your body produces wastes that it must remove. These wastes are removed by the organs of the excretory system.*

kidneys (KIHD neez), two bean-shaped organs that remove most of the extra water and cell wastes from your blood.

urine (YUR uhn), the liquid waste filtered from the blood by the kidneys.

How Does Your Urinary System Get Rid of Wastes?

The urinary system is made up of the kidneys, the bladder, and tubes. They all hold a waste liquid. In your back at about waist level, you have two bean-shaped organs called **kidneys.** The kidneys remove most of the cell wastes and extra water from your blood. The water and wastes combine to form a liquid called **urine.**

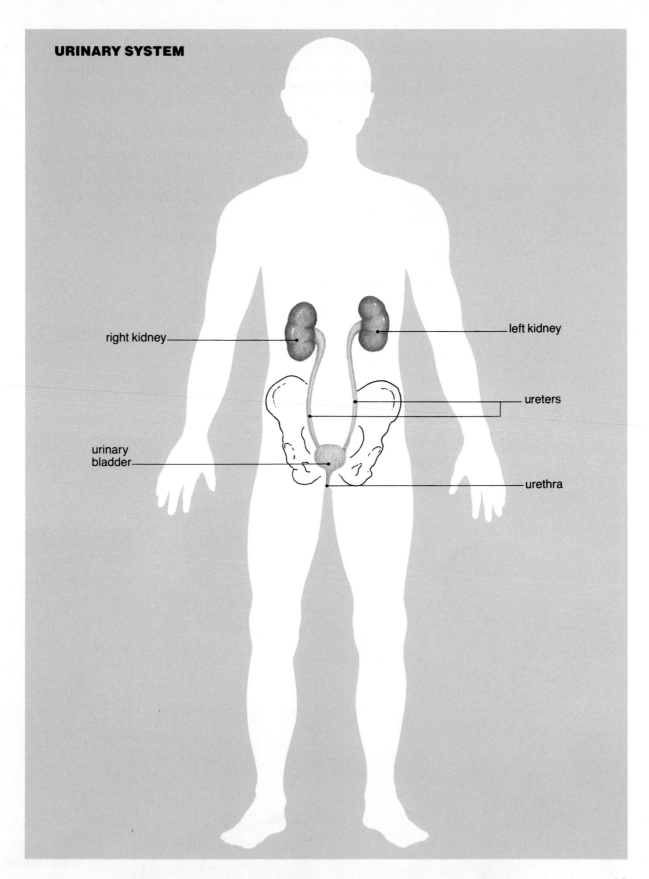

URINARY SYSTEM

right kidney

left kidney

ureters

urinary
bladder

urethra

A narrow tube called a *ureter* comes out of each kidney. As urine forms in the kidneys, it flows through the ureters to the *urinary bladder*. This is a baglike organ near your kidneys. It fills slowly with urine.

Your bladder has an opening at the bottom. A muscle around the bottom keeps the opening shut while the bladder fills. When you want the urine to leave your body, you relax the muscle. This allows the urine to leave your body through a tube called the *urethra*.

How Does Your Skin Help Get Rid of Wastes?

Some of your cell wastes and extra water leave your body through your skin. Your skin has tiny *sweat glands*. They remove water, salt, and some other wastes from your blood. The water, salt, and wastes form a liquid called *perspiration,* or sweat.

Sweat leaves your body through small openings in your skin called *pores*. The sweat moves out of your pores to the surface of your skin. The water in sweat evaporates. The other wastes stay on your skin until you wash them away.

■ Cell wastes and water leave the body when a person sweats. This lost water needs to be replaced to keep the body working as it should.

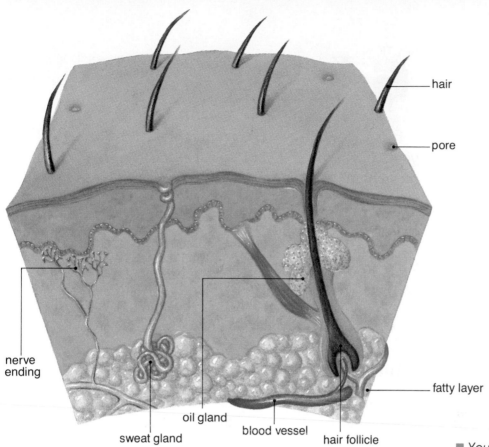

hair

pore

nerve ending

sweat gland

oil gland

blood vessel

hair follicle

fatty layer

The excretory system keeps wastes from remaining in your body. By removing your cells' wastes, your excretory system helps your cells stay healthy.

■ *Your skin is always working to help remove wastes from your body.*

STOP REVIEW
SECTION 5

REMEMBER?

1. What is the job of your excretory system?
2. What does your urinary bladder do?
3. How do the sweat glands remove wastes from your body?

THINK!

4. How might a breakdown of the excretory system affect a person's health?
5. What habit might help the urinary system do its job well?

6 Your Skeletal and Muscular Systems

Being able to move your body helps you take care of yourself. It would be hard to live without being able to move at all. Moving lets you interact with the world around you. It helps you work, write, eat, play, and do any physical action.

Two systems work together to move your body. Your skeletal system gives your body its size and shape. Your muscular system makes the body firm and moves your body parts. Sometimes these systems together are called the *musculoskeletal system.*

What Is Your Skeletal System?

If you were not wearing your clothes, they would fall into a heap. Most of the tissues in your body are as soft as cloth. But your body never falls into a heap because it has a framework of connected bones inside it. This framework is your **skeleton,** or skeletal system.

Your skeleton has more than 200 bones. The bones of your skeleton help protect your inner organs. Your skull, for example, is a hard case that protects your brain. Your ribs form a cage that protects your lungs, heart, and certain other organs.

skeleton (SKEHL uht uhn), the framework of connected bones in your body.

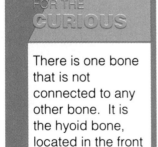

FOR THE
CURIOUS

There is one bone that is not connected to any other bone. It is the hyoid bone, located in the front of your neck.

■ *Your skeleton and muscles work together to help you move.*

SKELETAL SYSTEM

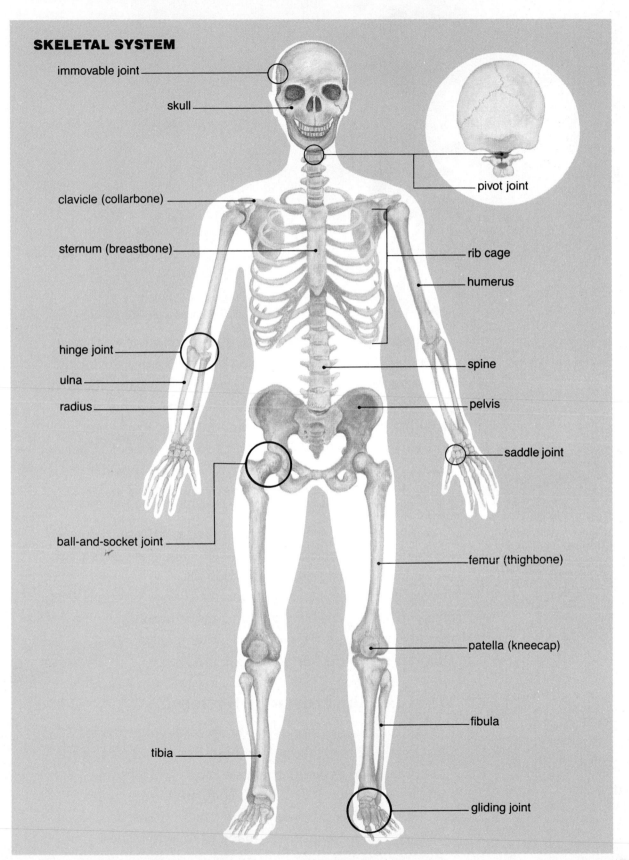

immovable joint

skull

pivot joint

clavicle (collarbone)

sternum (breastbone)

rib cage

humerus

hinge joint

spine

ulna

radius

pelvis

saddle joint

ball-and-socket joint

femur (thighbone)

patella (kneecap)

fibula

tibia

gliding joint

53

■ *The many bones, joints, and muscles in the hand allow various kinds of movement.*

cartilage (KAHRT uhl ihj), the stiff tissue between the bones in your movable joints.

Almost every bone in your body is connected to at least one other bone at a joint. At some joints, bones are locked into place and cannot move. There are immovable joints in your skull, for example. You also have many joints that allow the bones to move. At some movable joints, the bones can open and shut like the covers of a book. Your elbows and knees move in this way. At other movable joints, the bones can move around in a circle. You can move your shoulder in this way.

You have a stiff, smooth tissue called **cartilage** between the bones in your movable joints. The cartilage keeps your bones from grinding against each other.

Your movable joints let your bones change position. This ability makes it possible for you to move around and do things. But your skeleton cannot move by itself. Your muscular system makes your bones move.

What Is Your Muscular System?

Your muscular system is made up of all your muscles. Muscles are organs that pull on your bones and other parts of your body to make them move. You can feel some muscles just above your elbow. They are the soft parts around your bones. Some of your other organs, such as your heart and stomach, are made of muscle tissue.

54

MUSCULAR SYSTEM

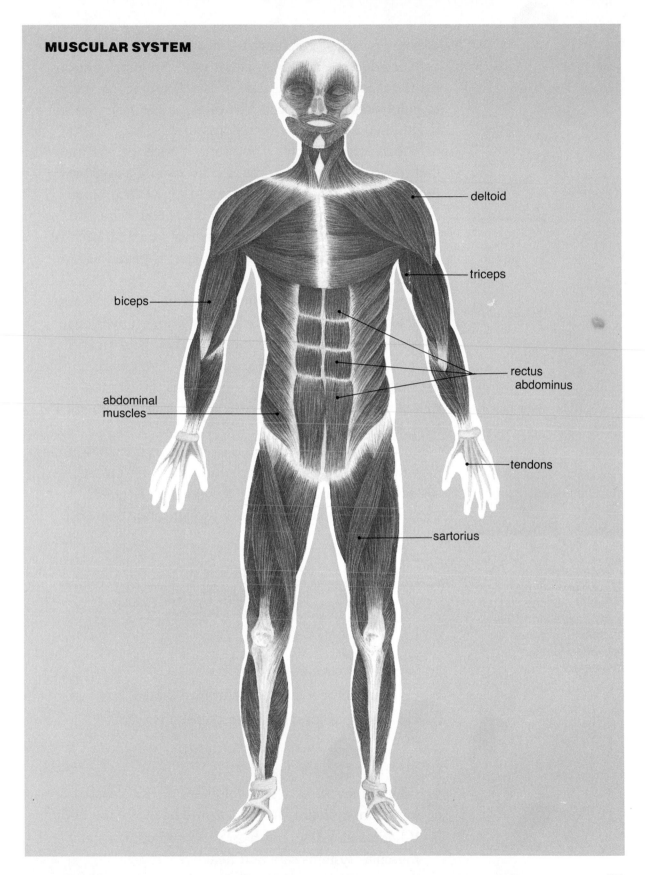

deltoid

triceps

biceps

rectus abdominus

abdominal muscles

tendons

sartorius

Some muscles stretch across movable joints. They are connected to the bones on either side of a joint by strong tissue called tendons. Muscles contract, or become shorter, to pull bones. Muscles can also relax, or return to the same length they were before they contracted.

Muscles can only pull. They cannot push. So the muscles that move your fingers to make a fist cannot straighten them again. Muscles work in pairs to move each bone. They pull the bone from opposite directions. When one muscle contracts, the other relaxes. For example, each of the muscles that straightens your fingers is paired with a muscle that curls your fingers.

Muscles that you have control over are your *voluntary muscles.* You also have muscles that work on their own. These are your *involuntary muscles.* They help most of your body systems work. For example, involuntary muscles in your digestive system cause peristalsis. Involuntary muscles make up the walls of your heart. These muscles keep it beating.

Muscles and bones help you sit up in your chair. Muscles move your eyes as you read. Your skeletal and muscular systems help you in many ways every day. Regular exercise, rest and sleep, and the proper foods help you keep these systems healthy.

■ *Try these actions at your desk to feel different muscles in your arms contracting. Many muscles are paired for opposing kinds of movement.*

STOP REVIEW
SECTION 6

REMEMBER?

1. What does your skeleton do?
2. How are some joints different from others?
3. How do your muscles make your bones move?

THINK!

4. Why are involuntary and voluntary muscles each important in their own ways to the health of the body?
5. What health habits can help you keep your skeletal and muscular systems safe and healthy?

56

7 Your Nervous System

David is reading a book. His hands are holding the book in front of his eyes. His eyes are looking at the words. He reads to the end of the page and then turns the page with his fingers. Various systems in David's body are working together to help him read.

■ *The nervous system controls the body parts needed for reading.*

All the parts of your body work together because one body system controls them all. The nervous system controls all the systems in your body. It gathers messages from all parts of your body. It helps you decide what you should do and how you should do it. The nervous system controls all your muscles.

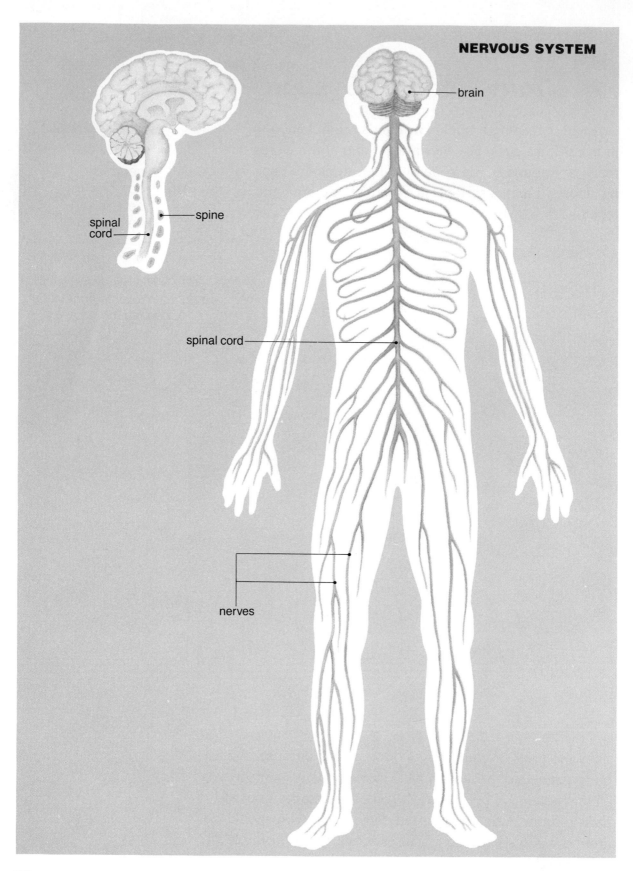

NERVOUS SYSTEM

brain

spine

spinal
cord

spinal cord

nerves

What Do Your Nerve Cells and Nerves Do?

The cells of your nervous system are called nerve cells, or **neurons.** Neurons have long branches coming out of them from both ends. Most neurons are very long and thin. Bundles of these long, thin neurons make up your nerves.

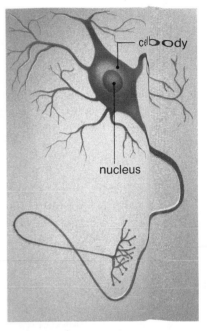

neurons (NOO rahnz), nerve cells, which make up your nervous system

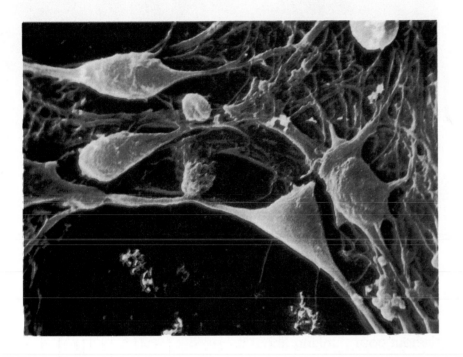

■ Nerves are made up of special branching cells called neurons.

Nerves receive and send messages. Some nerves carry messages to your brain to let it know what is happening in and around your body. These are *sensory nerves.* Other nerves carry messages from your brain to your muscles, telling your muscles what to do. These are *motor nerves.*

How Does Your Brain Work?

Your brain is the "control center" of your body. It is a soft organ that fills most of the space inside your skull. It is not much larger than a grapefruit. Your brain has three main parts. Look for these parts in the picture of the brain.

Your brain is always receiving messages. It sorts the messages and figures out what they mean. It lets you decide what you should do. Then it sends messages to the rest of your body. The messages from your brain make your body act.

■ *The brain works very quickly to let the batter decide to swing or not swing at the ball.*

cerebrum (suh REE bruhm), the largest part of the brain; where most of your thinking takes place.

cerebellum (sehr uh BEHL uhm), the part of the brain that makes your muscles work together; controls most movements that you do without thinking.

The largest part of your brain is your **cerebrum.** This is where most of your thinking takes place. Your cerebrum solves problems, forms emotions (feelings), makes decisions, and controls how you learn. It receives and answers messages from your senses.

Your **cerebellum** is the part of your brain that makes your muscles work together. It helps you move and keep your balance. Your cerebellum directs most of your moving without your thinking about it.

■ *All the parts of the brain work together so that the body can function.*

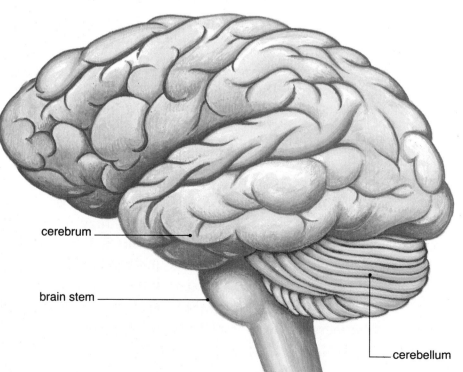

cerebrum

brain stem

cerebellum

The lowest part of your brain is the brain stem. Messages moving between your brain and the rest of your body pass through the brain stem. One part of the brain stem is the *medulla oblongata*. It takes care of critical life functions. These are breathing, maintaining heartbeat, swallowing, and controlling blood vessel size. Your whole brain stem helps control your inner organs. For example, it helps control how fast you breathe, even when you are not thinking about your breathing.

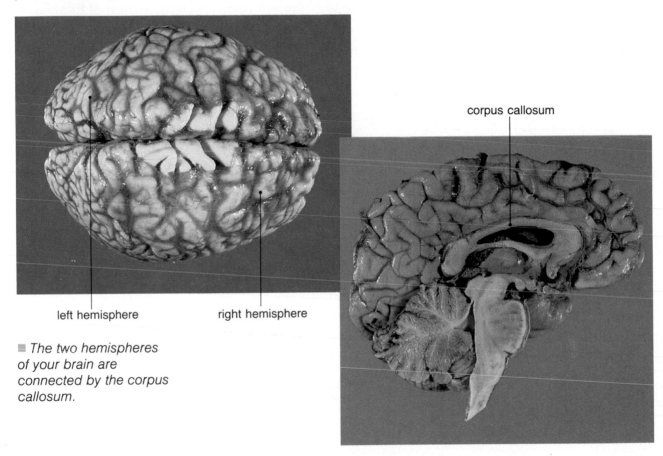

corpus callosum

left hemisphere   right hemisphere

■ *The two hemispheres of your brain are connected by the corpus callosum.*

The cerebrum is divided into two halves, or **hemispheres.** Scientists believe that the right and left halves of the brain are responsible for different tasks. The two halves of the cerebrum are connected by a band of nerve tissue that runs from front to back. This band is called the *corpus callosum*. Because of this connection, the two halves of the brain are able to exchange nerve messages. In this way, the two hemispheres work together. Your whole brain works to help you do all your daily tasks.

hemispheres (HEHM uh sfihrz), two halves of a sphere, or ball-shaped object, such as the brain.

REAL-LIFE
SKILL

Testing Reflexes

Have a partner sit with his or her legs dangling freely. Then strike the tendon just below the kneecap with the edge of your hand or a thin book. Determine how fast the knee jerks up for both your partner and you.

Researchers have found that one side of the brain sometimes takes the lead in certain tasks. For example, certain areas in the right hemisphere take care of dealing with how you see and your imagination. This hemisphere is working when you are enjoying art, music, or other forms of beauty. When you are setting the table, the right hemisphere is working. This is because you are thinking about the patterns in the placements of the forks, knives, spoons, plates, and glasses.

Certain areas in the left hemisphere take care of dealing with words and facts. This hemisphere takes the lead when you are using numbers and signs. When you are figuring out math problems, the left hemisphere is working.

Many people say artists are "right-brained" and math teachers are "left-brained." These terms are often used, but they are not correct. One side of the brain may lead in certain tasks. However, both sides always work together to produce our thoughts, decisions, and behaviors.

What Is the Job of Your Spinal Cord?

Your spinal cord starts at the base of your brain. It is the main path for messages entering and leaving your brain. Your spinal cord is soft and is protected by your "backbone," or spine. Your spine is a column of bones in the middle of your back that surrounds your spinal cord and protects it from damage.

Your spinal cord connects your brain to most of your nerves. The nerves bring their messages to your spinal cord. The messages then move through your spinal cord to your brain.

Sometimes your body makes very sudden actions that you do not even think about. These actions are controlled by your spinal cord. If you touched a hot iron by mistake, you would quickly pull your hand away before you even had time to think about it. This kind of fast action that you do without thinking is a *reflex*. Your spinal cord works many of your body's reflexes without your brain being directly involved.

Your nervous system makes you able to do everything you do. It controls all your other body systems. It lets you know what is happening around you. Your nervous system works to keep you alive and able to experience your world.

 **REVIEW SECTION 7**

REMEMBER?

1. What does your nervous system do?
2. How are sensory and motor nerves different?
3. What are the jobs of the cerebrum?
4. How are the hemispheres of your brain able to exchange nerve messages?

THINK!

5. How does your brain stem help you while you are sleeping?
6. How can you protect your nervous system so it can work as well as possible?

Thinking About Your Health

Caring for Your Body Systems

Answer the following questions to learn how proper health habits are related to your wellness and your body systems.

- What body systems are affected by the air you breathe? How might breathing smoky, dusty air affect these systems?

- What body systems are affected by the kind of food you eat? How might eating a balanced diet affect these systems?

- What body systems are affected by regular exercise, rest, and sleep? How do these habits contribute to your appearance and wellness?

An Interview with a Radiologic Technologist

> Ellen Leiter takes X rays of people to help physicians treat patients. She is a radiologic technologist in Orlando, Florida.

What is a radiologic technologist?

If you have ever had an X ray, it was likely taken by a radiologic technologist, or RT. Some people may call an RT an *X-ray technician* because at one time the only tool of an RT was an X-ray machine. Today, many RTs use X-ray machines, computers, and other equipment to look inside people.

Why would anyone want to look inside another person's body?

A physician often needs to see what is happening to the heart, bones, lungs, or other organs of a person who is ill or injured. Being able to see what is happening inside the body can help a physician decide on the best way to treat the person. Before there were X-ray machines, physicians had to guess or operate on a person to learn about the inside of the person's body. With the help of an RT, a physician today can "see" whether a person's broken bone is healing or whether something is blocking a person's digestive system.

How does an RT see inside the body?

Most X rays are snapshots of the inside of the body. Another kind of X ray shows movement inside the body. A physician may want to use this kind of X ray to see how well a person digests food. To take this kind of X ray, an RT has the person drink a certain liquid. As the person drinks, a camera films the drink moving through the person's body. There is another kind of X ray that is set up with a computer. It is called a *CAT scan*. With it a physician can see inside a person's body layer by layer, from front to back or from head to foot.

How does someone become an RT?

One way to become an RT is to study radiologic technology for two years in college. Another way is to study and work in a program at a hospital. The hospital program usually takes two years. It allows the student to be with patients more than the college program

■ Ms. Leiter uses computers in her work.

does. Students trained in the hospital program work with patients only a few weeks after starting their training.

Does an RT have to know a lot about photography?

An RT needs to know how to work the cameras. In the past, an X-ray technician needed to know how to process the film, using chemicals. The processing took longer then because the film came out wet and had to be dried. Today, RTs use an automatic machine to develop X rays. The RT just slides the film on a shelf. The X ray comes out dry in only ninety seconds.

What do you like about being an RT?

I like the variety of the work. No two days are the same. My work can be very interesting. One time I X-rayed a boy who had been bitten by an alligator. The X ray showed that the alligator had left a tooth in the boy's leg. Of course, the tooth was removed.

What is the most dangerous part of your job?

I have to protect myself and my patients from radiation. Too much radiation can be dangerous. A person cannot feel radiation, so RTs wear badges that measure the amount of radiation. Each RT gets a new badge each month. The old badge is sent to a laboratory that reports the amount of radiation. Careful records are kept. Also,

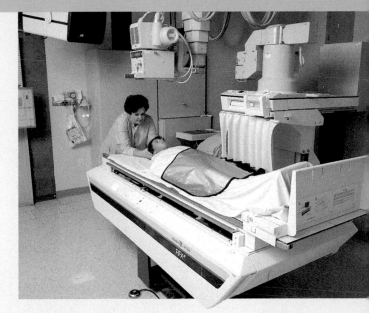

■ *An X ray is used to see inside a person's body.*

when taking some kinds of X rays, RTs wear lead aprons to protect themselves.

How is the work of the RT changing?

There is new technology all the time. Each machine seems so amazing when it first comes out. Then along comes another machine that is even more fantastic. The latest machines use magnetic forces in the body to make images. These new machines are better than the CAT scan and do not use radiation.

Learn more about people who use machines to study the inside of the human body. Interview a radiologic technologist. Or write for information to the American Society of Radiologic Technologists, 15000 Central Avenue, S.E., Albuquerque, NM 87123.

Main Ideas

- Your body is made up of many parts. Each part works to keep you healthy.
- Your circulatory system carries nutrients and oxygen to your cells and carries away the cells' wastes.
- Your respiratory system brings in oxygen and discharges carbon dioxide from your body.
- Your digestive system breaks down food so that your cells can use it.
- Your excretory system collects wastes and moves them out of your body.
- Your skeletal system protects parts of your body, gives your body its basic size and shape, and helps you move.
- Your muscular system works with your skeletal system to help you move and to protect your internal organs.
- Your nervous system carries messages through your body.

Key Words

Write the numbers 1 to 14 in your health notebook or on a separate sheet of paper. After each number, copy the sentence and fill in the missing term. Page numbers in ( ) tell you where to look in the chapter if you need help.

nucleus (28)	alveoli (41)
tissue (29)	saliva (43)
plasma (32)	peristalsis (45)
hemoglobin (33)	kidneys (48)
carbon dioxide (33)	urine (48)
platelets (34)	skeleton (52)
bronchial tubes (39)	cerebrum (60)

1. The gas ___?___ is one waste made by your cells.

2. Most of your blood is a clear, light-yellow liquid called ___?___ .

3. The ___?___ in your blood help it clot when you have a cut.

4. The small center of a cell is the ___?___ .

5. Most of the extra water and cell wastes are removed from your blood by the ___?___ .

6. A wavelike squeezing action called ___?___ moves food through the digestive system.

7. The part of your brain where most of your thinking takes place is the ___?___ .

8. Groups of cells that are alike and work together to do the same job form ___?___ .

9. A substance in your red blood cells that picks up oxygen in the lungs is ___?___ .

10. The trachea divides into two branches called ___?___ .

11. A liquid found in the mouth that helps break down food is called ___?___ .

12. A liquid waste filtered out of the blood by the kidneys is ___?___ .

13. The framework of connected bones inside the body is the ___?___ .

14. Your lungs contain many small air sacs called ___?___ .

Write the numbers 15 to 32 on your paper. After each number, write a sentence that defines the term. Page numbers in ( ) tell you where to look in the chapter if you need help.

15. cell membrane (28)
16. cytoplasm (29)
17. organ (29)
18. body system (30)
19. nutrients (30)
20. oxygen (30)
21. antibodies (33)
22. atrium (35)
23. ventricle (35)
24. lymph (38)
25. trachea (39)
26. pancreas (45)
27. bile (46)
28. gallbladder (46)
29. cartilage (54)
30. neurons (59)
31. cerebellum (60)
32. hemispheres (61)

Remembering What You Learned

Page numbers in ( ) tell you where to look in the chapter if you need help.

1. Name five kinds of tissues. (29)

2. What are the three main parts of the circulatory system? (32)

3. What do white blood cells do? (33–34)

4. What are three kinds of blood vessels? (36)

5. What body parts help clean the air as it travels to your lungs? (41–42)

6. Through what parts of the body does food travel as it is digested? (43–46)

7. What happens to the wastes in sweat on the surface of the skin? (50)

8. What are three areas of your body that have movable joints? (54)

9. What kind of nerve lets you know what is happening around you? (59)

10. For what kinds of skills is the right side of your brain specialized? The left side? (61–62)

Thinking About What You Learned

1. Why do you need to be responsible for taking care of your body systems?

2. How is your heart important to your respiratory and muscular systems?

3. How might your respiratory system be affected by cigarette smoke?

4. Why is peristalsis important?

5. How is the excretory system important to the circulatory system?

Writing About What You Learned

Select two body systems that affect each other. Describe the job of each system and how the job helps or influences the other system. For example, the nervous and muscular systems are both needed for the body to move.

Applying What You Learned

ART

Draw a picture of the heart, showing its four chambers and the major blood vessels that are connected to each chamber. Use arrows to show the direction of the blood through the heart.

Modified True or False

Write the numbers 1 to 15 in your health notebook or on a separate sheet of paper. After each number, write *true* or *false* to describe the sentence. If the sentence is false, also write a term that replaces the underlined term and makes the sentence true.

1. Your blood is red due to the presence of <u>hemoglobin</u> in red blood cells.

2. <u>Veins</u> carry blood away from your heart.

3. The exchange of oxygen and carbon dioxide is called <u>respiration</u>.

4. Water and everything else the cell needs is let in by the <u>cytoplasm</u>.

5. <u>Oxygen</u> is a waste made by cells.

6. <u>Platelets</u> are tiny parts of cells in the blood that help your blood to clot.

7. An upper chamber of the heart is called an <u>atrium</u>.

8. The lymphatic system is part of the <u>respiratory</u> system.

9. Air moves into your lungs through the <u>bronchial tubes</u>.

10. <u>Saliva</u> is a liquid that starts to break down food.

11. Most of the work of digestion takes place in the <u>pancreas</u>.

12. Cell wastes and extra water are removed from the blood by the <u>kidneys</u>.

13. Sweat leaves the body through <u>pores</u>.

14. <u>Tendons</u> keep your bones from grinding against each other.

15. Muscles can only <u>push</u>.

Short Answer

Write the numbers 16 to 23 on your paper. Write a complete sentence to answer each question.

16. What does the cell nucleus do?

17. Why must the blood pass through the lungs before circulating through the rest of the body?

18. What might happen to your lungs if you had no cilia?

19. What digestive fluid is made by the liver?

20. What part of the digestive system removes water from food?

21. What are three ways waste materials are removed from the body?

22. What is a body system?

23. How do white blood cells defend the body?

Essay

Write the numbers 24 and 25 on your paper. Write paragraphs with complete sentences to answer each question.

24. Explain how an organ can be part of more than one body system.

25. Summarize the layers of defense and protection provided by the human body.

Projects to Do

1. Touch the tip of your nose or the outside of your ear. The tissue you feel under the skin is cartilage. Write four sentences describing the feel of cartilage. Is it harder or softer than bone? Is it stiff, or can it bend? Write your description as though it were going to be read by someone who does not know what cartilage is.

2. Test your knee-jerk reflex. (It is also called the patellar tendon reflex.) Sit comfortably on a high chair or another place so that your legs hang loosely above the floor. Tap one leg just below the kneecap with the side of your hand, using the side where your little finger is. If you hit the spot that makes the reflex act, the muscles on top of your thigh will suddenly contract. Your lower leg will kick up. This reflex is one of many tendon reflexes in your body.

Information to Find

1. Ask your school nurse to teach the class how a person's blood pressure is measured. What tools are needed to measure blood pressure? What do the numbers mean? What are normal blood pressure readings for people your age and weight?

2. Some young people develop a curve in their spines at about age 11. For a few young people, special treatment is needed. The curve has no known cause. One S-shaped curve is called *scoliosis*. Many schools offer or require spinal screening. Ask your school nurse for more information about this condition. Ask if screening is done at your school.

■ *A knee-jerk reflex tells how well your nervous system is working.*

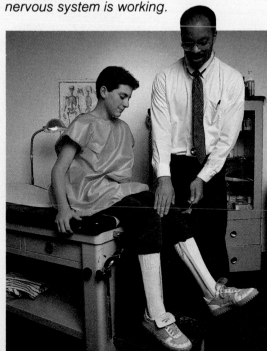

Books to Read

Here are some books you can look for in your school library or the public library to find more information about how your body systems work.

Donner, Carol. *The Magic Anatomy Book*. W. H. Freeman.

Facklam, Margery, and Howard Facklam. *The Brain: Magnificent Mind Machine*. Harcourt Brace Jovanovich.

Ward, Brian. *Skeleton and Movement*. Franklin Watts.

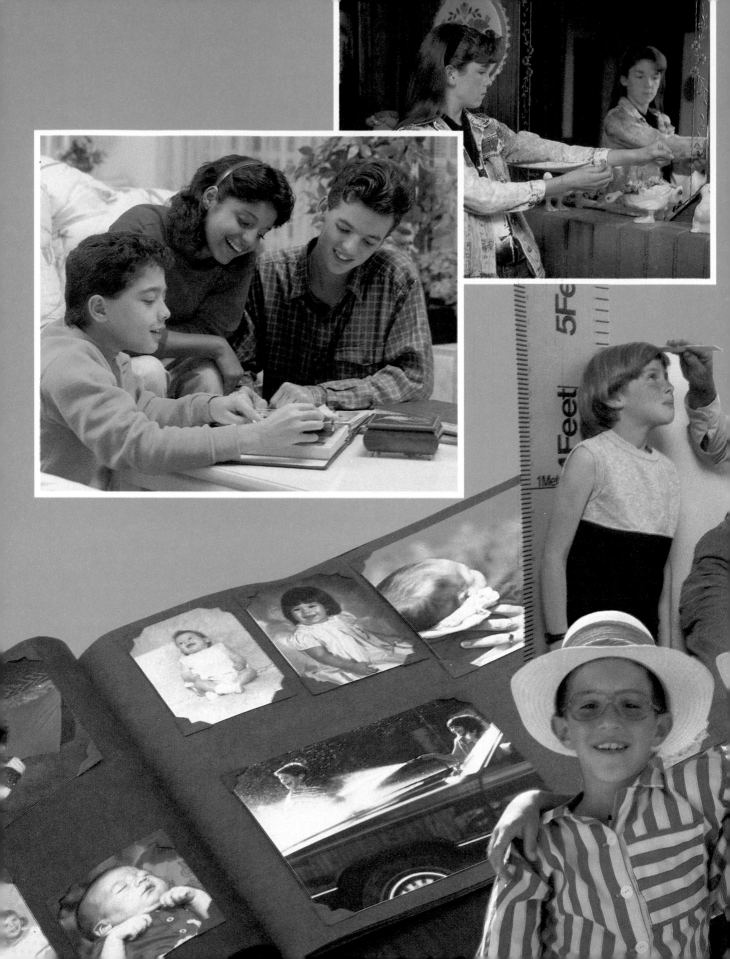

3

YOUR BODY GROWS AND CHANGES

During the next few years, your body will grow faster than before and will change in many ways. Some of the changes may make you feel uncomfortable about your body for a while. You may feel that you are becoming a completely different person. These body changes and feelings are normal.

As you enter these years of change, you probably have many questions about how your body grows. You may wonder if you are growing the way you should. What controls the way your body is changing? How fast will your body change? Finding answers to questions like these will help you understand the changes you are experiencing.

GETTING READY TO LEARN

Key Questions

- Why is it important to learn how your body grows?
- Why is it important to try to understand your feelings about how your body grows?
- What can you do to make responsible choices that will help your body grow as it should?

Main Chapter Sections

1 How Your Body Grows
2 How Your Body Changes
3 Heredity Affects Your Body
4 Being Aware of Your Changing Body

1 How Your Body Grows

Billy, his older brother Milt, and his older sister Nicki were looking at their family photograph album. Nicki laughed about a picture of herself taken at age 11. She remembered that she felt awkward because she was taller than most of the boys in her class. She said it was not until the eighth grade that the boys finally were as tall as she.

Nicki had noticed that people grow at different rates. People grow faster at some times during their lives than at others. Even when people belong to the same family, they grow at different rates. But certain facts about growth are the same for everyone. You and other people follow the same basic growth pattern. You grow in size because your body's cells increase in number.

When Does Growth Begin?

You began growing inside your mother's body as one tiny fertilized cell. A **fertilized cell** is formed by the combination of two reproductive cells, one from a male and one from a female.

fertilized cell (FUR tuhl yzd • SEHL), a cell formed by the combination of two reproductive cells, one from a male and one from a female.

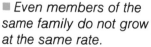

■ *Even members of the same family do not grow at the same rate.*

Males and females produce different kinds of reproductive cells. Male reproductive cells are called **sperm cells.** Sperm cells are so tiny that 500 of them placed end to end would measure only about 1 inch (2.5 centimeters). A female reproductive cell is called an egg cell, or **ovum.** An ovum is the largest of all human cells. The ovum is about the size of the period at the end of this sentence.

When a sperm cell and an ovum join, they form a single fertilized cell. This fertilized cell then divides and makes new cells. Cell division continues quickly. After about two weeks, the single fertilized egg cell has become more than 1 million cells.

sperm cells (SPURM · SEHLZ), male reproductive cells.

ovum (OH vuhm), a female reproductive cell; also called an egg cell.

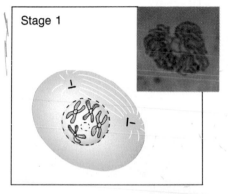

Stage 1

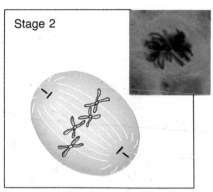

Stage 2

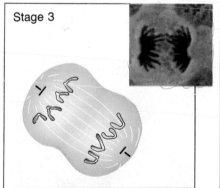

Stage 3

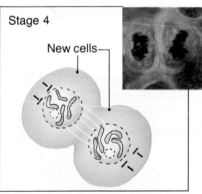

Stage 4

New cells

■ *Cell division takes place in four stages. Stage 1: The material within the nucleus makes an exact copy of itself. Stage 2: The nucleus disappears, and the material lines up in the middle of the cell. Stage 3: The material separates, half going to each side of the cell. Stage 4: The cell divides, and a nucleus forms in each of the new cells.*

In the first two months after a sperm cell and an ovum join, cells start to form specific layers that become tissues. These cells continue to grow and form a baby. After about nine months, the baby is fully formed, and it is born. Most newborn babies weigh between 5 and 10 pounds (between 2.3 and 4.5 kilograms). At birth a baby is about 3 million times bigger than the fertilized cell that began growing nine months earlier.

When Does Growth Speed Up?

Males and females have different patterns of growth. Until just before the teenage years, most males are taller than most females. But between the ages of 9 and 13, females start growing very fast. This rapid growth is called the **growth spurt.** It usually continues for about three years. From this time until about the mid-teens, most females are taller than most males of the same age.

Between the ages of 11 and 15, males begin their growth spurt. Some males grow as much as 4 inches (10 centimeters) in one year. By about the age of 15, most males are once again taller than most females.

Not everyone fits this pattern exactly. Some people start their growth spurt early. Others start late. Some people grow more than others. For these reasons, your classmates may be of many different heights and weights.

growth spurt, rapid growth.

■ All these students are the same age and in the same grade. However, they are not all growing at the same rate.

As you go through your own growth spurt, different parts of your body may grow at different rates. For example, your hands and feet may reach full size before the rest of your body does. Because of this, you may feel uncomfortable about your appearance. You may also feel clumsy sometimes. You may have times when you feel anxious or uncertain about how you will look when you are fully grown.

When Does Growth Slow Down?

Your growth slows down after your growth spurt. Each part of your body stops growing when it reaches its full, adult size.

In time you will stop growing taller. Females usually stop growing taller by about age 16. Males usually stop growing taller by about age 18.

After you reach your full, adult height, you will not grow any taller. But you may continue to grow in muscle size or in weight. Some cells in your body will continue to divide and make new cells. These new cells will replace dead or worn-out cells. Cells in your skin, muscles, blood, and some other body parts continue to divide all your life.

STOP **REVIEW SECTION 1**

REMEMBER?

1. When does a body start growing?
2. When do most males usually begin their growth spurt? Most females?
3. Why do some cells continue to divide after a person has reached full, adult height?

THINK!

4. How might a rapid growth spurt affect a growing person's emotions?
5. Why do you sometimes have strong opinions or feelings about some parts of your body, such as your skin, but not others, such as your feet?

76

2 How Your Body Changes

Your body has a system that directs activities such as growth and development. This system is called the **endocrine system.** Your endocrine system is made up of organs called **endocrine glands.** These glands are located in several parts of the body. They help control the way your body works. They also produce changes in your body.

Endocrine glands make hormones. **Hormones** are chemical messengers that help control some of your body's activities by changing the way your cells work. Hormones are carried by your blood from the endocrine glands to all your cells. Different endocrine glands in your body make different hormones.

KEY WORDS

endocrine system
endocrine glands
hormones
pituitary gland
thyroid gland
adrenal glands
gonads
puberty

endocrine system (EHN duh kruhn • SIHS tuhm), the body system that directs certain activities, such as growth and development.

endocrine glands (EHN duh kruhn • GLANDZ), organs that make up the endocrine system.

hormones (HAWR mohnz), chemical messengers that help control some of your body's activities by changing the way the cells work.

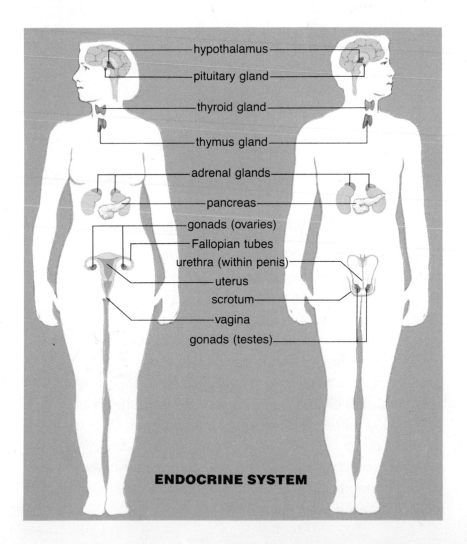

- hypothalamus
- pituitary gland
- thyroid gland
- thymus gland
- adrenal glands
- pancreas
- gonads (ovaries)
- Fallopian tubes
- urethra (within penis)
- uterus
- scrotum
- vagina
- gonads (testes)

ENDOCRINE SYSTEM

■ *Hormones from the endocrine system control many of the body's functions.*

77

Why Is the Pituitary Gland Important?

Perhaps the most important gland in the endocrine system is the **pituitary gland.** It is located at the base of the brain and is about the size of a kidney bean. The pituitary gland makes several hormones. One of these is *growth hormone.* Growth hormone makes your body grow. For example, the amount of growth hormone from your pituitary gland affects how tall you will grow. If your pituitary gland makes a large amount of growth hormone, your body will grow tall. If it makes a small amount, your body will be short.

During your growth spurt, the pituitary gland makes more growth hormone than usual. It stops making this hormone when you reach your adult height.

Which Endocrine Glands Does the Pituitary Gland Control?

The pituitary gland makes hormones other than growth hormone. Some of these hormones control other endocrine glands. They control the thyroid gland, the adrenal glands, and the gonads.

Shaped like a butterfly, the **thyroid gland** is located in the neck. This gland controls how fast your cells turn nutrients into energy. It also controls how fast nutrients are used for building and repairing cells.

The **adrenal glands** lie on top of the kidneys. These glands are shaped like triangles. The adrenal glands make many different kinds of hormones that control how the body uses nutrients. One adrenal hormone is called *epinephrine*. Epinephrine, also called adrenaline, helps make the body more alert and ready to react when a person is frightened or is angry. Epinephrine gives the body a short burst of extra energy and strength.

thyroid gland (THY royd • GLAND), the gland that controls how fast your cells turn nutrients into energy; also controls how fast nutrients are used for building and repairing cells.

adrenal glands (uh DREEN uhl • GLANDZ), glands that make many different kinds of hormones that control how the body uses nutrients.

■ *Being nervous before a big race may cause the adrenal glands to release adrenaline.*

The **gonads** are the reproductive organs. They produce the reproductive cells. Both females and males have gonads. In females, the gonads are called *ovaries*. Ovaries produce egg cells. In males, the gonads are called *testes*. Testes produce sperm cells.

When a girl or a boy reaches a certain age, hormones from the pituitary gland cause the gonads to begin growing and changing. As this happens, the gonads start making their own hormones. The time of life when the gonads start making their own hormones is called **puberty.** The word *puberty* comes from the Latin word for *adult*.

What Is Puberty?

Puberty is the time when a male or female begins developing reproductive cells. These cells make it possible for people to produce new human beings.

Girls usually begin puberty between the ages of 11 and 14. Boys usually begin puberty later than girls, between the ages of 13 and 16. During puberty, girls and boys start looking like adults.

When a girl begins puberty, changes happen inside her body. Her ovaries make a hormone called *estrogen*. Estrogen causes a girl's body to take on several adult features. For example, new hair begins to grow on different parts of her body. Hair already on her body may become darker and thicker. At the same time, the shape of her body begins to change. Fat tissue develops in places that define a female shape.

When a boy enters puberty, changes happen inside his body, too. His testes start producing sperm cells. The testes also make a hormone called *testosterone*. Testosterone has many effects. For example, it causes a boy's voice to change. The vocal cords become longer and the voice slowly deepens. It may "crack" sometimes when the boy talks. Another change during puberty is that new hair begins to grow on different parts of a boy's body. Some of this new hair is on the face. The shape of a boy's body also changes as he begins to look more like an adult male.

GROWTH PATTERNS OF BOYS AND GIRLS

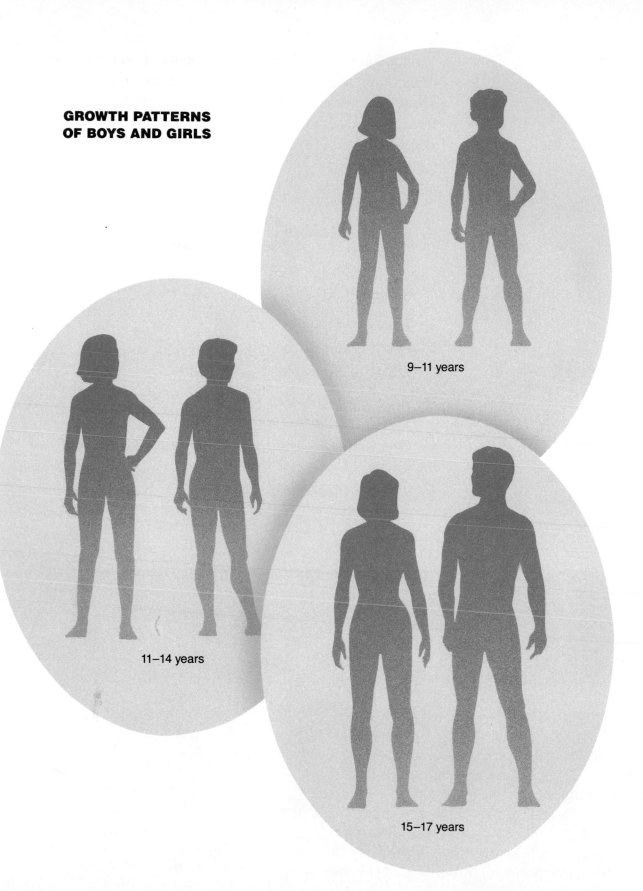

9–11 years

11–14 years

15–17 years

Although your body changes throughout your life, some of the most noticeable changes happen during puberty. These changes may sometimes make you feel that you have to get used to your body all over again. But this is normal.

REVIEW
SECTION 2

REMEMBER?

1. What do hormones do?
2. Which hormone controls your height?
3. What are the two kinds of gonads?

THINK!

4. Why is the bloodstream important to the endocrine system?
5. Why is it that people cannot control how tall or short they will be?

Making Wellness Choices

Karen realizes that her body is changing. She is feeling the effects of puberty. Karen knows that her body will go through many changes during puberty. But she still feels uneasy. Karen sees herself as a giant compared to most of the boys in her class. She even sees herself as different from many of the girls. Some of Karen's classmates tease her about being so tall. Karen does not feel good about herself. Her self-esteem is low.

? What could Karen do to help raise her self-esteem and feel good about herself again? Explain your wellness choice.

Heredity Affects Your Body

People's bodies grow and change at different rates and at different ages. People are of different heights, weights, sizes, and shapes. How you grow and change depends partly on the hormones your glands make. It also depends on what you eat and how much exercise and sleep you get.

The way your body grows is also influenced by heredity. **Heredity** is the passing of certain characteristics from parents to their children. These characteristics, called **inherited traits,** affect your appearance. You received inherited traits from your mother and father. Your parents, in turn, received their inherited traits from their mothers and fathers, your grandparents.

heredity (huh REHD uht ee), the passing of certain characteristics from parents to their children.

inherited traits (in HEHR uh tehd • TRAYTS), characteristics received from parents; they affect the way you look and act.

■ *In some families, members look alike because of inherited physical traits. Talents may also be inherited.*

Your adult height is one of the inherited traits you get from your parents. If your parents are tall, you are likely to grow tall, too. You will probably be short if your parents are short. Other inherited traits include eye color, hair color, skin color, and foot size.

How Are Cells Related to Heredity?

The nucleus in each cell in your body contains codes for all of your inherited traits. By means of chemicals, the codes direct your body's cells to do certain things or grow in certain ways. The codes are on long strands of matter called **chromosomes.** Chromosomes contain genes. **Genes** are tiny bits of information that influence heredity. Usually, one gene carries all the codes for a specific trait. But sometimes two or three genes together carry the codes for one inherited trait.

Almost every cell in a person's body has 23 pairs of chromosomes, or 46 chromosomes in all. The exceptions are the reproductive cells made by a person's gonads. A sperm cell and an ovum each have only 23 chromosomes. Instead of having a pair of each kind of chromosome, each of these cells has only one of each kind of chromosome.

chromosomes (KROH muh sohmz), long strands of matter located in cell nuclei; contain codes for all your inherited traits.

genes (JEENZ), tiny bits of information on chromosomes; influence heredity.

■ *The genes that influence heredity are carried on strands of matter called chromosomes.*

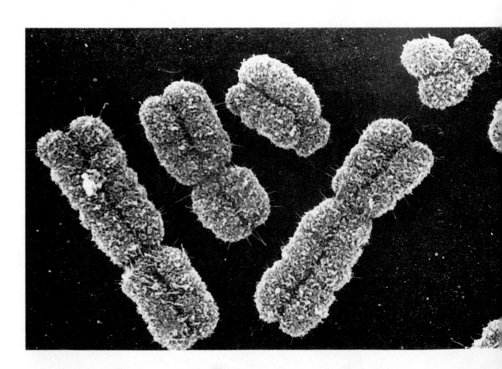

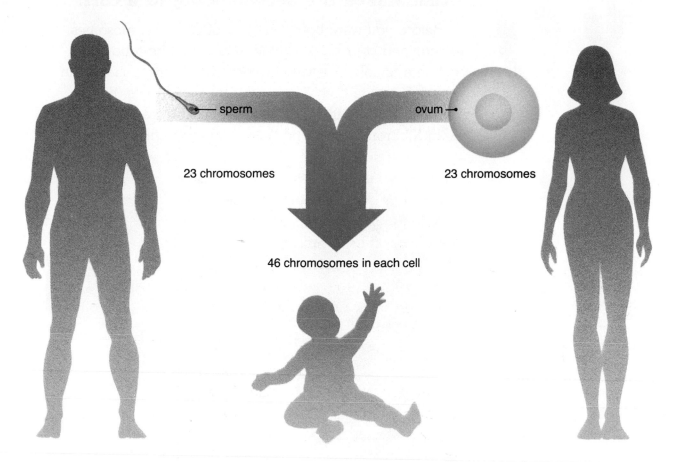

sperm

ovum

23 chromosomes

23 chromosomes

46 chromosomes in each cell

■ *A combination of the chromosomes from each parent makes an individual that is unique.*

When a sperm and an ovum join, they make one complete cell. That cell has 23 pairs of chromosomes, or 46 chromosomes in all. Of these 46 chromosomes, 23 are from the sperm cell, and the other 23 are from the ovum. The combination has chromosomes from the mother and the father. But it is a completely new combination that never existed before. It will make a unique individual.

The single cell made by the sperm cell and ovum divides and redivides many times. Eventually the single cell has grown and divided into millions of cells. Each of the person's cells has the same 46 chromosomes as the single cell that was made when the sperm cell and ovum joined.

As the body cells continue to divide, the chromosomes in each cell make exact copies of themselves. Each new cell gets an identical set of chromosomes. That is how codes for your inherited traits are passed on to all your cells.

What Makes You Become a Boy or a Girl?

Before you were born, one pair of your chromosomes determined your sex—whether you would be a boy or a girl. In a female, the two chromosomes of this pair are the same. They are both *X chromosomes*. In a male, the chromosomes of this pair are different from each other. One is an X chromosome, and the other is a *Y chromosome*.

■ *A person's sex is determined by a single pair of chromosomes. A male has an X and a Y chromosome, top. A female has two X chromosomes in the pair, bottom.*

■ *This baby girl received an X chromosome from both her mother and her father.*

Each sperm cell or ovum carries one chromosome for this particular pair. An ovum always carries an X chromosome. A sperm cell may carry either an X chromosome or a Y chromosome. If the sperm cell that joins with an ovum is carrying an X chromosome, the person will be a girl. If the sperm cell is carrying a Y chromosome, the person will be a boy.

What Are Dominant and Recessive Genes?

Half of a child's chromosomes come from the mother's ovum. The other half come from the father's sperm cell. When the ovum and sperm cell join, the chromosomes form new pairs. These new pairs of chromosomes result in new pairs of genes. Each pair of genes carries the codes, or directions, for a trait.

When the genes for a single trait carry different codes, one member of the pair may be stronger than the other. The stronger gene is **dominant.** The codes carried on the dominant gene keep the codes on the other gene from being carried out. The weaker gene is **recessive.** The codes on the recessive gene are "hidden" by the codes on the dominant gene. The codes on recessive genes are carried out only when two recessive genes are paired together.

The inherited trait for blue eyes, for example, is produced by a pair of recessive genes. Any other eye color is caused by dominant genes. People with blue eyes have received a recessive gene for blue eye color from each parent. People with brown eyes have received either one or two dominant genes for brown eye color from their parents.

Two brown-eyed parents can have a blue-eyed child only if both parents have the recessive gene for blue eye color. The diagram shows some of the possible combinations of genes for eye color.

dominant (DAHM uh nuhnt), describes the stronger gene of a pair; this gene's codes keep codes on the recessive gene from being carried out.

recessive (rih SEHS ihv), describes the weaker gene of the pair; its codes are "hidden" by the codes on the dominant gene.

■ *A recessive trait shows only when a person receives a recessive gene from both parents.*

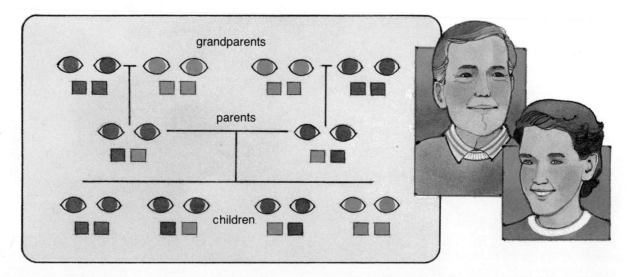

87

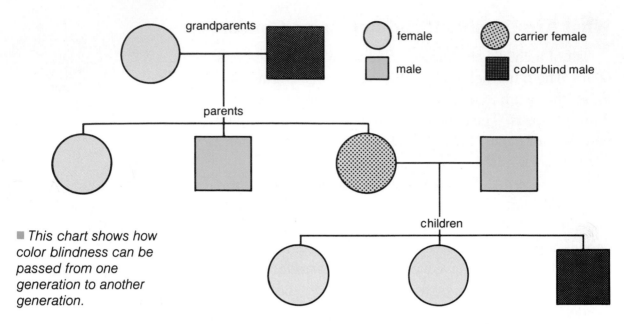

grandparents

female

carrier female

male

colorblind male

parents

children

■ *This chart shows how color blindness can be passed from one generation to another generation.*

For many of your inherited traits, neither gene of the pair is dominant. Some of your traits are a mixture of both your parents' traits.

Some inherited traits are called *sex-linked traits.* The genes for these traits are carried by the chromosomes that determine a person's sex. Color blindness is a sex-linked trait. A common kind of color blindness is difficulty in telling red from green. Usually only the males in a family are color-blind. Females who carry the gene for color blindness are often not color-blind themselves. Females who carry the gene may pass it to their children.

■ *Color blindness can be tested. If you can see the number 96, left, and the number 5, right, you are not color-blind.*

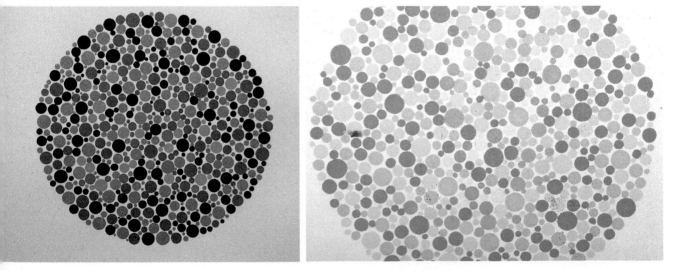

What Makes You Who You Are?

Your heredity is part of what makes you an individual. Heredity has a lot to do with how you look. It helps determine your personality—the ways you think, feel, and act. But not all of your traits are inherited. Many of them are ones that you develop. Who you are also depends on your life-style, or how you live. You form your life-style by what you learn from your parents, friends, teachers, and the world around you. Who you are depends on not just your heredity but also on the many choices you make about your life.

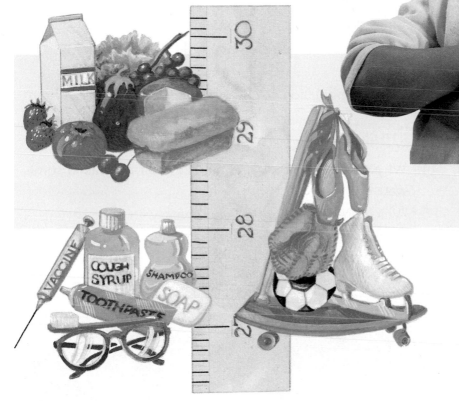

■ *Heredity only partly determines who you are. Many of your traits result from your environment.*

The way your body grows and changes also depends on more than your heredity. Your heredity determines your basic body build. Your environment—your family and the world around you—and your health habits affect how your body actually grows. Eating healthful foods, exercising regularly, getting enough sleep, avoiding harmful activities, and protecting yourself from illness are some ways in which you can help your body grow the best way it can.

The kinds of physical changes experienced in growth and puberty are much the same for one person as for another. The timetables are not the same, however. No two people grow in exactly the same way. The differences in how *you* grow and change are part of what makes you a special person.

REVIEW SECTION 3

REMEMBER?

1. What do chromosomes contain?
2. What two kinds of cells have only 23 chromosomes each?
3. What combination of chromosomes will result in a boy?

THINK!

4. Why do children look and act like their parents in some ways?
5. Which characteristics that you share with your parents result from heredity, and which result from making the same choices as your parents?

Thinking About Your Health

Do You Understand How Your Growth Is Affected by Heredity?

The growth of your body is influenced in many ways by your heredity. Characteristics, or traits, are passed from parents to their children. Make a list of your traits. These can be physical traits (eye or hair color) or sex-linked traits (gender or color blindness). From that list, see if you can identify the same inherited traits in other members of your family.

Health Close-up

Separated Identical Twins

Scientists are studying identical twins to find out how heredity and environment affect their growth and development.

Identical twins are born from a single fertilized egg that has split into two separate fertilized cells. Because identical twins come from a single fertilized egg, they have exactly the same genes.

Identical twins share the same inherited traits at birth. When they grow up in the same surroundings, they often act in similar ways. But scientists have found amazing likenesses between some pairs of twins who were separated shortly after birth. Here are some examples:

- One pair of separated twin brothers first met at age 39 after being separated at birth. They discovered they both drove the same kind of car and enjoyed woodworking. One had named his son James Alan; the other had named his son James Allan.

- Another pair of separated twins stand the same way and cross their arms and legs identically. They have the same interests and do the same kind of work. Both of these twins have wives named Betty!

Similar studies show that the health, physical development, and personalities of separated identical twins are often very similar. These studies are helping scientists learn more about how heredity and environment work together in making people the way they are.

Thinking Beyond

1. Why are identical twins better for these kinds of studies than any other group would be?
2. Suppose scientists could prove that most personality traits are the result of either genes or upbringing. What effect might each conclusion have?

■ *Identical twins separated at birth share traits other than physical traits.*

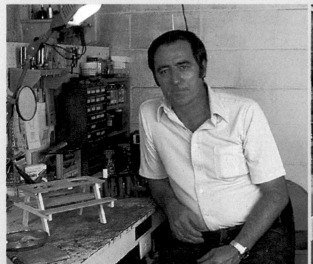

4 Being Aware of Your Changing Body

Think of all the ways you are changing. Some of these changes may be more confusing than others. Being aware of how you change during puberty can make the changes easier to handle.

Why Do Skin Problems Often Happen During Puberty?

When puberty begins, some glands in the skin enlarge very quickly. These glands include the oil glands that are connected to hair follicles. The oil glands, especially those on the face, begin producing much more oil than they did before puberty. The result is that the follicles get clogged with oil.

In many young people, blocked oil glands can become infected. This problem is called *acne*. Acne is common in both boys and girls. It is usually worse in boys because boys have a hormone that causes more oil to be made. Boys and girls who have acne need to wash their skin gently two or three times a day with soap and warm water. Shampooing hair when it feels oily also helps. Physicians also advise getting enough sleep and exercise. Some people find they have more pimples when they feel stressed or a few days after they eat certain foods.

■ *Some skin problems develop from blocked oil glands. Soap containing benzoyl peroxide helps control the microbes that cause acne.*

The most effective medicated soap that you can buy for acne contains benzoyl peroxide. It controls the growth of germs on the skin. If you have a severe problem with acne, you should see a special physician called a *dermatologist.* Dermatologists treat skin problems.

Sweat glands, especially those in the armpits, become more active during puberty, too. Hot weather, exercise, or excitement normally causes more perspiration. Perspiration by itself has no odor. Odor, however, can develop when perspiration reacts with bacteria on the skin. All people have a natural odor. Troublesome odor can be reduced by taking a bath or a shower every day and by using a deodorant.

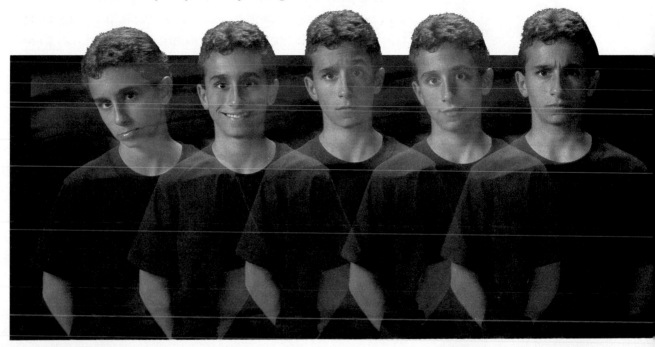

■ *Rapid mood changes are common during puberty.*

Are Mood Changes Common During Puberty?

During puberty you may have many different feelings about your body's changes. You may even have several different feelings at the same time. Sometimes you may think you cannot even control your moods or feelings. Mood swings are caused by physical changes. Endocrine glands give off hormones at an unsteady rate. Because of this unsteady rate, you can have a burst of energy and high spirits followed by a lack of energy and enthusiasm.

93

Your parents or other adults have already gone through puberty. They really do know what you are feeling. They can help you understand the changes you are experiencing. They want to teach you how to handle changes and discuss new ideas with you. They want to help you like yourself as you change. The changes you are going through now will help you learn to accept differences in other people as you become an adult.

Do Relationships Change During Puberty?

As you go through puberty, your relationships with your parents and friends go through many changes. Your parents and other family members are responsible for your well-being when you are young. You are dependent on them for many things, including food and shelter. Your parents are responsible for teaching you to take care of yourself.

There are probably times when you would like to be protected and cared for like a child. There are other times when you want to make your own decisions and be treated like an adult. During puberty you still need your family, but you may feel that you want to be more independent. You may go back and forth between wanting to be treated like a child and wanting to be treated like an adult. These feelings may be confusing to you. They may be confusing to your parents as well. As you grow and change, your parents do not always know exactly how you are feeling. They may treat you like a child when you want to be treated like an adult.

Talking to your parents during this time of change is very important. Tell them about the changes you are experiencing. Tell them that you want to be responsible for more of your own actions. But also listen to how they feel. You need to earn and keep their trust. Until you are an adult, a parent or guardian is legally responsible for your actions and safety. When you talk with them, you can share your feelings with them and find out how they feel. Talking usually makes it easier for all of you to get along. Talking also helps build a more adult relationship with a parent or guardian.

■ Describing your feelings in writing is one way to communicate with people who care about you.

94

Your relationships with your friends may change during puberty. You may begin to feel closer to people your own age who are going through similar changes. You may start to spend more and more time with one or two special friends. Having one or two special friends makes it easier to share experiences and feelings.

You may also join groups of people your own age who share common interests, have the same skills, or enjoy the same activities. Groups may meet at your school. You could decide to join a sports team or a youth group such as the Scouts. Being part of a group may help you feel more comfortable and secure. You can share ideas and experiences with other members of the group.

A possible problem is that you might become too much like the other group members. You may all try to dress alike, think alike, and act alike. If you try to be just like everyone else in the group, heavy pressures can be put on you. Be careful not to let the group become so important to you that you give up your right to make your own decisions.

REAL-LIFE
SKILL

Talking About Your Feelings

You do not need to talk about just your problems or bad feelings in order to feel better about yourself. Talk about your good feelings, too. Let your friends and family members know when you are excited and what makes you happy.

(STOP) **REVIEW SECTION 4**

REMEMBER?

1. What are three things you can do to take care of your skin?
2. What causes changes in your moods during puberty?
3. In what ways might your relationship with your family change during puberty?

THINK!

4. Imagine that you had an argument with your best friend. Describe two things that you could do to make yourself and your friend feel better.
5. Describe one advantage of belonging to a group of friends. Describe one disadvantage.

People in Health

An Interview with an Endocrinologist

> *Donald Brown understands how the endocrine system works with the other systems of the body. He is an endocrinologist in Los Angeles, California.*

What is an endocrinologist?

An endocrinologist is a physician who studies how the body grows and forms. Endocrinologists study the different hormones that the body's endocrine system makes. They try to understand problems that might happen when hormones are not made properly. They also look for ways to make the endocrine system work the way it should.

What are some problems of the endocrine system that might happen to young people?

There are several common health problems. One is diabetes. If a person has diabetes, the body is not making enough of a hormone called *insulin*. The pancreas makes insulin and releases it into the blood. Insulin helps the body process and store needed nutrients. If a person does not have enough insulin, body cells do not get the sugar they need. This can cause a person to faint.

In serious cases, it can cause a person to die. Endocrinologists can help people who have diabetes by having them take insulin by injection.

What is another problem of the endocrine system?

Another common problem among young people is thyroid disease. In this case, a person's body may not be making enough thyroid hormone. The thyroid hormone helps give the body energy. Without enough of this hormone, a person may feel very tired. Not having enough thyroid hormone in the body is like not having enough gasoline in an automobile engine. The engine starts to slow down. Soon it will stop completely.

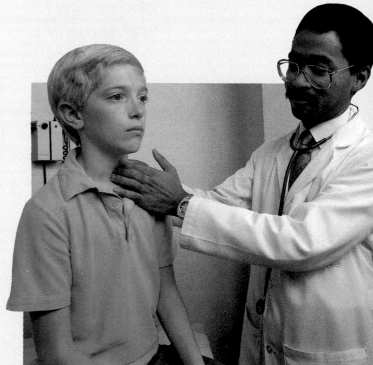

■ *Dr. Brown checks for possible thyroid problems by feeling the glands in a patient's neck.*

96

How does the endocrine system work with all the other body systems?

The endocrine system affects all the other body systems and helps them work as they should. The endocrine system has many glands. These glands make different hormones that go all through the body. Hormones reach every cell in the body and affect them in one way or another. For example, a thyroid problem can affect the circulatory system by making the heart beat faster.

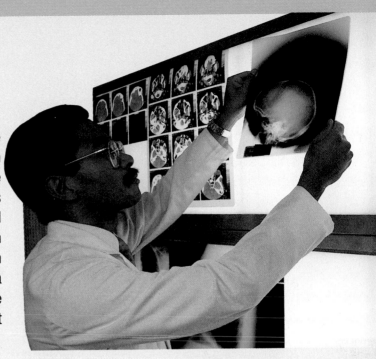

■ *X-ray photos are sometimes used to help locate endocrine problems.*

What can a young person do to maintain a healthy endocrine system?

Eating healthful foods and getting regular exercise are the main things to do. These things are important for weight control. When a person becomes overweight, the endocrine system is affected. When the system is affected, health problems such as diabetes might develop.

What do you like best about your work as an endocrinologist?

I like learning exactly how the body works. There is still so much that we do not know about the body. It interests me to see how the hormones interact with the different systems. There is so much more to learn. I want to help discover more of the ways in which the body works.

What education does a person need to become an endocrinologist?

A person must first finish high school. Then four years of college must be completed. After that a person must finish four years of medical school to become a physician. To become an endocrinologist, a person must then spend several more years studying this special area. Beyond all the education, however, the person needs to have an interest in how living things work.

Learn more about endocrinologists. Interview an endocrinologist. Or write for information to the Endocrine Society, 9650 Rockville Pike, Bethesda, MD 20814.

Main Ideas

- Your body grew from one fertilized cell that divided many times to form millions of new cells.
- Females usually begin their growth spurt sooner than males.
- Your growth slows down and each body part stops growing when it reaches adult size.
- During puberty you may have several different feelings at the same time about the physical changes that are happening to your body.
- People grow to be different heights, weights, sizes, and shapes, due partly to the hormones their glands make.
- The differences in how you grow and change are part of what makes you special.
- Who you are is determined only partly by your heredity. You are also affected by your environment and by the decisions you make.

Key Words

Write the numbers 1 to 9 in your health notebook or on a separate sheet of paper. After each number, copy the sentence and fill in the missing term. Page numbers in ( ) tell you where to look in the chapter if you need help.

sperm cells (73)	puberty (80)
endocrine glands (77)	inherited traits (83)
	genes (84)
hormones (77)	dominant (87)
adrenal glands (79)	recessive (87)

1. The ___?___ make up the endocrine system.
2. The weaker, hidden gene is ___?___ .
3. The stronger gene is ___?___ .
4. The time when your body changes and your gonads begin to produce hormones is ___?___ .
5. The male reproductive cells are called ___?___ .
6. The ___?___ control some of the body's activities by changing how cells work.
7. Tiny bits of information that are located on chromosomes and influence heredity are called ___?___ .
8. The many kinds of hormones that control how the body uses nutrients are produced by ___?___ .
9. Inherited characteristics, such as eye color and hair color, are called ___?___ .

Write the numbers 10 to 18 on your paper. After each number, write a sentence that defines the term. Page numbers in ( ) tell you where to look in the chapter if you need help.

10. fertilized cell (72)
11. ovum (73)
12. growth spurt (74)
13. endocrine system (77)
14. pituitary gland (78)
15. thyroid gland (79)
16. gonads (80)
17. heredity (83)
18. chromosomes (84)

Remembering What You Learned

Page numbers in ( ) tell you where to look in the chapter if you need help.

1. When does a fertilized cell begin to grow? (72–73)

2. Why are your classmates of many different heights and weights? (74)

3. How does the amount of growth hormone from your pituitary gland affect the way you grow? (78)

4. When do girls usually begin puberty? Boys? (80)

5. How does a boy's voice change when he enters puberty? (80)

6. What are inherited traits? (83)

7. What part of your cells contains codes for all your inherited traits? (84)

8. How many chromosomes do human cells other than sperm and egg cells contain? (84–85)

9. When a sperm joins with an ovum, what kind of chromosomes must the sperm be carrying for the child to be a girl? A boy? (86)

10. Describe how to take care of your skin to help control acne. (92–93)

11. Describe one emotional change that may happen during puberty and one way to handle it. (93–94)

12. Give one example of how a personal relationship may change during puberty. (94–95)

Thinking About What You Learned

1. Why are you not *exactly* like your mother or your father?

2. Is it possible for a person to become an artist if no one else in his or her family has any artistic talent? Explain your answer.

3. How does knowing about the changes that happen during puberty make it easier to deal with the changes as they take place?

4. The gene for red hair color is recessive to the genes for other hair colors. If both a mother and a father have red hair, what color hair could their children have? Explain your answer with words and a diagram.

Writing About What You Learned

Pretend you are a parent of a teenager going through puberty. Write a paragraph about how you might feel about your son or daughter growing up and becoming independent. You should include how your responsibilities to your son or daughter change as he or she grows and develops and how the son or daughter is responsible to the parent.

Applying What You Learned

SOCIAL STUDIES

Prepare a report about the social customs associated with puberty in other countries of the world. Present your report to the class.

Modified True or False

Write the numbers 1 to 15 in your health notebook or on a separate sheet of paper. After each number, write *true* or *false* to describe the sentence. If the sentence is false, also write a term that replaces the underlined term and makes the sentence true.

1. A <u>sperm</u> cell is formed by the combination of two reproductive cells.

2. The hormone <u>testosterone</u> causes a boy's voice to change.

3. <u>Glands</u> are tiny bits of information that influence heredity.

4. The sperm cell determines the <u>sex</u> of a fertilized cell.

5. Most girls have a <u>growth spurt</u> between the ages of 9 and 13.

6. Growth hormone is made by the <u>adrenal</u> glands.

7. In males, the gonads are called <u>testes</u>.

8. Another name for epinephrine is <u>adrenaline</u>.

9. <u>Puberty</u> is the passing of certain characteristics from parents to their children.

10. Two blue-eyed parents can have only a <u>brown-eyed</u> child.

11. Color blindness is a <u>sex-linked</u> trait.

12. Acne is usually worse in <u>girls</u>.

13. Because endocrine glands give off hormones at an unsteady rate, many teenagers have <u>mood swings</u>.

14. A female reproductive cell is an <u>ovum</u>.

15. The <u>pituitary</u> gland controls how fast your cells turn nutrients into energy.

Short Answer

Write the numbers 16 to 23 on your paper. Write a complete sentence to answer each question.

16. What physical changes occur in a female during puberty?

17. Why are hormones important to puberty?

18. How is the sex of a fertilized cell determined?

19. What factors make you who you are?

20. Why do young people get acne?

21. How do personal relationships change during puberty?

22. Why is the pituitary gland important?

23. How is puberty different in boys and girls?

Essay

Write the numbers 24 and 25 on your paper. Write paragraphs with complete sentences to answer each question.

24. How is your physical appearance affected by your parents' physical appearance?

25. Your friend Marcus complains that he feels ugly because he has acne. What could you say to Marcus that might help him feel better?

ACTIVITIES FOR HOME OR SCHOOL

Projects to Do

1. Write a paragraph or draw a picture that shows what you think you will look like as an adult. What physical traits might remain the same? What traits might be different?

■ *Think about how you might look as an adult.*

2. With your classmates, survey ten students about their responsibilities at home. Make charts of such items as different chores and home rules. Indicate the number of students who must do each chore and follow each rule. You may want to leave out students' names to protect privacy.

3. Make a list of simple ways people make changes in inherited traits. For example, some people with straight hair get permanent waves to make their hair curly. Some people wear contact lenses that change their eye color. Compare your list with those of your classmates. Why would people want to make these changes?

Information to Find

1. The pituitary gland makes growth hormone. Find out more about this gland and the other hormones that it makes.

2. Find out about DNA. What is the shape of DNA? Who discovered that shape? How does the shape help cells pass on directions for inherited traits? Books about heredity may help you find out about this substance.

3. Make a list of ten things parents do for their children to help keep them healthy during the first two years of life. How many things on the list are you partly or entirely responsible for now? How is learning to take care of yourself important?

Books to Read

Here are some books you can look for in your school library or the public library to find more information about growth and development.

Arnold, Caroline. *Genetics: From Mendel to Gene Splicing*. Franklin Watts.

Baldwin, Dorothy, and Claire Lister. *How You Grow and Change*. Franklin Watts.

Ward, Brian R. *Body Maintenance*. Franklin Watts.

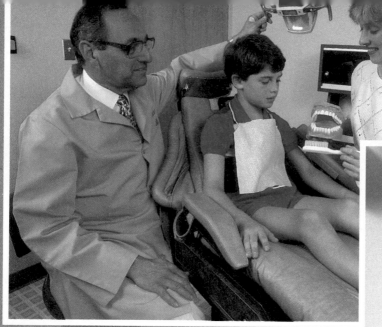

SHAMPOO

FO
OIL
HAI

NICE

16 FL. OZ.

TAKING CARE OF YOUR HEALTH

Parents are concerned about their children's health, as many young people know. Some young people may even depend on their parents' or family's concern rather than become more independent in caring for themselves. However, personal responsibility for health is a goal that many young people look forward to as they grow up. You may already be spending some of your own money on health products. Taking responsibility for caring for yourself is an important task. You are the key to your own good health. Learning good habits now can help you stay healthy all through your life.

GETTING READY TO LEARN

Key Questions

- Why is it important to learn how to care for your body?
- How does the way you feel about taking care of your body affect your health care and safety habits?
- How can you learn to make healthful choices about health products and services?
- What can you do to become more responsible for taking care of your own body?

Main Chapter Sections

1 Caring for Your Teeth, Skin, and Hair
2 Caring for Your Eyes and Ears
3 Choosing Health Products and Practitioners
4 Where to Find Information About Health Services

103

1 Caring for Your Teeth, Skin, and Hair

KEY WORDS

plaque
cavity
fluoride
calculus
epidermis
dermis

You can do things every day to take care of your own health. You can take responsibility for brushing and flossing your teeth and for keeping your skin and hair clean.

■ *You need to follow healthful habits every day to care for your teeth, hair, and skin.*

How Can You Take Care of Your Teeth?

Knowing about your teeth can help you understand how to protect them and why you should. The picture shows what a tooth looks like. You can see only the *crown*, the top part of the tooth, inside your mouth. *Enamel* covers each tooth. It is the hardest part of the tooth. Yet it can easily become damaged. The *root*, the bottom part, lies inside your gums and jawbone.

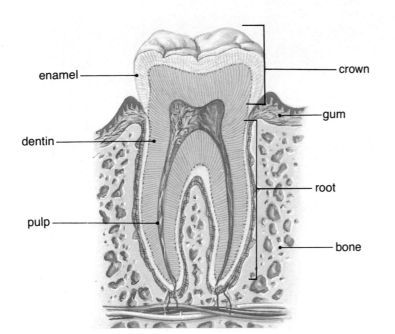

enamel —

dentin —

pulp —

— crown

— gum

— root

— bone

■ *Your teeth should last for your whole life.*

plaque (PLAK), a sticky substance that builds up on teeth.

cavity (KAV uht ee), a hole that forms in a tooth due to decay.

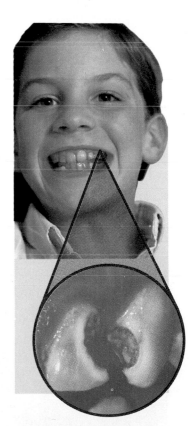

■ *A buildup of plaque between teeth can lead to cavities near the gum line.*

Every day a sticky substance called **plaque** builds up on your teeth. Plaque that has built up for several days can be seen. Fresh plaque, however, has no color and is invisible. Microbes that live in plaque digest the sugars found in certain foods and make a strong acid. The acid can slowly dissolve tooth enamel and can cause tooth decay. The result is a hole, or **cavity,** in the tooth. This process of forming cavities is called tooth decay.

Dentists work to help people prevent tooth decay. They tell people to eat fewer foods that have a lot of sugar in them. Those kinds of foods are candies, sugar-coated cereals, and many soft drinks. Sipping a sugary soft drink and keeping something sweet in your mouth for a long time can be more harmful to teeth and gums than drinking or eating such foods quickly.

Dentists tell people to keep their teeth clean and free of plaque. Teeth that are not kept clean can form cavities and produce sore gums. Dentists say that people should brush their teeth after every meal or sweet snack. You need to brush well, but gently, along your gum line. This is where many cavities begin. Your dentist or dental hygienist can show you a good kind of toothbrush to buy and ways to use it properly.

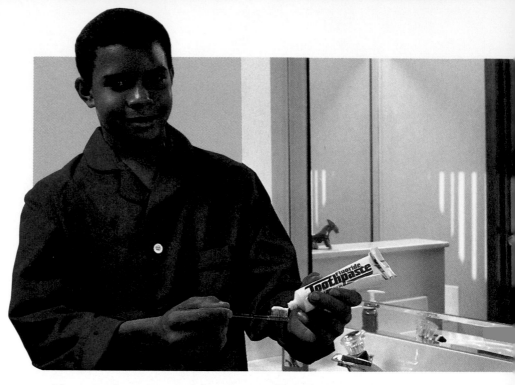

■ *Many toothpastes contain fluoride, which helps prevent tooth decay. Some communities add small amounts of fluoride to the drinking water.*

fluoride (FLUR yd), a substance that makes tooth enamel strong.

■ *Flossing removes plaque between teeth.*

Along with your toothbrush, toothpaste is another important tooth-cleaning aid. Toothpaste helps clean your teeth and stop tooth decay. Tests by the American Dental Association have shown that certain toothpastes, those that have fluoride, help prevent tooth decay. **Fluoride** keeps tooth enamel strong. Many toothpastes have fluoride. Fluoride is also added to or is naturally present in the water system in many communities. Fluoride can also be purchased at a pharmacy if ordered by a dentist.

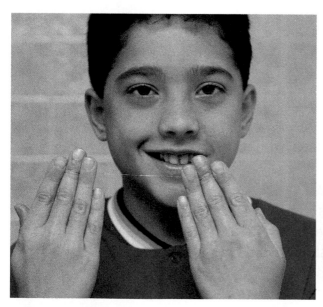

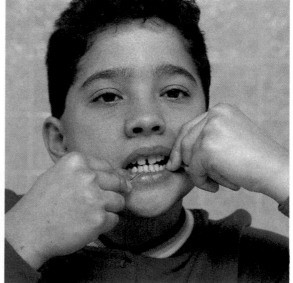

Another important tooth-cleaning aid is dental floss. Most dentists say you should use dental floss each day. Flossing helps you get rid of plaque. It also removes bits of food that get between teeth and under gums.

Some people do not brush and floss their teeth at all or do not do so enough. One problem that can result is bad breath. Another problem is that a hard, colored material called **calculus** can build up on the teeth. *Tartar* is another name for calculus. It can be removed only by a dentist or dental hygienist.

calculus (KAL kyuh luhs), a hard, yellow material that can build up on teeth; also called tartar.

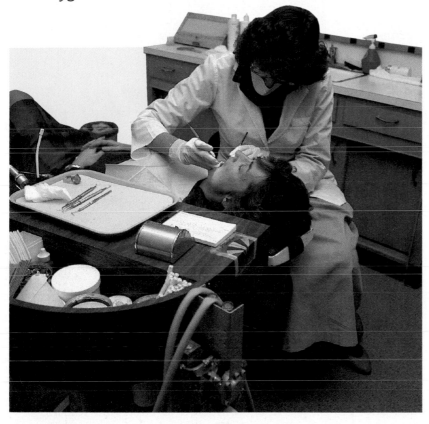

■ *Professional cleaning is one way to remove calculus.*

Regular checkups by a dentist are important to your plan for caring for your teeth and gums. When you visit a dental office, you may have your teeth cleaned. You may also have your teeth X-rayed. An X ray shows cavities or other problems the dentist may not be able to see otherwise. Most dentists and hygienists advise having your teeth cleaned and checked at least once a year to help you keep your teeth healthy. Follow your dentist's advice if more dental care is suggested.

How Can You Take Care of Your Skin?

Your skin is the largest organ of your body. Your skin has certain parts that help several body systems. For example, nerve cells that pick up signs of pain, touch, and temperature belong to the nervous system.

Your skin is made up of several layers. The outside layer is called the **epidermis.** It is your body's chief outer defense against infection. Under the epidermis lies the **dermis.**

epidermis (ehp uh DUR muhs), the outer layer of the skin.

dermis (DUR muhs), the layer of skin under the epidermis.

■ *Apply a sunscreen to your skin about 30 minutes before going out in the sun. This will protect your skin from the sun's rays.*

In the dermis are hair follicles. A single hair grows out of each one. An oil gland is connected to each hair follicle. The oil gland makes an oily substance that passes out of a tiny tube, or duct, to the surface of the skin. The oil helps keep your skin soft and waterproof.

The dermis also has sweat glands. These help the body's excretory system. Sweat glands get rid of some wastes in the form of perspiration. Perspiration leaves the sweat glands and passes to the skin's surface. There the water in perspiration evaporates into the air. This helps cool your skin. Perspiring is one way your body keeps a constant temperature.

FOR THE
CURIOUS

A person sheds about 1.5 pounds (0.7 kilogram) of skin in a year.

Dermatologists, physicians who care for the skin, tell people the following:

- *Wash!* Keep your skin clean by washing it gently with soap and warm water every day.
- *Protect!* Use sunscreen to protect your skin from sunburn.
- *Eat!* Eat the proper foods and drink plenty of water to help your skin build new cells and repair damaged ones.
- *Rest!* Get enough sleep to feel rested. Being well rested helps your skin look healthy.

How Can You Take Care of Your Hair and Nails?

Your hair is always exposed to the environment. The air carries dirt and dust that land on your hair. Oil from the many oil glands in your scalp helps keep your hair healthy. But the dirt and dust in your hair mix with the oil. Shampooing your hair removes the dirt and oil and keeps your hair looking clean. Hair that is not washed can have an odor and other problems.

Flakes of dandruff may be seen when oil from sweat glands in the scalp dries and mixes with dead skin cells. Dandruff often leads to an itchy scalp. If you have dandruff, you can probably cure it by using a special shampoo. Ask a pharmacist to help you select one. If the shampoo does not clear up the problem, you should see a physician.

Good hair care also means brushing your hair to get rid of remaining dandruff as well as tangles and loose dirt. Brushing also spreads out oil through the hair. Be sure to keep your brush and comb clean by washing them often in warm, soapy water and then rinsing them off.

Your hair is likely to become more oily during puberty. You may have to wash it several times a week to keep it clean. Whenever you wash your hair, you should rinse it well to remove all of the shampoo. Shampoo that is left on your scalp can irritate the skin and make it itch.

■ *Regularly brushing and shampooing your hair keeps it clean and healthy.*

Another way to care for both your appearance and your health is to care for your nails. Dirt collects under nails when you work or play. Cleaning your nails shows that you care about how you look to others. It also removes microbes that can collect under your nails. These microbes can be passed to your mouth or eyes if you bite your nails or rub your eyes.

You should trim your nails carefully. Trimmed nails are less likely to tear or break than long nails. Straight, trimmed toenails are less likely to become painfully ingrown.

STOP **REVIEW SECTION 1**

REMEMBER?

1. How often should plaque be removed from your teeth?
2. How can you keep your teeth and gums clean and healthy?
3. What are four ways to keep your skin healthy?
4. Why is it important to keep your nails trimmed?

THINK!

5. How might a buildup of tartar on your teeth affect your health?
6. How does the way you care for your hair and skin tell others how you feel about yourself?

2 Caring for Your Eyes and Ears

You learn a lot about your world through your eyes and ears. For example, seeing a division problem worked out on the chalkboard may help you better understand mathematics. Hearing sounds from a piano may spark an interest in learning how to play.

You can be responsible for much of the care of your eyes and ears. One way to care for them is by recognizing any problem and then seeking help to correct the problem.

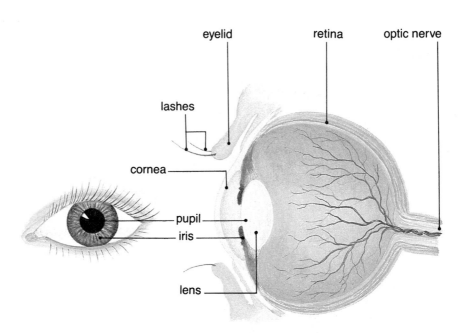

■ *The structures of the eye make vision possible.*

What Are Some Common Eye Problems?

People do not have control over some eye problems. Some serious vision problems are present at birth. Other problems can develop later in life. At any age, certain injuries and diseases can cause people to become blind or to have poor vision. Squinting and holding things close or far away to see them may be signs of vision problems.

Some vision problems are due to inherited disorders. Heredity most often determines the way the eye slowly

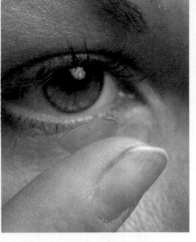

■ *Eyeglasses, left, and contact lenses, right, correct some kinds of vision problems.*

changes shape in early life and at puberty. Although the eye remains healthy, the way it works to focus light may change. It may produce blurred vision. Most eye problems in which vision is blurred are easy to fix with corrective lenses. **Corrective lenses** are eyeglasses or contact lenses.

Nearsightedness. For some people, nearby things look clear, but things far away appear blurred. These people have a common vision problem called nearsightedness. **Nearsightedness** is a condition in which the distance between the front of the eye and the retina is too long. The light from faraway things focuses in front of the retina instead of directly on it. Without corrective lenses, people may squint to help faraway things look a little clearer. But with corrective lenses, people who are nearsighted can see faraway things clearly.

Farsightedness. For some people, faraway things look clear and nearby things are blurred. These people have another common vision problem called farsightedness. **Farsightedness** is a condition in which the distance between the front of the eye and the retina is too short. Light from nearby things reaches the retina before it comes into focus. People with farsightedness often need corrective lenses to see nearby things clearly, as in reading or doing close work.

Astigmatism. Some people have a vision problem called astigmatism. **Astigmatism** is a condition in which the cornea or the lens of the eye is curved unevenly.

corrective lenses (kuh REHK tihv • LEHNZ uhz), eyeglasses and contact lenses used for adjusting vision problems.

nearsightedness (NIHR syt uhd nuhs), a condition in which the distance between the front of the eye and the retina is longer than normal.

farsightedness (FAHR syt uhd nuhs), a condition in which the distance between the front of the eye and the retina is shorter than normal.

astigmatism (uh STIHG muh tihz uhm), a condition in which either the cornea or the lens of the eye is curved unevenly.

113

■ *To a person who is farsighted, objects at a distance are in focus. Nearby objects appear blurred.*

■ *To a person who is nearsighted, objects nearby are in focus. Distant objects appear blurred.*

114

This unevenness causes incoming light to focus at different points in the eye instead of at just one point. As a result, vision is blurred. A person with nearsightedness or farsightedness can also have astigmatism. Astigmatism can also be treated with corrective lenses.

Eye Infections. Unlike vision focus problems, eye infections usually happen quickly and are often painful. Microbes are the cause of eye infections. Microbes can enter the eyes and infect them in different ways. The most common way is by people touching their eyes. Two common eye infections are pinkeye and sties.

Conjunctivitis is the medical name for pinkeye. It is an infection of the lining of the eye and the tissues under the eyelid. The eye and eyelid get red and swell. Conjunctivitis can be spread if a person who has it shares personal things such as face towels or eye makeup. Conjunctivitis needs to be treated by a physician.

Sties are infections of the oil or sweat glands in the eyelids. A sty is like a pimple on the edge of the eyelid. The same microbes that cause boils cause sties. Sties are not as easily spread as conjunctivitis. However, a person with a sty should still keep his or her washcloth and face towel separate from those of other family members. A clean, warm, wet cloth applied to the eye two to three times a day will help a sty heal faster. A person who often gets sties needs to be treated by a physician.

conjunctivitis (kuhn juhngk tih vyt uhs), an infection of the lining of the eye and the tissues under the eyelid; also called pinkeye.

sties (styz), infections of the oil or sweat glands in the eyelids.

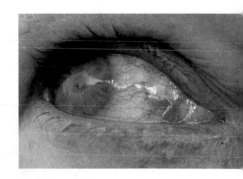

■ *Pinkeye, above, is an infection of the lining of the eyelid. A sty, left, is an infection of the oil or sweat glands along the edge of the eyelid.*

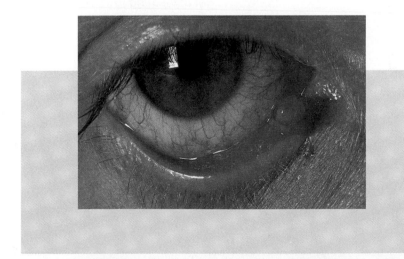

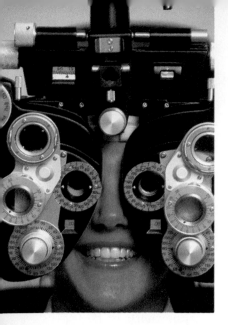

■ *Vision tests can detect problems before they become serious.*

How Can You Take Care of Your Eyes?

You can take care of your eyes in three ways. You can protect them from injury. You can protect them from infection. You can also make sure that your vision is clear.

To check your vision, you can have your eyes tested. Many schools give free vision screening tests each year. Health clinics and health departments regularly offer free vision tests, too. Talk with a parent or guardian, your teacher, or your school nurse if you think you might have an eye problem.

The following list tells you what practices can protect your eyes from injury and infection:

- Keep sharp things away from your eyes.
- Wear safety glasses or goggles when mowing the lawn, working with tools, or playing certain sports.
- Try not to touch or rub your eyes.
- If you feel something in your eye, ask an adult for help. Blink quickly to cause more tears to flow. Tears might wash out the object. Do not try to remove the object yourself. Also, do not rub your eye. You might scratch the cornea.
- Wear sunglasses outdoors on bright days. Wearing sunglasses near snow or water helps reduce the glare that can hurt your eyes.

■ *Have an adult help you if you get something in your eye.*

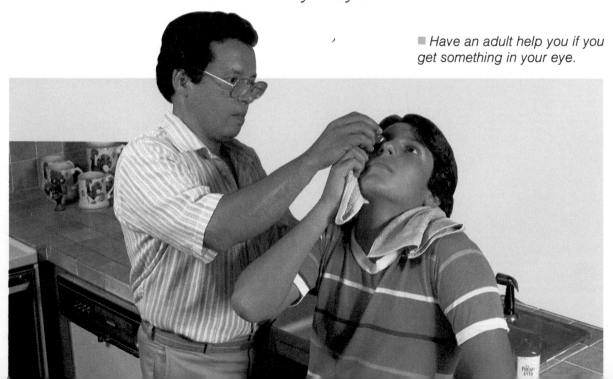

What Causes Hearing Loss?

Your outer ear is shaped to catch sound waves. It directs them through your ear canal to your eardrum. When sound waves reach your eardrum, it vibrates. This causes the three tiny bones in your middle ear to vibrate. In this way, the energy of sound reaches the hearing part of the ear—the cochlea—in the inner ear. The cochlea is filled with a fluid. The sound vibrations cause the fluid to move. The motion of the fluid causes hairlike nerve endings in the cochlea to send messages through the auditory nerve to your brain. Your brain interprets the messages as the sounds you hear.

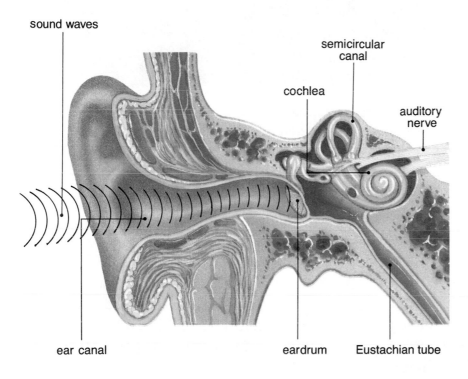

sound waves

semicircular canal

cochlea

auditory nerve

ear canal

eardrum

Eustachian tube

■ *The structures of the ear make hearing possible.*

Sound is measured in **decibels.** The higher the decibel level, the louder the sound is to you. For example, a clap of thunder is about 140 decibels. Loud music can be just as intense. Normal speech is about 60 decibels. The rustling of leaves is about 20 decibels. Being around sounds as low as 85 decibels for a long time can cause hearing loss. In fact, even one very loud sound, such as from an explosion, can cause complete hearing loss. Very loud sounds cause hearing loss by making parts of the ear vibrate so hard that they are damaged. This damage cannot be repaired.

decibels (DEHS uh behlz), units of measure for the loudness of sound.

117

There are also other causes of hearing loss. Head injuries can damage the middle ear, the inner ear, or both. Infections in the middle ear can reduce hearing. They cause fluid to replace air in the middle ear. Hearing loss from infections most often lasts for only a short time if the infection is treated. Long-term hearing loss can happen when any damage is done to the eardrum, to the bones in the middle ear, or to the inner ear.

Some people are born with ear damage that keeps them from hearing well. Some elderly people may also have a hearing loss. If you know someone who has a hearing loss, you can help him or her understand you better by following some simple practices:

- Speak clearly, but do not shout.
- Face the person directly. Keep your hands away from your face when you talk. Do not talk while you are eating. Do not talk to the person from another room.
- Reduce background noises when you talk to a person who has some hearing loss. Turn off the radio or television, for example.
- Remember that people with hearing problems do not hear and understand as well when they are distracted, tired, ill, or upset.

How Can You Take Care of Your Ears?

You can guard your hearing by protecting your ears from injuries. A safety helmet can protect your ears from heavy blows that could damage hearing. Helmets should be worn when you play sports such as baseball or football or when you ride a bicycle or a skateboard.

If you have a cold, do not blow your nose too often or too hard. If you blow your nose too hard, harmful microbes could be forced into the tubes of your ears. The microbes could then cause an ear infection. When you blow your nose, leave both nostrils open and blow gently.

Earplugs can reduce loud sounds and protect the ears. Many musicians wear earplugs when they play very loud music. Plugs or earmuffs are also necessary when using power mowers or other power tools.

To take good care of your ears, do not put anything into them. Even cotton swabs can push earwax against the eardrum, which would make it less able to vibrate. When the eardrum cannot vibrate well, a hearing loss results. However, such hearing losses can be prevented.

■ *Hearing tests are given each year at some schools.*

119

To find out if you are hearing everything you should, you may want to take a hearing test. Most schools give tests to screen for hearing problems. You can also call your health department to find out if your community offers this service. If you think you might have a hearing problem, talk with a parent or guardian, your teacher, or your school nurse.

REVIEW
SECTION 2

REMEMBER?

1. What is the difference between nearsightedness and farsightedness?
2. How are eye infections different from focus problems?
3. What are three ways by which young people can protect themselves from hearing loss?

THINK!

4. How might ignoring a vision problem affect you?
5. Why should you have your hearing tested?

Making Wellness Choices

Doug likes to sit in the front row in all his classes. That way, he can see the writing on the chalkboard clearly. During the second week of school, Doug's class went to the school nurse's office for a vision screening test. After Doug took his turn looking at the eye chart, the nurse said Doug should have his eyes tested by a specialist. The nurse gave Doug a note for his parents. It described signs of possible vision problems. On the way home from school, Doug told his friends that he was not going to give the note to his parents. He said he could see just fine from his desk.

 What could you tell Doug? Explain your wellness choice.

Health Close-up

Modern Technology for Hearing Loss

About 20 million people in the United States have some kind of hearing problem. Nearly 2 million of those people have a serious problem or total hearing loss.

Until recently, people with hearing problems had one of two choices. They could wear a bulky hearing aid. Or they could just miss most of the sound around them. Some people were willing to put up with their hearing loss. They would do anything to avoid the clumsy hearing aids.

New developments in technology now offer better solutions to the problem of hearing loss. Many modern hearing aids are small enough to be worn in or behind the ears. All hearing aids include a microphone that will pick up sound, an amplifier that will make sounds louder, and a speaker that directs the sounds to the ears.

One of the latest developments helps people who once had total hearing loss. This special type of hearing aid is called an electronic ear. The first step in getting this electronic ear is minor surgery. A surgeon places a tiny receiver inside the ear. The receiver is connected to wires that go into the inner ear.

The receiver picks up sounds and sends them to a sound processor. The processor is about the size of a credit card. In fact, it can be carried inside a shirt pocket. The job of the processor is to change the sounds into electrical signals. When that is done, the signals

■ *Hearing aids improve the hearing of millions of people.*

can be sent through the wires that extend from the receiver. The wires carry the signals to the inner ear. The brain recognizes the signals as sounds— sounds somewhat like those a person hears with a normal ear.

Thinking Beyond

1. Aside from missing a lot of enjoyment, what other problems might a person face as a result of a hearing difficulty?
2. Bionics is the science of building replacements for body parts. In what way is the electronic ear bionic? In what way is it not a bionic ear?

3 Choosing Health Products and Practitioners

Think of the last time you bought something. What was it that influenced your choice? It may have been the price. Did you buy the product quickly without careful thought? Did you really need the product?

Every time a person buys or uses goods or services, that person is a **consumer.** A wise consumer knows the things that influence a choice. He or she knows how to make sound consumer choices by using facts. A wise health consumer follows a plan for choosing health products and services.

How Do Product Labels Give Information to Consumers?

When you choose a health product, you may want to ask yourself these questions:

- Do I really need this?
- Which kind of this product best fills my needs?
- Which brand should I buy?
- What size is the best for me?
- Can this product harm me?

consumer (kuhn soo muhr), a person who buys or uses goods or services.

REAL-LIFE
SKILL

Making Decisions

1. Find out all you can about your possible choices.
2. Think of the results of each possible choice.
3. Select what seems to be the best choice.
4. Think about what happens as a result of this choice.

■ *Carefully reading labels is a wise way to shop for health products.*

One way to answer these questions is to read labels. Like food labels, labels on health products give several facts: the kind of product, the brand name, and the name and address of the manufacturer. Many labels also describe what the product does. They may use phrases like "stops wetness and odor" or "helps fight dandruff." They may also use advertising phrases such as "leaves hair soft and shiny" or "makes teeth whiter and breath fresher."

■ *Health product labels describe what products do and warn about possible health problems.*

Most labels on health products list the ingredients. **Ingredients** are the things from which the product is made. By reading the list of ingredients, you can compare one product with another. You can also see if one brand has anything in it that you do not want to use. For example, your physician might have told you not to use a certain ingredient because you have an allergy to it.

ingredients (ihn GREED ee uhnts), the things products are made from.

Many health products can harm your health if not used properly. That is why most labels have directions for use. For example, the label on a cough medicine might say, "Take one teaspoonful every 4 to 6 hours."

Labels often give warnings about possible dangers. For example, the labels on products in spray cans warn against storing the cans near heat. At high heat, the cans might explode.

Labels often give directions to follow in case of an accident. The label on a skin ointment bottle might say, "If skin ointment gets into eyes, rinse thoroughly with water."

How Does a Wise Consumer Use Advertising?

advertising (AD vuhr tyz ihng), process of giving people information that encourages them to buy something.

Advertising is one way health consumers get information. Advertising gives useful facts that can help you shop wisely. However, some advertising may suggest benefits that products do not have.

One kind of advertising uses the endorsement, or recommendation, of a famous person. An actor or athlete, for example, may say he or she always uses a certain brand of deodorant. Without exactly saying so, the advertising hints that by using this deodorant, the consumer can be like the famous person. It may hint that the person is letting the company use his or her name because the product is so good. In fact, the main reason may be the large amount of money the company paid the actor or athlete to talk about the product.

■ *A responsible consumer is careful not to believe every claim made in advertising.*

Johnny Steam always stays cool!

He works hard, like you. He plays hard, like you. But he keeps his cool, no matter how hot he rocks.

COOL ANTI-PERSPIRANT DEODORANT 4 FL. OZ

You can too.

Some advertising uses the so-called unfinished comparison. You may see phrases like "costs pennies less," "makes breath fresher," or "faster-acting." The questions you must ask yourself are: Less than *what*? Fresher than *what*? and Faster than *what*?

Much advertising is based on the concern people have about how others feel about them. Advertising for hair and skin products often hints that, by using these products, the consumer will become more popular. Ask yourself these questions: How could the product in fact make a difference? How is one brand of product any better than another?

Health products and services are heavily advertised. A wise consumer needs to use advertising as part of a plan for choosing these products and services.

■ *Choosing a dentist or physician is an important decision.*

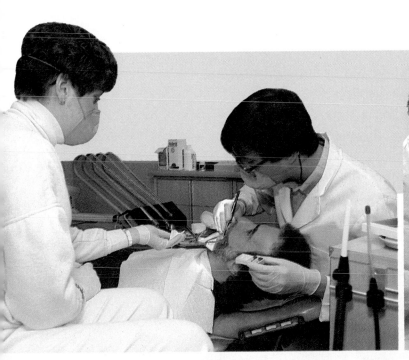

How Can You Choose a Physician or Dentist?

The choices people make about health care professionals are some of their most important consumer decisions. Choosing qualified physicians and dentists can help people protect their wellness. A qualified physician or dentist has passed state tests. He or she has earned a license from a state to practice medicine or dentistry there.

The kind of physician a family chooses depends in part on their medical needs. Most people go to a family physician for checkups and when they are ill. Your family physician has been trained to treat almost all things for which you may need medical attention. Sometimes, however, a certain illness or condition calls for more tests and care. In these cases, the family physician will send you to a specialist. A **specialist** is a physician who has continued his or her training for two or more years to study certain problems of the body.

Some specialists focus on particular conditions of the body and how to treat them. Some specialists, called surgeons, do operations. There are many kinds of medical specialists. Their titles describe the body systems or kinds of conditions they treat. Here are the titles of a number of specialists and the areas in which they work.

- dermatologist—skin
- neurologist—brain and nervous system
- obstetrician—childbirth
- ophthalmologist—eyes
- orthopedist—bones and joints
- otologist—ears
- pediatrician—children and young adults
- psychiatrist—mental and emotional health

specialist (SPEHSH uhl luhst), a physician who has continued his or her training in a certain medical field.

■ *There are many kinds of medical specialists.*

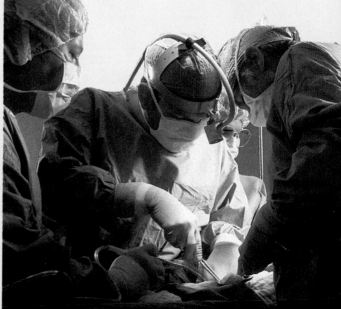

126

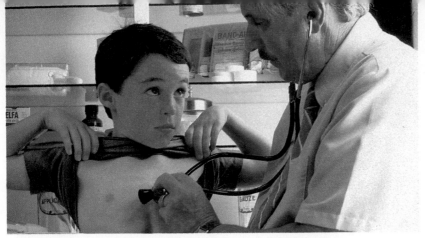

■ *Pediatricians specialize in the treatment of children and young teenagers.*

Most people go to a general dentist rather than to a specialist for dental checkups. General dentists fill cavities and take care of some dental problems. If you need certain kinds of dental work, however, your dentist may send you to a dental specialist. Orthodontists straighten crooked teeth. Periodontists treat gum diseases.

When people move to a new city or town, they need to find a new physician and dentist. They can check several places for information. Before they move, they can ask the physicians and dentists they have been seeing. After they move, they can call the local medical and dental societies. The societies can provide names of their members in the town. All members of such societies are licensed to practice. Another place to get information is the health department.

STOP REVIEW SECTION 3

REMEMBER?

1. What are five questions you can ask yourself when choosing health products?
2. What are two reasons for studying the ingredients on a product label?
3. How does a wise consumer use advertising?

THINK!

4. What problems could happen if a consumer does not read the ingredients on a product label?
5. Why is choosing a physician or dentist important to your health?

127

4 Where to Find Information About Health Services

You may want more information about the health services in your community. Or you may have a question about a certain health problem. Your health teacher, a physician, a school nurse, or health workers at a clinic can answer many health questions. But you can get health facts from other sources, too.

Where Can You Find Information About Local Health Services?

Your telephone book lists most of the health services in your city or town. Telephone numbers for emergency health care are printed in the front of the book. The services of your local health department are listed under the name of your town, city, or county.

Your public library may have books prepared by local, state, or national health agencies and by private health groups. It is likely to have many books and magazines about health care. Before you follow any health advice from books or magazines, check with a parent or a guardian.

■ *Your public library and local telephone book provide information about most of the health services offered in your community.*

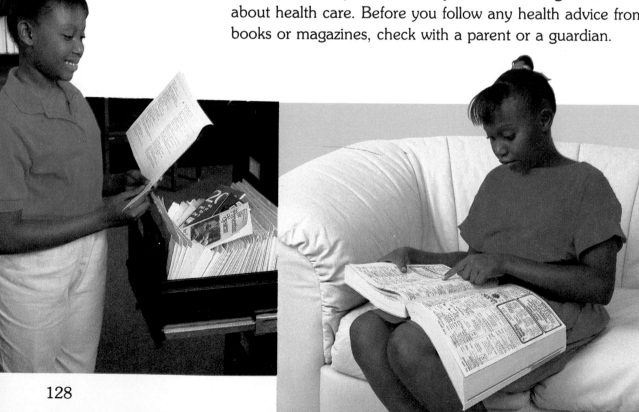

128

Where Can You Find Information About State Health Services?

The health department in your state works with the local health department in your community. The state office takes care of health services such as disease control and food inspection. It also provides public health nursing and health education. It may run homes and hospitals for the needs of certain people, such as elderly patients or people who have emotional problems. The addresses and telephone numbers for offices of your state health department are listed in the telephone book under the name of your state.

■ *Information about health services is available from your state or local health department.*

HEALTH DEPT.

Where Can You Find Information About National Health Services?

The chief national health department is the Department of Health and Human Services. One part of this department is the Food and Drug Administration. It is responsible for the safety of foods and medicines. Another part is the Public Health Service. It studies diseases and works to control them.

Research into the causes of diseases such as AIDS, cancer, and diabetes is done at the laboratories of the National Institutes of Health in Maryland.

The Environmental Protection Agency (EPA) is separate from the Department of Health and Human Services. The EPA works to protect community health by fighting pollution. The addresses and telephone numbers for offices of these agencies are most often listed in your telephone book under "United States Government."

The National Institutes of Health (NIH) in Bethesda, Maryland, studies diseases such as cancer, diabetes, and heart disease. The NIH has many parts. Each part has people who study a different health problem.

The Centers for Disease Control (CDC) is a branch of the Public Health Service. The CDC, based in Atlanta, Georgia, works to prevent and control communicable diseases in the United States. It keeps records on cases of diseases that occur all across the country. CDC workers can spot outbreaks of a disease before it becomes an epidemic. The CDC may then help local health departments fight the disease.

The CDC also acts as a kind of health detective agency. Sometimes people show symptoms of a disease that physicians cannot explain at first. The CDC helps track down the cause of the problem.

The CDC has many other jobs. It helps train physicians to study the spread of disease. It works with foreign governments and international groups to control disease and improve health around the world.

■ *The Centers for Disease Control keeps records on cases of certain diseases from all over the world.*

Where Can You Find Information About Private Health Organizations?

Many private health organizations are backed by the work and money of volunteers. These organizations often deal with health education and research. Some of them, such as the American Cancer Society, the American Heart Association, and the American Lung Association, deal with only one kind of health problem. Others, such as the American Red Cross, offer many kinds of health care and training.

Some private health groups are made up of people who are professional health workers. The members of the American Medical Association, for example, are physicians. The American Public Health Association is made up of physicians, nurses, dentists, and many other health workers. Associations such as these set standards and goals for making sure their members keep current in their special field of health.

Private health groups have offices in most large cities. You can write or call a nearby office if you want to learn more about how a group works. To find the address or telephone number of the office, look in your telephone book under the name of the group. The yellow pages has a section called "Health Agencies." This section lists groups concerned with a variety of health problems and services.

Many private health groups provide special 800 telephone numbers for help or free information. A person can call these groups from anywhere in the United States. The National Child Safety Council, for example, answers questions on safety for people calling 1-800-222-1464.

■ *Participating in fund-raising events is one way to help the voluntary health organizations in your community.*

Your community has many health services and groups that can help you and your family with your health needs. Your telephone book, the public library, and your school nurse can give you health information. They can tell you about the kinds of community health care available in your area.

STOP **REVIEW SECTION 4**

REMEMBER?

1. Where are telephone numbers for emergency health care printed?
2. What kinds of health information might you find in your public library?
3. What does a state health department do?

THINK!

4. Why is it important to check with a parent or guardian before you follow health advice you find in a magazine?
5. How can the telephone book help a wise consumer?

Thinking About Your Health

Are You Practicing Good Health Care Habits?

To stay healthy, you need to follow certain health practices each day. On a sheet of paper, make a one-week calendar. Then, as each day of the week passes, record your own health practices for the day by using the following coding system:

- brushed teeth and gums = TEETH (B)
- flossed teeth = TEETH (F)
- showered or bathed = BATH
- washed hair = HAIR
- cleaned nails = NAILS
- washed hands = HANDS
- ate a balanced diet = DIET
- participated in a physical activity = EXERCISE

At the end of the week, study your list. Decide which health practices you need to improve. Also, notice the ones that you do regularly.

133

An Interview with an Optometrist

> *Jorge Won, O.D., knows about eye care and treatment. He is an optometrist in New York City.*

What does an optometrist do?

An optometrist takes care of people's eyes. Optometrists examine eyes. They identify vision focus problems and treat them. This may mean ordering corrective lenses such as eyeglasses or contact lenses.

Are there eye-care practitioners other than optometrists?

Another practitioner is a medical doctor called an ophthalmologist. An *ophthalmologist* is a specialist in medical eye care. An ophthalmologist can order corrective lenses. He or she can also prescribe medicine to treat the eyes and do surgery when it is needed. Some eye specialists are physicians who treat only eye problems of children or older adults.

How do you decide what kind of corrective lenses someone should wear?

With the help of certain instruments and tests, I check a person's vision. I consider many things. I ask the person questions about his or her life-style, and I listen to his or her concerns. If the person is young, we discuss the options for corrective lenses with his or her parent or guardian.

■ *Optometrists check eyes and order corrective lenses for patients.*

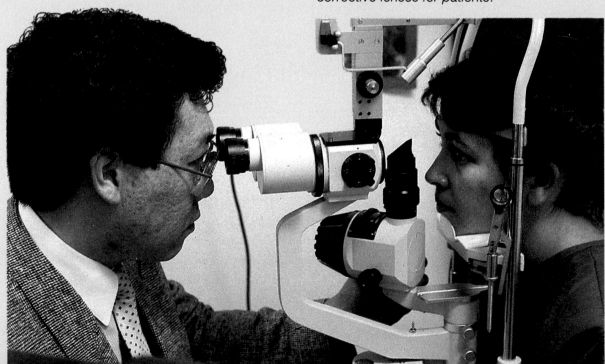

How old does someone have to be to wear contact lenses?

Age is not the most important thing to consider for wearing contact lenses. However, contact lenses are not for everyone. A person may not be able to insert and remove the lenses. Some people have dry eyes or other medical problems that would make wearing lenses difficult. If a person is physically able to wear the lenses, I must also think about other things. Some people may not be responsible enough to take care of their lenses properly. Sometimes I notice that a patient has dirty hair and fingernails. I might tell that person that he or she would have fewer problems with glasses. Contact lenses must be handled with care. They must be kept very clean. Otherwise, the person may develop serious eye problems.

What can young people do to keep their eyes healthy?

Young people can follow good vision habits. For example, they should use adequate lighting when they read. Using proper lighting will make it easier for them to read for longer times. They also need protective eye wear while playing certain sports or working with tools.

How many years of school does it take to become an optometrist?

It takes between seven and eight years of schooling past high school to become an optometrist. All optometrists

■ Dr. Won uses special instruments to test a person's vision.

also must be licensed. In most states, optometrists must keep taking courses to renew their licenses.

What else should young people know about optometrists?

Optometrists check eyes and order the corrective lenses that some people need. They also can detect signs of other problems. They can refer a person to the proper physician. I want my patients to have good vision and eye health all their lives.

Learn more about people who care for eyes and treat them. Interview an optometrist or an ophthalmologist. Or write for information to the Better Vision Institute, 1800 N. Kent Street, Suite 1210, Rosslyn, VA 22209.

CHAPTER REVIEW 4

Main Ideas

- Caring for your teeth means brushing and flossing daily, eating few sugar-sweetened foods, and visiting a dentist regularly.
- Washing your skin with soap and your hair with shampoo helps keep them healthy.
- You can take care of your eyes by protecting them from injury and infection and by having your vision tested.
- You can take care of your ears by protecting them from injury and by having your hearing tested.
- A wise consumer knows the many kinds of influences that affect a choice.
- There are many ways to learn about the health services in your community.

Key Words

Write the numbers 1 to 8 in your health notebook or on a separate sheet of paper. After each number, copy the sentence and fill in the missing term. Page numbers in ( ) tell you where to look in the chapter if you need help.

plaque (105)
fluoride (106)
epidermis (108)
corrective lenses (113)
farsightedness (113)
conjunctivitis (115)
decibels (117)
specialist (126)

1. A person who sees objects clearly only in the distance has ___?___ .

2. A substance that makes tooth enamel strong is ___?___ .

3. The outer layer of the skin is called the ___?___ .

4. Another term for pinkeye is ___?___ .

5. A dermatologist is an example of a ___?___ .

6. A sticky substance that builds up on the teeth is ___?___ .

7. Units for measuring the loudness of sound are called ___?___ .

8. Eyeglasses are called ___?___ .

Write the numbers 9 to 17 on your paper. After each number, write a sentence that defines the term. Page numbers in ( ) tell you where to look in the chapter if you need help.

9. cavity (105)
10. calculus (107)
11. dermis (108)
12. nearsightedness (113)
13. astigmatism (113)
14. sties (115)
15. consumer (122)
16. ingredients (123)
17. advertising (124)

Remembering What You Learned

Page numbers in ( ) tell you where to look in the chapter if you need help.

1. What substance made in plaque causes tooth decay? (105)

2. What are three examples of sugar-sweetened foods that can cause tooth decay? (105)

3. What are three important tooth-cleaning aids? (105–107)

4. How does oil from your oil glands help your skin? (108)

5. What causes dandruff? (110)

6. How is brushing your hair helpful? (110)

7. What is one reason for blurred vision? (112–113)

8. List five ways to protect your eyes and vision from harm. (116)

9. Name the parts of the ear through which vibrations pass before the brain interprets a sound. (117)

10. What might happen if a person blows his or her nose too hard? (119)

11. What are three things a person needs to do to be a wise consumer? (122)

12. How should a wise consumer use advertising? (124–125)

13. What can a family in a new community do to find a physician or dentist? (127)

Thinking About What You Learned

1. Why should you brush and floss your teeth each day?

2. Why are clean skin, hair, and nails important to your health?

3. Why is it important to be able to recognize problems with your vision and hearing?

4. How can a person have astigmatism and be nearsighted at the same time?

5. Why should you be careful not to tear or damage the label on a medicine container?

6. Why should consumers be aware of how they feel about themselves when thinking about buying a product or using a service?

Writing About What You Learned

1. There is a saying "Out of sight, out of mind." This saying can describe someone who has a poor attitude about his or her health. Write a paragraph using the meaning of this saying to tell about someone who does not care about his or her dental health.

2. Write a story about someone your age who believes that all the advertising words used to describe grooming products are true. Tell how this person is influenced by what others say about grooming products in magazines or on television. Tell what this person needs to do to become a wise consumer.

Applying What You Learned

ART

Design a personalized T-shirt that promotes good health care habits. Your design should try to encourage others to start or keep their good health habits. You may wish to use one or more of the health topics presented in this chapter.

Modified True or False

Write the numbers 1 to 15 in your health notebook or on a separate sheet of paper. After each number, write *true* or *false* to describe the sentence. If the sentence is false, also write a term that replaces the underlined term and makes the sentence true.

1. A <u>cavity</u> in a tooth is a hole caused by acid dissolving the enamel.

2. If faraway things look clear but nearby things look blurred, you may be <u>farsighted</u>.

3. You should floss your teeth at least <u>twice</u> a day.

4. A <u>sty</u> is like a pimple on the edge of the eyelid.

5. An obstetrician is a <u>specialist</u>.

6. You can get information on pollution from the <u>National Institutes of Health</u>.

7. The body's outer defense against infection is the <u>epidermis</u>.

8. A very loud sound for a short time is <u>less</u> damaging than a very soft sound for a long time.

9. <u>Ingredients</u> are the things from which a product is made.

10. <u>Plaque</u> can cause cavities.

11. Perspiring is one way your body <u>varies</u> its temperature.

12. If the cornea of the eye is curved unevenly, the person has a condition called <u>astigmatism</u>.

13. The <u>American Medical Association</u> is a private health organization.

14. The <u>EPA</u> would know how many cases of polio occurred last year.

15. <u>Tartar</u> helps keep tooth enamel strong.

Short Answer

Write the numbers 16 to 23 on your paper. Write a complete sentence to answer each question.

16. Why is the cochlea filled with a fluid?

17. Why do manufacturers put their addresses on their products?

18. What is the cause of most eye infections?

19. What is the value of having your teeth X-rayed?

20. How could long, dirty nails lead to an infection?

21. How is nearsightedness different from astigmatism?

22. What are two things you can do to keep your ears healthy?

23. Before you buy a product, what should you ask yourself?

Essay

Write the numbers 24 and 25 on your paper. Write paragraphs with complete sentences to answer each question.

24. Why is it important to learn how to care for your body?

25. What community services contribute to your personal health?

ACTIVITIES FOR HOME OR SCHOOL

Projects to Do

1. Make a simple instrument for testing how sensitive your ears are. Tie a piece of string or yarn about 12 inches (30 centimeters) long around each end of a coat hanger. Then wind the other end of each piece of string around each index finger, so that one string is on each finger. Place your index fingers in your ears. Have someone tap on the hanger while you listen to the sounds. Take one finger out of an ear and listen to how the sound changes. Does the sound change if you change the shape of the hanger?

■ *Try testing how sensitive your ears are.*

2. With a partner, review store ads for personal-care products. Prepare a shopping list of goods you think would help with grooming and health. Discuss the items, and group them into the following categories: items needed for health, items needed for grooming, items that are not needed at all. Discuss your groupings with a parent or an older family member.

Information to Find

1. Some people with cavities do not go to a dentist until they feel pain in a tooth. Find out why a tooth can be painful. Years ago dentists had to remove a tooth that ached. Today dentists can save badly damaged teeth by doing root-canal treatment. Find out what root-canal treatment is.

2. *Cataracts* are a serious disorder of the lens in the eye. Find out how the lens is affected and what can happen if it is left untreated. What can be done to help a person who has cataracts?

3. Some hair-grooming products contain a certain kind of alcohol. Find out from a hairdresser how hair products containing alcohol should be used on the hair. Find out if alcohol can damage the hair.

Books to Read

Here are some books you can look for in your school library or the public library to find more information about health and consumer choices.

Bains, Rae. *Health and Hygiene.* Troll Associates.

Ward, Brian. *Dental Care.* Franklin Watts.

White, Laurence B., Jr., and Ray Broekel. *Optical Illusions.* Franklin Watts.

CHOOSING AND PREPARING FOODS WISELY

Food choices and ways of cooking have changed a lot since the days when people ate only what they could grow or hunt. People in the United States today can choose from many different foods. They can prepare these foods according to methods brought to this country from all over the world.

This wide variety of foods and ways of cooking presents you with many choices. How can you choose foods that give your body what it needs? How much and what kinds of food are necessary for good nutrition? How can you prepare foods in healthful ways? Choosing and preparing foods wisely will help you achieve and maintain wellness.

GETTING READY TO LEARN

Key Questions

- Why is it important to learn about food?
- How can you develop more healthful eating habits?
- How can you learn to make healthful food choices?
- How can you take more responsibility for the foods you choose to eat?

Main Chapter Sections

1 Choosing Foods for Variety and Balance
2 Choosing Foods in the Right Amounts
3 Knowing About Modern Foods
4 Preparing Foods in Healthful Ways

1 Choosing Foods for Variety and Balance

KEY WORDS

recipe
proteins
fats
minerals
vitamin
carbohydrates
fiber
balanced diet

Gloria's favorite lunch food is a tuna salad sandwich. Her brother Jeff likes a peanut butter sandwich better. When Gloria and Jeff went to Angela's house for lunch, Angela surprised them with a meal that was not a sandwich. Angela and her mother were making chicken burritos.

To make the burritos, Angela cooked shredded chicken with onions, green chili peppers, and spices. Then she warmed some thin, flat flour cakes called *tortillas* on a griddle. She put a scoop of the chicken mixture on each tortilla and then rolled up the tortillas.

■ *A lunch of chicken burritos can be a nutritious choice that is a change from sandwiches.*

recipe (REHS uh pee), a set of directions for making a certain food.

The children each ate two burritos. Gloria and Jeff liked the taste. Jeff asked Angela how to make the burritos. A set of directions for making a certain food is called a **recipe.**

People have come to the United States from many countries. They have brought many favorite recipes from their homelands. They have taught their ways of cooking to other families. Many people in the United States today use recipes from all around the world.

142

Some recipes are better known in one part of the United States than in others. Angela's recipe for chicken burritos, for example, comes from New Mexico. Ordinary foods found in the United States can be combined in many ways to make healthful meals.

How Does Chinese Cooking Meet Food Group Needs?

Mei-Ling's parents grew up in China. A Chinese meal at Mei-Ling's house most often has small servings of many different foods. The food on Mei-Ling's table is arranged carefully. In Chinese cooking, foods are chosen to look beautiful as well as taste good.

Mei-Ling's family is having a big dinner tonight. The meal begins with egg rolls filled with chicken and vegetables. Then the family has cabbage soup with small pieces of beef in it. Next come two main dishes. One is stir-fried shrimp served in a sauce of Chinese black beans. The other is sweet-and-sour pork, a dish that contains pieces of green pepper, pineapple, and tomato. Steamed rice is served with the shrimp and pork dishes. The family also eats spinach cooked in soy sauce. The meal ends with a dessert of sesame cookies. Mei-Ling's family drinks milk with their meal. They also drink Chinese tea.

■ *Recipes from another country, such as China, provide variety and balance in food choices.*

Chinese and other Asian foods are often prepared in a special pan called a wok.

The food in this meal gives Mei-Ling and her family many nutrients. Nutrients are the materials in food that help keep your body healthy. You need about 50 different nutrients. Most foods have more than one kind of nutrient, but no single food has all the nutrients you need. For this reason, you need to eat a variety of foods every day, as Mei-Ling's family does.

Healthful foods each belong to one of the five basic food groups. A food group has foods in it that have similar nutrients. By eating foods from all five basic food groups every day, you can get the nutrients your body needs.

One of the five basic food groups is the Meat, Poultry, Fish, Dry Beans, Eggs, and Nuts Group. What foods in Mei-Ling's meal belong to this group?

Food Guide Pyramid
A Guide to Daily Food Choices

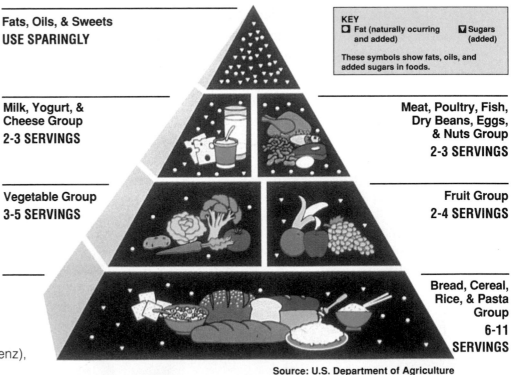

Source: U.S. Department of Agriculture

proteins (PROH teenz), nutrients that your body's cells need for growth and for repairing themselves.

fats, nutrients that give your body energy.

Foods in the Meat, Poultry, Fish, Dry Beans, Eggs, and Nuts Group give you many different kinds of nutrients. These include proteins and fats. **Proteins** provide energy and help your body grow and help repair body cells. **Fats** help give your body energy.

144

How Does Norwegian Cooking Meet Food Group Needs?

Erik's grandparents came to the United States from Norway. His family still makes many Norwegian dishes.

Tonight's meal begins with soup made from fish, carrots, onions, and milk. The soup is followed by a salad of cucumbers and fresh onions. The main dish is lamb, served with cabbage. Peas with mushrooms is another vegetable dish served with the meal. For dessert, Erik's family enjoys orange diamond cakes. These cakes are made with flour, orange peel, raisins, and almonds. Erik's family drinks milk with their meal.

Erik's meal has foods from several food groups. The lamb, fish, and almonds are from the Meat, Poultry, Fish, Dry Beans, Eggs, and Nuts Group. The milk that is in the soup and that the family drinks belongs to the Milk, Yogurt, and Cheese Group. This group is another of the five basic food groups. It has foods in it made from milk.

Foods in the Milk, Yogurt, and Cheese Group, like those in the Meat, Poultry, Fish, Dry Beans, Eggs, and Nuts Group, give you proteins, fats, and minerals.

■ *Nutritious meals from many cultures can be prepared with foods from the five basic food groups.*

Minerals are used by the body to build some body parts and to help control nerve and muscle activity. Most foods in the Milk, Yogurt, and Cheese Group contain calcium and phosphorus. These two minerals help make your bones and teeth strong.

Erik's meal includes foods from two more basic food groups. The cucumbers, carrots, onions, cabbage, peas, and mushrooms belong to the Vegetable Group. The raisins and orange peel in the orange diamond cakes belong to the Fruit Group.

Foods in the Fruit Group, the Vegetable Group, the Meat, Poultry, Fish, Dry Beans, Eggs, and Nuts Group, and the Milk, Yogurt, and Cheese Group give you nutrients called vitamins. Each **vitamin** helps a specific reaction happen in the body. Vitamin C, for example, helps your body fight off illness. Vitamin C also helps your body use the mineral iron. Fruits and vegetables also have carbohydrates in them. **Carbohydrates,** like fats and proteins, are nutrients that give your body energy.

How Does Caribbean Cooking Meet Food Group Needs?

Aston and his parents came from Jamaica, an island in the Caribbean Sea. They moved to New York when Aston was a baby. Now they are back in Jamaica for a family party. At the party, Aston's aunt and uncle are serving some Jamaican dishes that Aston has never tasted before.

■ Trying new foods from different cultures widens your choices for healthful nutrients.

The dinner begins with bits of spiced fish served on wheat toast. Then comes roast chicken stuffed with sweet potatoes, sausage, and spices. The meal also includes cucumbers cooked with black pepper and paprika. The dish Aston enjoys the most is made from rice, kidney beans, and milk. The drink served with the meal is fruit juice.

Aston's meal has foods from all five basic food groups. The rice in Mei-Ling's and Aston's meals and the wheat toast in Aston's meal belong to the Bread, Cereal, Rice, and Pasta Group. So do tortillas, oatmeal, spaghetti, and rolls. Foods in this group are rich in carbohydrates. These foods also supply some vitamins and minerals.

What Gives Meals Variety and Balance?

Mei-Ling, Erik, and Aston had very different meals. But the meals were alike in one way. Each meal had foods from all, or nearly all, of the five basic food groups. Because of this variety of foods, each meal supplied many different nutrients. The meals gave Erik, Aston, and Mei-Ling what their bodies need to stay healthy.

The meals also supplied two other important nutrients. These are water and fiber. Drinks such as milk and fruit juice have some of the water that you need each day.

■ Many different drinks contain water. You need eight glasses of water each day.

What foods are good sources of certain nutrients? This chart shows the calories and nutrient values of certain foods in the five basic food groups.

Key

As a source of a certain nutrient, the food is:

— poor   □ fair   ◿ good   ◪ excellent   ■ outstanding

Milk, Yogurt, and Cheese Group

Food	Calories	Protein	Vitamin A	Vitamin C	Calcium	Iron
Cheese, American 1 slice	106	good	fair	—	good	—
Cheese, Cottage 1/2 cup	109	excellent	—	—	fair	—
Cheese, Swiss 1 slice	107	good	fair	—	good	—
Milk 1 cup	150	good	fair	—	good	—
Milk, Lowfat 2% 1 cup	121	excellent	excellent	—	outstanding	—
Yogurt, Plain 1 cup	144	excellent	—	—	outstanding	—

Meat, Poultry, Fish, Dry Beans, Eggs, and Nuts Group

Food	Calories	Protein	Vitamin A	Vitamin C	Calcium	Iron
Beef, Ground 3 ounces	186	outstanding	—	—	—	excellent
Chicken, Baked Leg and thigh	188	outstanding	—	—	—	good
Egg Large	80	good	fair	—	—	fair
Peanut Butter 2 tablespoons	186	good	—	—	—	—
Pork Chop 3 ounces	308	outstanding	—	—	—	excellent
Tuna 3 ounces	168	outstanding	—	—	—	fair

Fruit Group

Food	Calories	Protein	Vitamin A	Vitamin C	Calcium	Iron
Apple Medium	80	—	—	good	—	—
Orange Medium	65	—	fair	outstanding	fair	—
Banana Medium	127	—	fair	good	—	fair
Grapefruit 1/2	41	—	—	outstanding	—	—
Peach Medium	38	—	—	good	—	—
Pear Medium	122	—	—	good	—	—

Vegetable Group

Food	Calories	Protein	Vitamin A	Vitamin C	Calcium	Iron
Asparagus 1/2 cup	17	—	excellent	outstanding	—	—
Potato, Baked Large	132	fair	—	outstanding	—	fair
Broccoli 1/2 cup	20	—	outstanding	outstanding	fair	—
Carrots 1/2 cup	24	—	outstanding	good	—	—
Spinach 1/2 cup	20	fair	outstanding	good	outstanding	excellent
Brussel Sprouts 1/2 cup	28	fair	good	outstanding	—	fair

Bread, Cereal, Rice, and Pasta Group

Food	Calories	Protein	Vitamin A	Vitamin C	Calcium	Iron
Bagel	165	good	—	—	—	fair
Bread, White 1 slice, enriched	61	—	—	—	—	—
Bread, Whole Wheat 1 slice	55	—	—	—	—	—
Raisin Bran 1 cup, enriched	144	fair	outstanding	outstanding	—	outstanding
Rice 1/2 cup	112	—	—	—	—	fair
Tortilla, Corn 6 inch, enriched	63	—	—	—	fair	fair

But you need to drink plenty of plain water, too. In fact, you should drink about eight glasses of water a day to keep your body working as it should.

Water helps your body use other nutrients. It helps your body digest food. Then water helps carry nutrients to the cells. Water also helps remove wastes from the body.

Fiber is another part of food that helps in digestion. Fiber comes from the parts of plants that give the plants shape. Grains, seeds, and many fruits and vegetables have fiber. Without enough food fiber, the digestive process may slow down. This can cause your intestines to feel uncomfortable. Getting enough fiber helps your digestive system work at its best.

fiber (FY buhr), a part of food that helps in digestion.

■ Sources of fiber include grains, seeds, and many fruits and vegetables.

Thinking About Your Health

What Influences Your Food Choices?

Why do you choose certain foods to eat? List on a sheet of paper 20 foods that you enjoy eating. Next to each food, try to describe what determined your choice. You may use one or all of the following code symbols next to each item.

P = physical factors (food selected because of its taste or color)

I = intellectual factors (food chosen based on your knowledge about healthful foods)

E = emotional factors (food selected to make you feel happy)

S = social factors (food chosen because of advertisements, friends, culture)

Study your food list. Then decide what other foods could be added to the list to make your diet balanced.

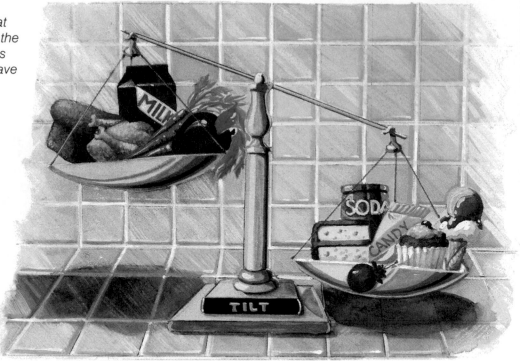

■ *This scale is unbalanced. If you eat too many foods from the Fats, Oils, and Sweets Group, you will not have a balanced diet.*

balanced diet (BAL uhnst • DY uht), a variety of foods in amounts that meet your nutritional needs.

No matter what kinds of foods you like, you can choose and combine foods wisely. The combination of all the foods you eat is your diet. A **balanced diet** is one that has a variety of foods from each of the five basic groups. Eating foods from all the groups gives you the nutrients you need to grow and stay healthy. A balanced diet also includes plenty of water and fiber.

 **REVIEW**
SECTION 1

REMEMBER?

1. Name the five basic food groups.
2. What are the main nutrients in foods?
3. What is a balanced diet?

THINK!

4. Describe foods you could eat in a balanced breakfast.
5. Name a single dish that has ingredients from at least four food groups. What is the food group for each ingredient?

2 Choosing Foods in the Right Amounts

To stay healthy, you need to eat a balanced diet. A balanced diet has foods from all five food groups in the amounts that meet your nutritional needs. If you eat too little food, you may not get enough nutrients. But if you eat foods with more of the energy nutrients than you need, you may gain weight. Getting too little or too much of the nutrients you need can cause health problems.

<table>
<tr><td>KEY WORDS</td></tr>
<tr><td>nutritional
   deficiency
calories
cholesterol</td></tr>
</table>

People need different amounts of nutrients at different times in their lives. If you are growing quickly and are very active, you need more of certain nutrients than does someone whose growth has slowed or who is not physically active. The amount of each kind of food you eat is also important. Eating too much of some foods and too little of others can mean you are not getting the proper nutrients in balance.

■ *Both meals have the same kinds of foods. However, even though the meal on the left has more food, it is not a balanced meal. The meal on the right is well balanced and contains more nutrients because of the way the food was prepared and served.*

What Problems Can Occur from Eating Too Little Food?

Some people do not have enough food. Others choose to eat very little. All these people can suffer from health problems caused by eating too little food.

■ *Citrus fruits, such as oranges, lemons, limes, and grapefruits, contain large amounts of vitamin C, as well as other nutrients.*

nutritional deficiency
(noo TRIHSH uhn uhl • dih FIHSH uhn see), lack of a certain nutrient in the diet.

Missing Nutrients. When only a few kinds of food are available, people may not get enough of certain nutrients. Too little of a certain nutrient in the diet could result in a **nutritional deficiency.**

Nutritional deficiencies can cause many health problems. For example, a disease called *scurvy* is caused by a lack of vitamin C. Before the 1700s, sailors who stayed at sea for many months at a time often got scurvy. This disease caused their gums to bleed and their teeth to become loose. James Lind, a Scottish physician, experimented and noticed that sailors who had scurvy got better if they ate fresh lemons and limes. Lemons, limes, and other citrus fruits have vitamin C. Vitamin C in the diet prevents scurvy.

Nutritional deficiencies still exist today. When a person eats too little protein, he or she may experience muscle weakness and weight loss. A lack of calcium in the diet can cause soft bones and weak teeth.

152

Skipping Meals. People sometimes skip meals because they think they are too busy to eat or they want to lose weight. Skipping meals may keep people from getting all the nutrients they need. Some people feel better with three meals a day. Other people find that eating five small meals keeps them feeling alert and strong. Your regular meals should include a healthful breakfast every morning.

Last year, Raymond often skipped breakfast. He would say he was not hungry. However, by the middle of the morning, he often felt tired, had a headache, and did not want to do his schoolwork. By lunchtime, he was so hungry that he ate too fast. The school nurse talked with him about planning meals that would help him feel better all day.

Now Raymond eats a healthful breakfast every morning. He most often has a glass of orange juice, a piece of wheat toast, and cereal with skim milk. Raymond's breakfast gives him energy to begin his day.

■ *When Raymond skips breakfast, he often feels tired in school, left. When Raymond eats a nutritious breakfast, he does much better in class, right.*

153

What Problems Can Occur from Eating Too Much Food?

Food is the body's source of energy. When you eat too much food, your body receives more energy than it can use. The extra energy is stored in the body as extra fat. Extra fat gives the body extra weight. When you eat the right amount of food and get enough exercise, you use the energy you get from your food. You help control your weight and help your body stay healthy.

■ *An apple or other fruit makes a nutritious after-school snack.*

Low-Nutrient, High-Calorie Foods. Being overweight and certain other health problems can be caused by eating too many fatty or sweet foods. To control your weight and stay healthy, it is important to limit the amounts that you eat of these foods.

You need fat in your diet. In a balanced diet, no more than one-third of your daily calories should come from fats. **Calories** are units of energy produced by food. Fat is high in calories, so a little fat gives your body a lot of food energy. However, a high-fat diet over a long time raises the chance that you will have problems with your heart when you are older. Also, a person gains weight faster on a high-fat diet. Limiting fatty foods, such as potato chips, ice cream, bacon, and lunch meats, is a good health habit to follow. It is also a good idea to limit fried foods. Fat is added to them during the cooking process.

calories (KAL uh reez), units of energy produced by food.

154

You should limit animal fats and dairy fats because they are the dietary sources of cholesterol. **Cholesterol** is a waxy substance that is found naturally in a person's blood. However, too much cholesterol can lead to problems with the heart and the blood vessels. Many foods that come from animals, such as butter, fatty meats, beef liver, shrimp, and egg yolks, add to the body's natural cholesterol level. Excess cholesterol clings to the inside walls of blood vessels. As a result, the flow of blood may be slowed or blocked.

A balanced diet includes carbohydrates. Starchy foods, such as potatoes, certain vegetables, and grains, provide carbohydrates. So do sugars, but it is a good idea to get most of your carbohydrates from starches. This is because starches offer more nutrients per calorie than do sugar products. For example, sweets and sweetened soft drinks contain a lot of sugar. While they provide calories for energy, they may offer no other useful nutrients. Sweets can cause health problems, too. For example, eating too much sugar can damage your teeth. And many sweets, such as cakes and cookies, also contain a lot of fat.

Your body needs a little salt. But many nutritionists believe that most people in the United States eat too much salt. Eating too much salt may lead to problems with your heart and blood vessels. Too much salt may cause high blood pressure.

cholesterol (kuh LEHS tuh rohl), a waxy substance that is found naturally in a person's blood; also is contained in animal fats.

MYTH
AND
FACT

Myth: All cholesterol is bad for your health.

Fact: Cholesterol is important for maintaining a healthy body. Too much cholesterol is not good for your health.

■ *Maintaining a healthful weight requires regular exercise, enough rest, and a balanced diet.*

Too Little Exercise. When you exercise, your body burns up the energy it gets from the food you have eaten. If you get too little exercise, you will gain weight. The two keys to weight control and good health are eating a balanced diet and exercising regularly.

People who are overweight sometimes go on "crash diets" or "fad diets" that do not give them enough nutrients to stay healthy. To lose weight in a healthful way, a person should combine a balanced low-fat diet with exercise. Before trying to lose weight, however, a person should talk with a physician. Eating a balanced diet, limiting low-nutrient foods, and exercising regularly can help you maintain a proper weight and stay healthy.

STOP | **REVIEW**
SECTION 2

REMEMBER?

1. Why should people not skip meals?
2. What is the key to weight control?
3. Why should people cut down on eating fatty foods?

THINK!

4. Why should a person eat a healthful breakfast every morning?
5. How can a person eat a variety of foods and still avoid foods that are unhealthful?

Health Close-up

Anorexia Nervosa and Bulimia

Anorexia nervosa and bulimia are two common eating disorders. They are connected with food intake and body weight.

Anorexia nervosa is an eating disorder of people who limit their intake so much that they become ill. At the same time, they push themselves to exercise far too much. Bulimia is an eating disorder of people who binge, or eat large amounts of food, and then get rid of the food before it can be digested. To get rid of the food, they make themselves vomit or they take laxatives. Sometimes a person suffers from both anorexia nervosa and bulimia.

Scientists are not sure what causes eating disorders. However, anorexia nervosa and bulimia occur most often in teenage girls and young women. Some scientists think that these people may be very worried about staying thin. Other scientists think that emotional problems connected with growing up may cause the disorders.

Anorexia nervosa damages the body by starving the cells. Without healthful foods, the body cells suffer from serious nutritional deficiencies. These deficiencies cause the body to be less able to fight infections. Bulimia damages the body, too. The sudden, large amounts of extra food force the digestive system to work very hard. Vomiting over and over again can damage tissues in the digestive system. The stomach acid present in vomit can decay tooth enamel, causing dental problems.

People who have one or both of these serious eating disorders do need treatment. Physicians, psychologists, and nutritionists can help the people work on their emotional problems and follow healthful diets. When the people are able to gain a good self-concept and feel more in control of their lives, they can break their harmful eating habits.

■ *Some people wrongly see themselves as being overweight, even when their weight is ideal.*

Thinking Beyond

1. What might cause some people to care so much about being thin?
2. How could someone with an eating disorder get the treatment he or she needs?

157

Knowing About Modern Foods

In the past 50 years, the variety of foods available to most people in the United States has increased. Today, you most likely eat many foods that your grandparents could not get. Even greater changes may be coming in the future.

How Have Foods Changed?

In the past, people could eat only the foods that were grown or raised where they lived. They could buy fresh fruits and vegetables only when the fruits and vegetables had just been picked. They had no way to store these foods.

Today, food is shipped all over the world. People in Kansas can eat fruit from Hawaii. A variety of fresh fruits and vegetables are available all year long in most places in the United States.

■ *Dependable methods of transportation allow a variety of fresh fruits and vegetables to reach markets around the country.*

convenience foods
(kuhn VEEN yuhns • FOODZ), foods that are partly or completely prepared when you buy them.

Preparing a meal no longer has to take as long as it did in the past. People can buy many **convenience foods.** These are foods that are bought partly or completely prepared. Frozen vegetables, canned soups, and frozen dinners are some common convenience foods. These foods often cost more than fresh foods. They cost more because you pay for the maker's time. However, convenience foods can save preparation time for busy people. Convenience

foods can also add variety to the diet. Some of these foods are prepared according to recipes from all over the world. Some of the foods are prepared for people with special dietary needs.

Most convenience foods can be stored for a long time. Chemicals called **preservatives** may be added to the foods to keep them from spoiling. Preservatives and other substances added to food are called **additives.**

Additives in food may improve the color or taste of the food. Or they may change its texture. For example, dye is often added to cheddar cheese to make the cheese orange instead of white. Some fruit drinks, ice cream, canned soups and stews, and lunch meats contain flavoring additives. Ice cream, soups, and salad dressings may contain additives that make them thicker. Some foods have natural thickeners, such as cornstarch or seaweed-based products, added to them.

Modern foods have other kinds of artificial treatments, too. For example, fruit and vegetable growers often use chemicals called *insecticides* to kill certain insects. Some insects destroy foods before they ripen. Insecticides help keep fruits and vegetables healthy. Sometimes these chemicals are still on the fresh fruits and vegetables that you buy. This is one reason it is important to wash fresh fruits and vegetables before you eat them.

preservatives (prih ZUR vuht ihvz), chemicals added to foods to keep them from spoiling.

additives (AD uht ihvz), preservatives, dyes, flavorings, and other substances added to food.

■ *Always wash fresh fruits and vegetables before eating them.*

How Can You Choose Modern Foods Wisely?

If you buy convenience foods or other foods that are packaged, read the labels carefully to find out the ingredients—the things from which the food is made. The label lists the ingredients in the order of how much of each ingredient is contained in the food. The list begins with the ingredient there is most of, and ends with the one there is least of. By law, the list must include everything that is in the food.

Try to choose foods that have the fewest chemical additives. To identify these additives, look for the words *artificial colors* and *artificial flavorings*. Also look for unfamiliar words that may be the names of dyes and flavoring chemicals.

Most package labels also list the nutrients in the food. The list lets you compare the nutrients in different foods or in different brands of the same food. You can then choose the food with the most nutrients.

The nutrition facts on package labels also include

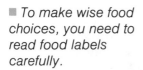

■ *To make wise food choices, you need to read food labels carefully.*

information called *Percent Daily Value.* These numbers can help you see how a food fits into your overall diet. For example, a value of 30 for one nutrient means one serving of that food provides 30 percent of your daily need for that nutrient. You could then eat other foods that would provide the remaining 70 percent of that nutrient for one day.

When a food receives little processing, few of its original nutrients are lost. This is particularly true for vitamins, which are easily destroyed by heat. A good rule to follow in food selection and preparation is "the fresher, the better."

STOP REVIEW
SECTION 3

REMEMBER?

1. Why are additives put into some foods?
2. What kinds of information can be found on food labels?

THINK!

3. Why should convenience not be the main reason to select foods?
4. Why is it important to be able to understand a food label?

Making Wellness Choices

Steve and Cindy often shop for groceries with their parents. On this trip, their parents ask them to select a breakfast cereal that will be tasty and nutritious for the whole family. Steve and Cindy walk up and down the long aisle lined with shelves full of different cereals. There are dozens of cereals from which they must make one selection. Some cereals they do not know. Others they have tried, and some they have heard about in advertising.

? How could Steve and Cindy select one cereal? Explain your wellness choice.

4 Preparing Foods in Healthful Ways

William invited his friend Sal for dinner. Sal thought that William would heat frozen dinners for them. Instead, with the help of his father, William made a *frittata*. It was like a baked spinach-and-cheese omelette. It tasted delicious! And making it took only a little longer than heating a frozen dinner.

William chopped an onion and put it in a nonstick pan. He heated and stirred the onion over low heat until it became brown. Then he added a crushed clove of garlic. He stirred and heated the garlic and onion for five minutes.

Earlier, William had thawed a package of frozen spinach. He squeezed the water from the spinach. When the onion and garlic had cooked, he put the spinach into the pan with the onion and garlic. Then he stirred in the juice squeezed from a lime, a teaspoon of crushed basil leaves, a bit of black pepper, and a bit of nutmeg.

■ *Although it took longer to make, William's frittata is more nutritious than a fast-food hamburger.*

William set the pan aside and beat five eggs in a bowl. Then he added the spinach mixture to the eggs. He also stirred in a quarter pound of grated Parmesan cheese.

William poured the whole mixture into a 9-inch (22.5-centimeter) baking pan. He baked the frittata in the oven at 350 degrees Fahrenheit (177 degrees Celsius) for 20 minutes.

Many foods, like the frittata, are quick and simple to make. They help a person make a balanced meal easily. All William needed to add was a whole-grain bread. Then his meal included foods from each of the five food groups.

■ *Nutritious meals can be fun to make and delicious to eat.*

How Can You Prepare Foods Wisely?

Some ways of preparing foods are more healthful than others. Broiling fish, poultry, and meat reduces fat because none is added and much drips off as the food cooks. Poaching cooks fish and poultry very quickly without added oil or fat. Stir-frying is also a low-fat choice if you use only a small amount of vegetable oil or a nonstick spray coating. Microwave cooking also requires little or no fat.

■ Grilling chicken, as well as other meats, is better than frying because much of the fat drips away while grilling.

When you prepare fruits and vegetables, wash them carefully to remove dirt, harmful microbes, and insecticides. Eat fruits and vegetables raw, or cook them just long enough to make them tender. Steam them, or cook them in the smallest amount of water possible. Steaming vegetables preserves their nutrients.

164

Why Do People Use Seasonings in Cooking?

Flavorings and seasonings add variety to the taste of foods. Salt is often used for seasoning. However, too much salt in the diet is not healthful. Too much salt may cause blood pressure to rise.

Seasonings other than salt can give your food interesting flavors. Using them can help you limit the use of salt, too. Lime juice, basil, pepper, and nutmeg, for example, were the seasonings in William's frittata.

You can sweeten your food without adding sugar. Fruits such as apples and bananas contain sugar naturally. Adding pieces of fruit to cereal or to other foods will sweeten them.

Today's variety of foods and variety of ways of preparing foods present you with many choices. If you choose foods wisely and if you prepare your meals carefully, you can limit your intake of low-nutrient foods. This will help you give your body the nutrients it needs for good health without extra calories.

STOP REVIEW
SECTION 4

REMEMBER?

1. What happens to nutrients in vegetables that are steamed?
2. Why should you wash fruits and vegetables before eating them?

THINK!

3. What are two advantages of using fresh foods when cooking?
4. Why are foods that are called "natural" becoming more popular?

People in Health

An Interview with a Certified Dietary Manager

Kathy Orgeron knows about planning and preparing balanced meals for students. She is a certified dietary manager for a school in Metairie, Louisiana.

What does a certified dietary manager do?

A certified dietary manager oversees daily food preparation, orders and

■ *Certified dietary managers order food, plan menus, and oversee food preparation.*

purchases food, and plans menus. A certified dietary manager is concerned with the nutritional needs of people in a school, hospital, nursing home, or business. He or she must also be aware of new developments in the field of nutrition, including new recipes and new ways of preparing foods.

When you started your job, what was one of the first things that you did?

When I started my job, I made an effort to find out what foods the students liked and disliked. I saw that many students threw away cafeteria food. It upset me to see so much food being wasted. Before I could plan and prepare balanced meals, I had to find out what foods the students wanted and needed. I held a general meeting with school administrators, parents, and students to discuss this problem. We agreed to add new items to the menu. Now students enjoy their food more.

What things do you think about in planning a balanced meal?

I look at more than the nutritional value of foods. I also think about the colors and temperatures of various foods. For example, I would not want to serve a meal of turkey, cauliflower, mashed potatoes, and pears. The colors of these foods are too much alike, so the meal would not look appetizing. It is also more appetizing to have a mixture of hot and cold foods and not just one or the other.

■ *Ms. Orgeron talks with students to find out what foods they like.*

Some students may not realize that if food does not look good, they are less likely to eat it. Also, foods taste better if they have some seasoning.

What can seasonings do for food?

Seasonings can enhance the flavor of food, but they should not be overused. Lunches at our school are not dull. The students here are used to eating spicy food, and they like some seasoning added to their food. People in different parts of the country tend to use different kinds of seasoning. I do add a little salt during cooking.

Are you concerned with the amount of additives in foods that you order?

I try to get items that contain very few preservatives. However, to get the best prices and serve large numbers of people, I need to order very large quantities of food. Food sold in bulk must often be stored for a long time, so there are very few items I can purchase that do not contain any preservative at all. I do try to get the highest-quality food available.

How do you plan your menus?

I use a large calendar, and I schedule the menus for a whole month at a time. This is not as easy as it sounds. I have to make sure I use all the food groups in each meal, and I must try not to repeat foods too often.

How did you prepare for your career as a certified dietary manager?

I thought about what I wanted to do and what jobs were available. It occurred to me that everyone has to eat! So I spent a year studying dietary management at a vocational technical school. While I was in school, I studied the science of nutrition. I also studied food production, food storage, food preparation, and food service, as well as many other subjects.

Learn more about people who work as certified dietary managers. Interview a certified dietary manager in a school or hospital. Or write for information to the American Dietetic Association, 216 W. Jackson Boulevard, Suite 800, Chicago, IL 60606.

Main Ideas

- Many people in the United States today use recipes from around the world.
- The foods containing the nutrients needed to stay healthy are classified in five basic food groups.
- To stay healthy, you need to eat a balanced diet.
- If you buy food in a package, read the label carefully; it lists the ingredients and may list nutrients in the food.
- Food preservation and preparation methods have changed a lot since the days when people ate only what they could grow or hunt.
- Some ways of preparing foods are more healthful than others.

Key Words

Write the numbers 1 to 8 in your health notebook or on a separate sheet of paper. After each number, write the letter of the definition below that best describes each term. Page numbers in ( ) tell you where to look in the chapter if you need help.

1. recipe (142)
2. minerals (146)
3. fiber (149)
4. balanced diet (150)
5. nutritional deficiency (152)
6. cholesterol (155)
7. convenience foods (158)
8. additives (159)

a. waxy substance that is naturally in a person's blood; it also is in animal fat

b. nutrients, such as calcium, that help build some body parts and control nerve and muscle activity

c. diet that contains a variety of foods from each of the five basic food groups

d. foods that are partly or completely prepared when you buy them

e. lack of a certain nutrient in the diet

f. part of food that helps in digestion

g. preservatives and other substances added to food

h. set of directions for making a certain food

Write the numbers 9 to 14 on your paper. After each number, write a sentence that defines the term. Page numbers in ( ) tell you where to look in the chapter if you need help.

9. proteins (144)
10. fats (144)
11. vitamin (146)
12. carbohydrates (146)
13. calories (154)
14. preservatives (159)

Remembering What You Learned

Page numbers in ( ) tell you where to look in the chapter if you need help.

1. How can you get most of the nutrients your body needs? (142–150)
2. What do the nutrients in foods from the Meat, Poultry, Fish, Dry Beans, Eggs, and Nuts Group do for your body? (144)

3. What nutrients do foods from the Fruit Group and the Vegetable Group give you? (146)

4. What can happen if you eat too little food? (151–153)

5. What is scurvy? (152)

6. Why should your regular meals include a healthful breakfast every morning? (153)

7. How can extra nutrients cause a person to gain weight? (154–155)

8. Why do people use convenience foods? (158–159)

9. Why do convenience foods often cost more than fresh foods? (158)

10. Why are preservatives often added to convenience foods? (159)

11. What are two ways of cooking that keep nutrients in food? (164)

12. Why should you wash fresh fruits and vegetables before eating them? (164)

Thinking About What You Learned

1. Why are some recipes more common in one part of the country than in another?

2. Why is it important to have enough exercise as well as a balanced diet?

3. Why is it not good to have too much fat in your diet?

4. Why is it important to know what preservatives or chemicals have been added to packaged foods?

5. How can cooking vegetables too long or in too much water remove some nutrients?

Writing About What You Learned

1. Write a menu for one day. This menu should follow the guidelines of the food pyramid. It should involve ways of preparation that are healthful and do not remove nutrients or add fat.

2. Compose a letter to a classmate, your parents, or your teacher that includes an invitation to dinner. Explain that you are going to prepare a meal of healthful and nutritious foods from another culture.

Applying What You Learned

SOCIAL STUDIES

Research a region of the world to learn about some of its traditional foods. Plan a lunch or dinner that is a traditional and balanced meal from that region.

Modified True or False

Write the numbers 1 to 15 in your health notebook or on a separate sheet of paper. After each number, write *true* or *false* to describe the sentence. If the sentence is false, also write a term that replaces the underlined term and makes the sentence true.

1. A TV dinner is a <u>convenience food</u>.

2. <u>Cancer</u> is a disease caused by a vitamin deficiency.

3. You should limit low-nutrient, <u>high-calorie</u> foods.

4. <u>Cholesterol</u> is a waxy substance found naturally in blood.

5. In a balanced diet, most of your daily calories come from <u>protein</u>.

6. The two keys to weight control are eating a balanced diet and <u>exercising regularly</u>.

7. A set of directions for making a certain food is called a <u>recipe</u>.

8. <u>Vitamins</u> help control nerve and muscle activity.

9. For your digestive system to work at its best, you should eat enough <u>fat</u>.

10. <u>Calories</u> are units of energy produced by food.

11. Eating too much <u>salt</u> can damage your teeth.

12. <u>Preservatives</u> in foods keep them from spoiling.

13. The first ingredient on a label is the ingredient present in the <u>largest</u> amount.

14. Chicken that is broiled is lower in fat than chicken that is <u>fried</u>.

15. Dye put in food to make it look better is a <u>preservative</u>.

Short Answer

Write the numbers 16 to 23 on your paper. Write a complete sentence to answer each question.

16. Why is it important to wash fresh fruits and vegetables before eating them?

17. What is the difference between a vitamin and a mineral?

18. Which food group is rich in carbohydrates?

19. How are water and fiber alike?

20. How is skipping meals different from dieting?

21. What is a nutritional deficiency?

22. What are two ways people can gain weight?

23. Why is too much cholesterol bad for your health?

Essay

Write the numbers 24 and 25 on your paper. Write paragraphs with complete sentences to answer each question.

24. Describe the factors you would need to consider in establishing a balanced diet.

25. Why is it important to learn about food?

Projects to Do

1. Survey at least two sections of a large grocery store. Notice which foods have little added sugar and have had little processing. For example, look in the cereal aisle. What ingredients and additives are in cereals that are at your eye level? What cereals are on the top shelf? What cereals are on the bottom? Why, do you think, are certain products at young people's eye level?

2. Make a breakfast suggestion box for your class. Write down ideas for healthful foods that may not be common breakfast meals. Include recipes if possible. Put your ideas in the suggestion box. Ask your classmates to add their own suggestions. You may want to create new breakfast menus using some of your classmates' ideas.

■ *Food preparation and the variety of foods available have changed a lot over the years.*

3. Talk with an adult about the ways some foods have changed since he or she was your age. (If you can, talk with a grandparent.) Is a wider variety of foods available now? Were any convenience foods available then? Why or why not?

Information to Find

1. Select one country other than the United States. What are some foods that may appear in a traditional meal eaten by a family in that country? Recipe books in the library can help you find out about foods in other countries. List at least four dishes. To which food group or groups does each dish belong?

2. Name at least three foods, besides lemons and limes, that are good sources of vitamin C. Nutrition books in your library will have this information.

Books to Read

Here are some books you can look for in your school library or the public library to find more information about food, diet, and cooking.

Matthews, Dee. *The You Can Do It! Kids Diet*. Holt, Rinehart & Winston.

Paul, Aileen. *The Kids' Diet Cookbook*. Doubleday.

Waters, Marjorie. *The Victory Garden Kids Book*. Houghton-Mifflin.

EXERCISE, REST, AND SLEEP

You may know that your body needs exercise, rest, and sleep to stay healthy. But you may not know why you need to exercise, why your body needs to rest, and why you need a certain amount of sleep.

In what ways does exercise help your body? How much exercise is right for you? What happens to your body when you sleep? Why do you need to sleep and dream to stay healthy? The answers to these questions will help you plan for a balance of exercise, rest, and sleep in your daily and weekly schedules. This balance will help you maintain personal wellness.

GETTING READY TO LEARN

Key Questions

- Why is it important to learn about balancing your exercise, rest, and sleep?
- How do you feel about the ways you now exercise, rest, and sleep?
- How can you learn to make healthful choices about your exercise, rest, and sleep?
- What can you do to have a healthful daily schedule of exercise, rest, and sleep?

Main Chapter Sections

1 How Exercise Helps You
2 Planning an Exercise Program
3 Your Need for Rest and Sleep

1 How Exercise Helps You

exercise (EHK suhr syz), any activity that strengthens or develops some body part or your whole body.

physically fit (FIHZ ih klee · FIHT), having a body that is able to work at its best.

A few months ago, Mark noticed that he had gained weight. He became tired and out of breath after a few minutes of swimming. His muscles did not have as much strength when he carried heavy things. He did not sleep well, and he did not feel good about himself.

Mark's brother, Dennis, said that Mark needed to get more exercise. **Exercise** is activity that strengthens or develops some body parts or your whole body. A sport such as swimming or playing soccer is exercise. Some work, such as raking leaves or shoveling snow, acts as exercise. Walking, dancing, and bicycling are also exercise.

Regular *vigorous* activity helps people of all ages stay healthy. It helps you control your weight. It makes many body systems work better. It stretches and strengthens your muscles, particularly the heart muscle. In all these ways, regular exercise makes you **physically fit.** That is, it makes your body able to work at its best. Physical fitness helps you feel good about yourself.

■ *Regular vigorous exercise helps people keep physically fit.*

How Can Exercise Help You Control Your Weight?

To help keep your body weight within a healthful range, you need to keep the calories you take in balanced with the calories you use up. The number of calories in a food depends on the kinds of nutrients the food has. Fat in food has more than twice the calories of protein or carbohydrates. One gram of fat has nine calories, while one gram of protein or carbohydrate has four calories. Most fresh fruits and vegetables are low in calories because they are high in water and fiber and low in fat. When you take in more calories than your body is able to use, the extra food is changed to fat that is stored in your body. You gain weight when extra fat builds up in your body.

Your body is constantly burning calories all day. Each of your daily activities burns calories at a different rate.

CALORIES USED IN AN HOUR BY PEOPLE OF DIFFERENT WEIGHTS

Activity	77 lbs.	99 lbs.	110 lbs.
Basketball	345	405	435
Bicycling	150	175	190
Running	405	480	515
Skating	215	255	275
Skiing	370	435	465
Soccer	375	435	470
Swimming	185	220	235
Tennis	265	310	335
Walking	165	205	225

By including regular exercise in your daily routine, you use up even more calories. Calories are constantly burned to keep your heart beating and your lungs working.

How Can Exercise Help Make Your Body Efficient?

Mark changed his schedule so that he could jog every other day and become more fit. At first he was short of breath after only a few minutes of jogging. He could feel his heart pounding. He could not talk while he jogged. Mark's body had to take in more air, and his blood had to move faster. More oxygen and nutrients had to reach his muscles. Jogging made Mark's muscles and his respiratory and circulatory systems work harder than they were used to working.

Mark slowly began to lose weight. He also began to fall asleep faster at night. Now he is able to run farther without getting tired. His body has become more **efficient.** He is able to do more with less effort. The extra strain he has been putting regularly on his body's muscles has improved his fitness.

efficient (ih FIHSH uhnt), able to do more with less effort.

■ *As Mark continues to exercise, he gets stronger and improves his physical fitness.*

With more exercise, Mark's lungs have become able to hold more air. Lungs that hold more air help your body work more efficiently. You do not have to breathe as hard or as often to get the oxygen you need. Deeper breathing also lets you get rid of more carbon dioxide each time you breathe out. Carbon dioxide in your body can make you feel tired. The faster you can get rid of carbon dioxide, the sooner you feel rested.

Jogging has also made Mark's heart muscle stronger. A strong heart helps make the circulation more efficient. It pumps more blood each time it beats. It can move the same amount of blood with fewer beats.

Regular, vigorous exercise expands your blood vessels so that blood can flow more easily. Exercise keeps cholesterol and blood fats from building up on the inside walls of blood vessels. Continuing to exercise regularly can help your blood pressure stay normal all your life. **Blood pressure** is the force of blood against the walls of your arteries.

blood pressure (BLUHD · PREHSH uhr), the force of blood against the walls of your arteries.

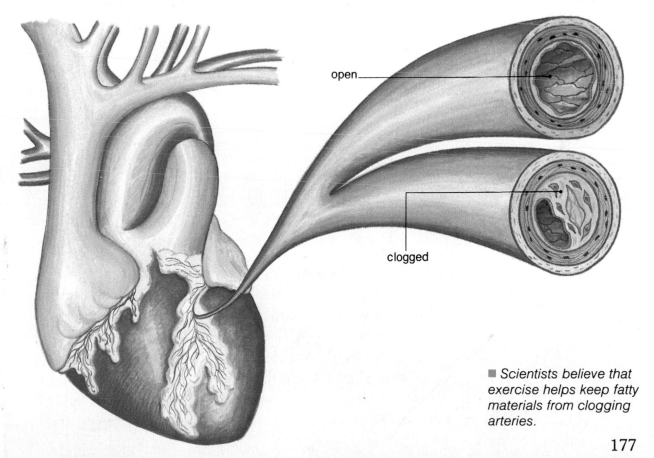

open

clogged

■ *Scientists believe that exercise helps keep fatty materials from clogging arteries.*

Lifting Safely

To lift a heavy object, crouch down. Keep your back as straight as possible. Take the object in your arms, and hold it close to your body. Then use your leg muscles to push your body up. Never try to lift an object that is too heavy for you.

When blood vessels have little cholesterol and blood fats deposited on them, it is easier for blood to reach all your cells. Your cells then receive more oxygen and nutrients, so you get more energy when you need it. When your blood flows more easily, it can also carry away wastes more quickly. Your whole body works more efficiently when your circulatory system is healthy. Mark's blood keeps flowing more easily because of his jogging.

How Can Exercise Improve Your Muscles and Posture?

Exercise gives you added muscle strength. Stronger muscles can do more work for a longer time. The harder you make your muscles work, the stronger they become.

■ *Exercising strengthens muscles in the body.*

Certain kinds of exercise help strengthen certain muscles. For example, push-ups make the muscles in the chest and the back of the upper arms strong. Running makes the leg muscles strong.

By strengthening your muscles, exercise helps improve your posture. **Posture** is the way you hold your body. Strong muscles help you hold yourself up straight. They help you sit or stand for a long time without becoming tired.

posture (PAHS chuhr), the way you hold your body.

Good posture helps your whole body work at its best. There is less crowding of your inner organs when your posture is good. Good posture tells other people that you feel good about yourself. It is an important body message.

It is never too late to practice good posture. If you have poor posture, you may be able to change it. The two suggestions that follow can help you make good posture a habit.

First, stand with your back against a wall. Your head, shoulders, and feet should be touching the wall. Keep your chest high and your chin and shoulders level. Keeping your knees slightly relaxed, point your feet straight ahead. When viewed from your side, your ear, shoulder, and hip should be in a straight line. Try to keep this posture when you stand or walk.

The second suggestion will help you improve your sitting posture. Sit so that your upper spine is against the back of the chair. Keep your back straight, and rest your feet on the floor for balance. Your weight should be supported by your hips and thighs. You should be able to feel the back of the chair supporting your spine.

Try to remind yourself to use good posture at all times. If you practice standing and sitting up straight, good posture will soon become a habit. Good exercise habits strengthen the muscles, making good posture easier to maintain.

"Pot bellies" are due to weak abdominal muscles. When the muscles sag, the pot belly pulls the spine into a curve, causing poor posture.

■ *Good posture helps your body work at its best. Remind yourself to use good posture while sitting, standing, and walking.*

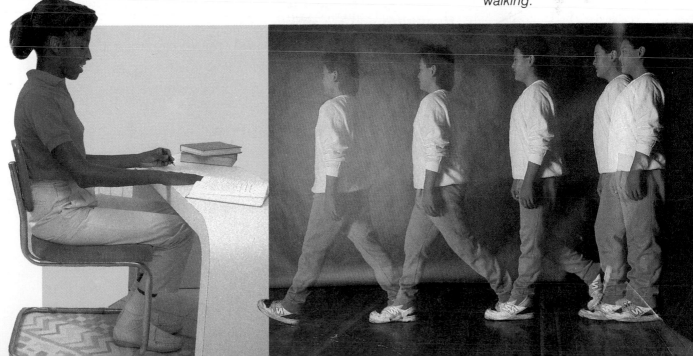

How Can Vigorous Exercise Improve Your Endurance and Flexibility?

Vigorous exercise gives you more endurance. With **endurance** you are able to keep working for a long time without becoming tired. When you have more endurance, you have the energy to be active for longer periods. You can play a sport or dance longer without getting tired. Endurance comes mostly from exercise that gives you stronger muscles, deeper breathing, and more efficient circulation.

endurance (ihn DUR uhns), the ability to keep working for a long time without becoming tired.

■ *Swimming improves endurance. Stretching develops flexibility.*

Some exercises also give your body more flexibility. With **flexibility** you are able to bend, turn, and stretch easily. Exercises such as side twists and lying-down knee lifts improve your flexibility by stretching your muscles. These exercises make your joints able to move more freely.

flexibility (flehk suh BIHL uht ee), the ability to bend, turn, and stretch easily.

How Can Exercise Improve Your Self-Esteem?

Having self-esteem means liking and respecting yourself. Regular exercise can help you feel good about yourself by helping you look the best you can. Physical activity builds strong muscles that help you have good posture. Exercise also helps control your weight. You can look and feel your best if your posture is good and your weight is right for you.

There is another way exercise can help you build self-esteem. You can take pride in working toward the goals you set for physical fitness. Having realistic goals for fitness helps you work hard to reach them. Goals that are too easy for you do not challenge you to do your best. Goals that are too hard for you are discouraging because you think you cannot succeed. When your goals are realistic, you try hard to reach them. Trying hard helps you build and maintain your self-esteem.

■ *Reaching goals for physical fitness helps improve your self-esteem.*

STOP REVIEW SECTION 1

REMEMBER?

1. What are three benefits of regular exercise?
2. How does regular exercise help your heart and blood vessels?
3. What effect does exercise have on your muscles?

THINK!

4. Why is some physical activity exercise, and some not?
5. What is one exercise for improving endurance, strength, and flexibility all at once?

Measuring Body Fat

Scientists divide total body weight into two parts: lean body weight and body fat. *Lean body weight* is the combined weight of your muscles, your bones, your organs, and the tissues that hold your body together. *Body fat* is what remains.

Some body fat is normal and needed. Fat stores some vitamins, such as A, D, E, and K. Fat also provides needed calories if you become ill or for some other reason cannot eat normally for a few days. Fat surrounds your organs to help protect them from injury. It helps keep your body warm in cold weather. Too much body fat, however, can cause health problems.

By standing on a bathroom scale, you find out your total body weight. One way to get a measurement of just your body fat is to have a trained person use a tool called *skinfold calipers*. Skinfold calipers have two movable jaws hinged together. Squeezed around folds in the skin, the calipers measure body fat directly under the skin. That is where most of your body fat is found.

Skinfold measurements for body fat are taken at several places on the body. One place to measure is on the back of the upper arm, at the triceps. A second place is on the inner calf, halfway down the lower leg. Another is on the back, under the shoulder blade. All the caliper measurements taken on a person are added together. Then the amount is compared with a reference chart to determine what percentage of the person's weight is body fat.

The amount of body fat most sixth-grade girls need is 15 to 20 percent of total body weight. Boys the same age need 10 to 15 percent. The percentages will increase some as you go through puberty. Knowing your percentage of body fat tells you more about your body composition than just knowing your total weight. Too much or too little body fat, not weight, increases a person's chance of developing health problems.

■ *Skinfold calipers measure body fat.*

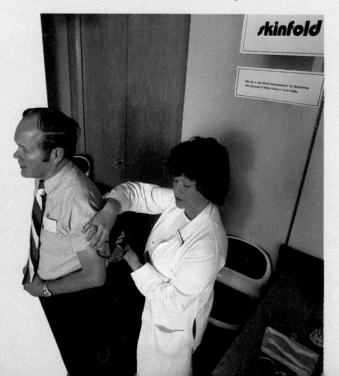

Thinking Beyond

1. Why is having body fat normal and necessary?
2. After it has been determined that a person has too much body fat, what can be done to reduce the amount?

2 Planning an Exercise Program

Peggy wanted to keep her body trim and healthy. So she decided to set up an exercise program. An **exercise program** is a plan of the exercises that you want to do for a certain amount of time several days a week. Peggy took some tests to learn how physically fit she was. She used her scores to set exercise goals for herself. Then she chose several kinds of exercises to help her meet her goals and improve her overall fitness. She selected some exercises that she liked and others that she wanted to learn more about. She planned her schedule to include exercise every day. Peggy set up a program of different activities to make her body stronger, more flexible, and more efficient.

KEY WORDS

exercise program
cardiorespiratory
  fitness
workout
warm-up
aerobic exercise
target heart rate
cool-down

exercise program (EHK suhr syz • PROH gram), a plan of the exercises that you want to do for a certain amount of time several days a week.

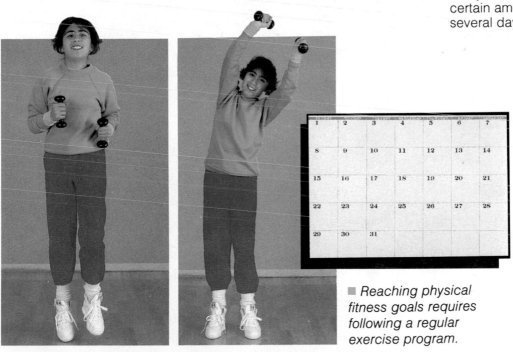

■ *Reaching physical fitness goals requires following a regular exercise program.*

Ready: How Fit Are You?

The first step in planning an exercise program is to find out how physically fit you are. Your school may give physical fitness tests. The YMCA, the YWCA, or another community organization in your area may give such tests.

Do not take these tests if your physical activity is limited for any medical reason. Do not take the test for endurance, the steady state jog, unless you have been doing endurance exercises for at least eight weeks.

The following tests, taken together, measure overall physical fitness. Separately, the tests measure muscle strength, endurance, and flexibility.

■ *Bent-knee curl-ups* are used to test abdominal muscle strength and endurance. Do this test with knees bent and arms crossed at the chest, as shown below. Count the number of curl-ups done in 2 minutes. If the number is equal to or higher than 36, you have an acceptable level of fitness. If the number is lower than 36, your muscle-strength fitness might need improving.

■ *The bent-knee curl-up is complete when the student's lower shoulder blades return to the testing surface.*

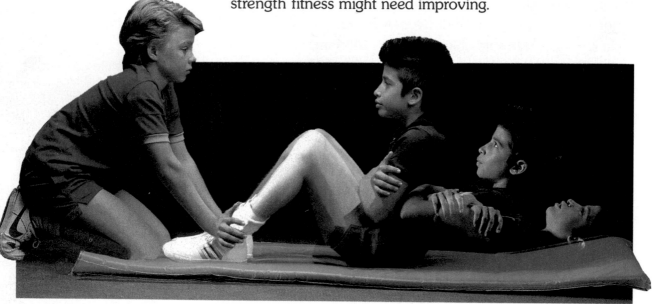

cardiorespiratory fitness (KAHRD ee oh RES puh ruh tohr ee • FIHT nuhs), the condition of your heart and lungs.

■ *A steady state jog* is used to test **cardiorespiratory fitness,** or the condition of your heart and lungs, which is an important part of endurance. A *steady state* is a pace you can keep up for 20 minutes. On a track that has distances marked, run or jog for 20 minutes. At the end of this time, compare the distance you jogged with the distances listed in the table on page 185. If your distance is equal or higher, you have achieved an acceptable level of endurance. If your distance is lower than the distance for your grade level on the table, your endurance fitness might need improvement.

STEADY STATE JOG TEST
DISTANCES COVERED IN 20 MINUTES

Grade Level	Miles	Yards	Meters
Males			
4	1.8	3,170	2,900
5	2.0	3,520	3,220
6	2.2	3,870	3,540
7–12	2.4	4,220	3,860
Females			
4	1.6	2,820	2,570
5	1.8	3,170	2,900
6	2.0	3,520	3,220
7–12	2.2	3,870	3,540

Source: The American Health and Fitness Foundation

■ A steady state jog tests cardiorespiratory fitness.

■ The *sit-and-reach* is a test of lower-back function and joint flexibility. Sit with your legs extended, and reach as far forward as possible without bending your knees. You should be able to reach 9 inches (22.5 centimeters) from where you started. If the distance you can stretch is equal to or greater than this, you have achieved an acceptable level of fitness. If the distance is lower than the standard, your flexibility fitness might need improving.

■ The sit-and-reach is used to test lower-back function and joint flexibility.

Set: What Fitness Goals Can You Set?

After you have found out how physically fit you are, you need to set realistic exercise goals for yourself. Suppose you can do only 20 bent-knee curl-ups the first time you try the strength test. After two weeks of practicing every other day, maybe you could do 30 curl-ups. But you probably could not do 40 curl-ups after so short a time. Being able to do 40 curl-ups would not be a realistic exercise goal for you. Doing 30 curl-ups would be more realistic. You do not have to break sports records to be physically fit. Your goals should help you improve your overall fitness just a little at a time. Your goals will be different from other people's goals. Like everything else about you, your level of physical fitness will always be different from the levels of other people.

■ Different people have different goals for attaining physical fitness.

Go: How Can You Have a Good Exercise Workout?

The activities you do during one session of *exercise* make up a **workout.** A workout has three important parts. Each part can help make you more physically fit. All three parts are needed to prevent certain problems.

The first part of a workout is called the **warm-up.** A warm-up prepares your body little by little for strenuous exercise by increasing your heart and breathing rates. During a warm-up, you also stretch your muscles and tendons so that you will not strain or tear them. You need at least 5 minutes to warm up properly.

workout, an exercise routine.

warm-up, the first part of a workout; prepares your body for strenuous exercise by gently increasing heartbeat and breathing rates; stretches your muscles.

■ *A complete workout needs to have three parts.*

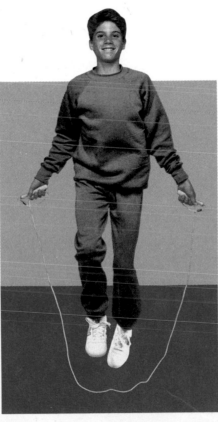

The second part of a workout is **aerobic exercise.** For aerobic exercises, think of the word *fit. F* stands for *frequency* (how often); the exercise must be done at least three times a week to improve fitness. *I* stands for *intensity* (how hard); the exercise must be done at a speed that keeps your heart at its target heart rate.

aerobic exercise (air OH bihk • EHK suhr syz), the second part of a workout; is frequent and intensive, and lasts at least 20 minutes.

187

target heart rate (TAHR guht • HAHRT • RAYT), the rate at which your heart beats when your cardiorespiratory system is working hard enough to make the system stronger.

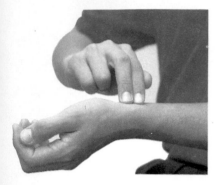

■ Check your target heart rate by taking your pulse.

■ Aerobic exercises require steady, vigorous movement for at least 20 minutes.

Your **target heart rate** is the rate at which your heart beats when your cardiorespiratory system is working hard enough to make the system stronger. *T* stands for *time* (how long); the exercise must last at least 20 minutes during each workout.

You can find out whether you are reaching your target heart rate by checking your pulse halfway through your aerobic exercise. Feel a pulse point in your wrist. Count the number of beats in 6 seconds. Then add a zero to the number. For example, if your pulse rate is 15 beats in 6 seconds, your heart is beating about 150 times a minute. For a person less than 20 years old, a target heart rate range of 145 to 185 beats per minute is an aerobic exercise goal.

Swimming, cross-country skiing, jogging, skating, bicycling, and skipping rope are some good forms of aerobic exercise. Any game with steady, continued running or movement can also be aerobic exercise if it is played for at least 20 minutes.

You can use the *talk-sing test* to know if you are exercising at a good intensity. You should be able to talk to another person, but you should not be able to sing. If you are breathing too fast to talk, slow down a bit. If you can sing, you are not working vigorously enough.

The third part of a workout is called the **cool-down.** A cool-down gradually reduces your body movement to slow your heartbeat and breathing to normal. The gradual change prevents cell wastes from being trapped in the muscles and causing muscle cramps. A cool-down should last at least 5 minutes. It should consist of gentle, slow stretching exercises.

cool-down, the third part of a workout; gradually reduces your heartbeat and breathing rates to normal.

How Can You Exercise Safely?

The best time of day to exercise depends on your own needs. Some people have more energy for exercising in the morning; others, in the evening. Your exercise time may depend on your meal schedule at home. It is better not to exercise for at least an hour before eating.

You need to dress for the weather if you exercise outdoors. Dress right for heat, cold, and wind. Notice what experienced exercisers wear.

During any workout, you need to wear the right kind of shoes for the kind of exercise you are doing. Many injuries, such as sprains and strains, can be prevented by wearing the proper shoes. Walking or jogging shoes, for example, will properly cushion the heels and support the ankles.

■ *Safety during exercise requires using proper form, dressing for the weather, and drinking plenty of water.*

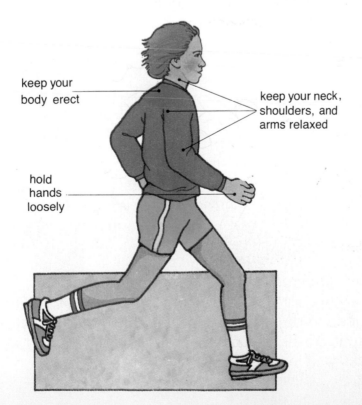

keep your body erect

keep your neck, shoulders, and arms relaxed

hold hands loosely

Choose walking or running surfaces that are smooth and a little soft, such as grass, dirt, or sand. Soft surfaces may keep you from getting foot and leg injuries.

To have a safe workout, you need to drink enough water. The water you lose as perspiration during exercise must be replaced. Experienced exercisers drink some water before exercising. They may carry water to sip at times while they bike, run, dance, or play a sport. Sometimes they drink fruit juice along with water after exercise.

STOP **REVIEW SECTION 2**

REMEMBER?

1. What do the three physical fitness tests measure?
2. Why should you begin with stretching activities each time you exercise?

THINK!

3. Design an exercise program for developing cardiorespiratory fitness.
4. How can an activity such as walking be a good aerobic exercise?

Making Wellness Choices

Yoshi's family has decided to go on a bicycle tour of a state park during spring vacation. That will be about two months from now. The trip will last 4 days and cover about 20 miles (32 kilometers) a day. Yoshi thinks that the plan sounds exciting, but she knows that the days will be long and tiring. She will need to be physically fit to enjoy the tour. Yoshi decides she needs to prepare herself by planning a daily schedule of exercise, rest, and sleep to improve her physical fitness.

? What might Yoshi's schedule include? Explain your wellness choice.

190

3 Your Need for Rest and Sleep

Edward has worked hard helping his father with yard work. Edward's muscles moved and stretched a lot as he pushed a mower, trimmed hedges, and carried leaf bags. Now that Edward has finished, he feels pleased that he could help. But he is also tired and needs to rest.

KEY WORDS

fatigue
stress

■ *After working hard, Edward is tired and needs to rest.*

Nancy has had a busy day. She walked to and from school, went to ballet class, and then studied for several hours. Now she is ready to refresh her body and her mind by getting some sleep.

Everyone needs rest and sleep. Most adults spend about one-third of their lives sleeping. Scientists do not know exactly why people need to sleep. But they agree that being tired or sleepy is a way the body helps protect itself from working too hard.

What Makes You Feel Tired?

Your body lets you know when it needs to rest. Your eyelids may feel heavy. You may start yawning. You may not be able to concentrate on a task. Your muscles may feel weak, and you may begin to slow down. These are some signs of **fatigue,** or tiredness.

fatigue (fuh TEEG), tiredness.

191

You may feel fatigue for many reasons. One reason may be that you did not get enough sleep the night before. Another may be that your body needs food to give it more energy. You may feel fatigue because you need a change from what you are doing. The different reasons cause different kinds of fatigue.

Sitting or riding for a long time with little chance to move can be physically tiring. The reason you get tired is that your body is breathing slowly and is circulating less oxygen than it would if you took breaks to walk or stretch.

■ *Resting during vigorous exercise, such as hiking up a steep hill, helps reduce physical fatigue.*

Physical Fatigue. When your muscles are tired, you feel physical fatigue. Perhaps you have been exercising for a long time. As your muscles work, their cells use oxygen and nutrients, and they produce wastes. After a while, wastes are made faster than your blood can carry them away. When wastes build up in your muscles, your brain receives a signal that you are tired. Then you need to do something less active so that your muscles can rest.

Mental Fatigue. When your mind is tired, you feel mental fatigue. Maybe you have been studying for several hours. When you have been thinking hard for a long time, your whole body may feel tired. Then you need to rest your mind and refresh your body by doing something different. Physical exercise can help you recover from mental fatigue. The change can sometimes even help you think more clearly.

Rest from mental fatigue can be a refreshing quietness or a quiet change from other activities. Being still or calm is restful. People often listen to music to relax.

Emotional Fatigue. When strong feelings make you tired, you feel emotional fatigue. Sometimes you feel you have too much to do or to think about. You may start to worry and feel tense. This tension is called **stress.** Too much stress can lead to emotional fatigue. Sometimes long-lasting emotional fatigue is like feeling sad without a particular cause. Sleep may not help you overcome this kind of fatigue. But exercise or some other activity you enjoy can help you relax from stress and overcome emotional fatigue. Often it helps to talk to a parent or another trusted adult about your feelings. By talking about your feelings, you are making a positive wellness choice.

■ *Taking breaks to stretch can reduce mental fatigue.*

stress (STREHS), tension caused by worrying or strong feelings.

■ *Exercising or doing a chore can reduce emotional fatigue.*

193

Other Causes of Fatigue. Even when you do nothing at all, you may feel tired. Boredom can cause fatigue. The solution to boredom is any kind of activity that interests you. It can be creating something, helping someone, learning a skill, or playing a sport or game.

If you feel tired without knowing why, you may be ill. Many illnesses cause fatigue. Try to rest more than usual for a day or two. If you still feel fatigue after that, talk with a parent, a guardian, or the school nurse.

There are different kinds of fatigue and different reasons for it. There are also different ways to help prevent it and recover from it. Three habits that can help are exercise, rest, and adequate sleep.

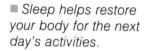
■ *Sleep helps restore your body for the next day's activities.*

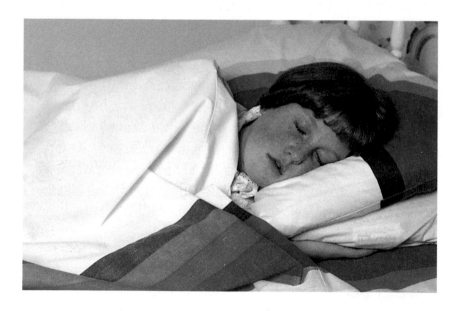

What Happens When You Sleep?

When you fall asleep, many of your body's activities change. Your muscles relax. Your heartbeat and your breathing slow down. Your senses are dulled. Your brain has times of quiet activity.

This slowdown in the way your body works saves energy. Your body uses the energy to repair itself. It builds new cells to replace worn-out ones. It clears away the wastes that have collected in your tissues during the day. Sleep gets your body ready for the next day's activities.

How Much Sleep Do You Need?

Different people need different amounts of sleep. A person's need for sleep is affected by age. Some babies sleep as much as 16 hours out of every 24. Many adults sleep 7 or 8 hours a night. People your age need about 9 or 10 hours of sleep each night. You may need more sleep than that when you are ill or when you have exercised hard during the day.

Everyone needs to sleep each day to stay alert when awake. If you do not get enough sleep several nights in a row, you may have trouble thinking during the day. You may become irritable. People who have had very little sleep for a long time see or hear things that are not really there. Eventually they fall asleep no matter how hard they try to stay awake.

What Happens When You Dream?

When you first fall asleep, you do not dream. After about 90 minutes, your eyes begin to move around very quickly under your closed eyelids. You are in a period of rapid eye movement (REM) sleep. REM sleep is sleep with dreams. Most people have four or five periods of REM sleep a night. Periods of REM sleep last from 5 to 15 minutes. After each period, you go back into dreamless sleep.

During REM sleep, some of your muscles twitch. Your brain waves show that your mind is very active during this period. Brain waves are tiny waves of energy that your brain produces as it works.

Scientists do not know why people dream, but they have several ideas. One idea is that dreams are made up of bits of memory in no certain order. When you dream, your brain may be sorting through those bits of memory and deciding which ones to store.

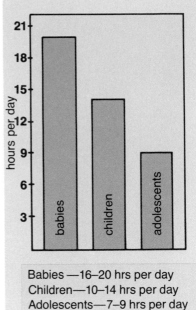

Babies —16–20 hrs per day
Children—10–14 hrs per day
Adolescents—7–9 hrs per day

■ The amount of sleep you need will change as you grow older.

■ During REM sleep, your body is at rest. However, as the pattern of brain waves shows, your mind is very active.

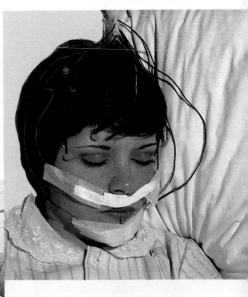

195

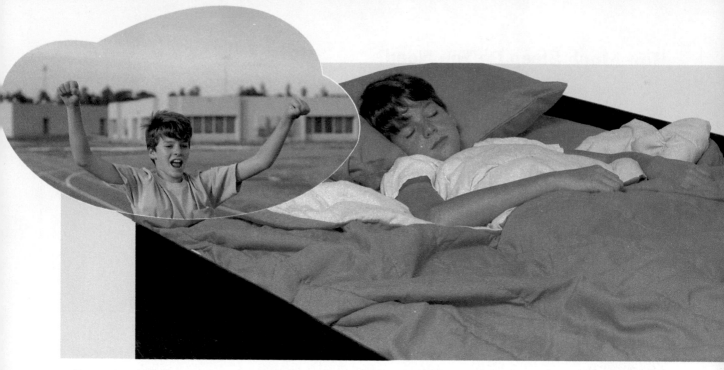

■ *Dreaming may be a way of seeing your wishes come true.*

■ *A good night's sleep is usually accompanied by dreams. They can help you wake up feeling mentally and physically refreshed.*

Another idea is that dreams contain thoughts and feelings that you do not want to know about when you are awake. They may be problems you do not want to face, secret fears, or wishes for things you cannot have. In your dreams, you go through those thoughts and feelings. You may dream that your problems have been solved or that some wishes have come true. For example, you may be worried about a test the next day. You may dream about taking the test and doing well on it.

Scientists have learned that everyone needs to dream. If people do not dream enough one night, they often make up for it by dreaming more the next night.

How Do Exercise, Rest, and Sleep Work Together?

Dreaming and sleeping help keep your mind and your body healthy. When you sleep well, you wake up rested and refreshed. Your mind and your body are ready to work and play hard. A day of exercise and activity uses energy. You take breaks from activity to rest for a while. Then you can continue your activities. You work, play, and rest all through the day. At some point, you feel so tired that you sleep again. Exercise, rest, and sleep work together to help you stay healthy.

196

REMEMBER?

1. How do tired or sleepy feelings help protect your body?
2. What can help you recover from mental fatigue?
3. What happens to your body when you fall asleep?
4. What may happen if you do not sleep enough?

THINK!

5. What kinds of activity might cause physical, mental, and emotional fatigue?
6. Design a daily schedule that includes at least 20 minutes of exercise, a restful break, and adequate sleep. The schedule should also allow you to complete your schoolwork, your chores, and other important activities.

Thinking About Your Health

Creating a Weekly Schedule

Create a 24-hour schedule for 7 days like the one shown here. Mark on your schedule the times when you are at school, eating meals, doing chores, studying, and playing. Mark the times you usually exercise and sleep. What does your schedule look like? Now consider how to add times for rest to your schedule. What are some good times for you to rest?

AM	Sunday	Monday	Tuesday	Wednesday	Thursday	Friday	Saturday
12							
1							
2							
3							
4							
5							
6							
7							

197

People in Health

An Interview with a Sports Coach

Morgan Wootten knows about the importance of exercise and physical fitness. He is a high school basketball coach in Hyattsville, Maryland.

What does a sports coach do?

A sports coach teaches players the rules of a sport and the skills for playing that sport. He or she directs the plans of the team and makes decisions that will help the team win in competition. A coach also helps players learn the meaning of cooperation, confidence, and concentration. But before players can learn any of these things, they must be physically fit. A coach uses different exercises to help players become physically fit.

Do you have certain exercises for the players?

In basketball, which is the sport I coach, these exercises are called drills. A *drill* is a way of teaching or training players by having them do the same exercise again and again. After trying many different kinds of drills, I have found the right ones to help my players improve their physical condition. Also, before my players practice, I have them do exercises for flexibility.

Why is flexibility important in sports?

The ability to stretch helps a player perform better. It also reduces the chance of injury. Flexibility makes it easier for the body to move. Stretching exercises help get the muscles ready to play a sport.

What exercise helps build endurance for basketball players?

One exercise to build endurance is running. Playing basketball well requires fast running from one end of the court to the other. Running dashes is good for building up quickness. But running long distances is important because it increases overall endurance. I encourage my players to participate in long-distance running before the basketball season.

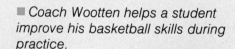
■ *Coach Wootten helps a student improve his basketball skills during practice.*

■ *Basketball helps players both mentally and physically.*

Is sleep important for your players?

The proper amount of sleep is very important. I believe it is also important to go to bed at almost the same time each night. The body needs a chance to rest and relax. Sleep helps prepare the body for the next day.

Is a balanced diet important too?

There is an old saying in basketball: What you eat today will run, jump, and shoot for you tomorrow.

Can exercising ever be harmful?

If exercises are not done properly, they can be harmful. It is important to learn to exercise correctly. Young people should also know that it can be harmful to exercise before an injury has completely healed. The biggest mistake some players make is that they try to play too soon after an injury. I would rather see a player come back a week too late than one day too soon.

Why is playing basketball good for a person?

Many young people know that playing basketball helps them get into excellent physical condition. What they might not know is that physical and mental conditioning go hand in hand. The beauty of playing basketball is that it helps both your physical condition and your mental condition. The skills a person learns in basketball can be used throughout life. Basketball is a great way to work off energy. It is also a way to use spare time wisely. The players on a team learn about teamwork. They learn how to get along with one another. They learn about dedication. They learn how to handle both success and failure. That's why basketball is so much like the game of life.

Learn more about people who work as sports coaches in schools. Interview a coach. Or write for information to the National High School Athletic Coaches Association, P.O. Box 941329, Maitland, FL 32794-1329.

Main Ideas

- Your body needs a balance of exercise, rest, and sleep to stay healthy.
- Exercise makes your whole body look, feel, and work the best it can.
- For your body to weigh the amount that is right for you, you need to balance the calories you take in with the calories you use.
- Regular exercise expands your blood vessels so that blood can flow more easily, gives your muscles strength, improves your posture, builds up your endurance, and gives your body more flexibility.
- Exercise can help you build self-esteem. You can take pride in meeting the goals you set for physical fitness.
- Your body lets you know when it needs rest.

Key Words

Write the numbers 1 to 8 in your health notebook or on a separate sheet of paper. After each number, copy the sentence and fill in the missing term. Page numbers in ( ) tell you where to look in the chapter if you need help.

exercise (174) workout (187)
efficient (176) aerobic exercise
flexibility (180) (187)
cardiorespiratory fatigue (191)
  fitness (184) stress (193)

1. The condition of your heart and lungs is called ___?___ .

2. If you feel tired, you are experiencing ___?___ .

3. Your body is ___?___ if it is able to do more with less effort.

4. Your body's ability to bend, turn, and stretch easily is called ___?___ .

5. You experience ___?___ if you worry and are tense.

6. Any activity that makes your body work hard is ___?___ .

7. A ___?___ is an exercise period made up of three parts.

8. The longest and most intense part of a workout is ___?___ .

Write the numbers 9 to 16 on your paper. After each number, write a sentence that defines the term. Page numbers in ( ) tell you where to look in the chapter if you need help.

9. physically fit (174)
10. blood pressure (177)
11. posture (178)
12. endurance (180)
13. exercise program (183)
14. warm-up (187)
15. target heart rate (188)
16. cool-down (189)

Remembering What You Learned

Page numbers in ( ) tell you where to look in the chapter if you need help.

1. What does being physically fit mean? (174)

2. What causes your weight to stay about the same? (175)

3. How does exercise improve your posture? (178)

4. How do certain exercises improve your flexibility? (180)

5. How can exercise improve your self-esteem? (180–181)

6. How can you find out how physically fit you are? (183–185)

7. When you follow an aerobic exercise program, how often should you exercise? How hard? How long? (187–188)

8. Why should drinking water be part of a safe exercise workout? (190)

9. What are three kinds of fatigue? (192–193)

10. How can you overcome mental fatigue? (193)

11. What can help you relax from stress? (193)

12. How does your body use the energy it saves while you sleep? (194)

13. How much sleep do most people your age need? (195)

14. What do your muscles do during REM sleep? What does your mind do? (195)

15. What happens if a person does not dream enough one night? (196)

Thinking About What You Learned

1. What is an advantage of having three or four aerobic exercises in one exercise program?

2. What do you need to consider when trying to improve your endurance and flexibility?

3. Why is it important to set realistic goals for physical fitness?

4. How may your needs for physical fitness be different from those of your friends and family members? How might they be the same?

5. How might exercise help some people who are having problems in their daily lives?

Writing About What You Learned

1. Select one kind of vigorous exercise activity you do. Describe how you prepare for it. Mention any special clothing or equipment that is needed. Describe the warm-up needed. Is the activity done alone, in pairs, or in groups? Describe the cool-down.

2. Write about exercise, rest, and sleep. How are they related?

Applying What You Learned

MATHEMATICS

Keep a record of what you eat and what you do for one day. Determine the number of calories in the foods you have eaten using a food/calorie chart. Also determine the number of calories used in your activities. Compare the calories you take in with the calories you use.

Modified True or False

Write the numbers 1 to 15 in your health notebook or on a separate sheet of paper. After each number, write *true* or *false* to describe the sentence. If the sentence is false, also write a term that replaces the underlined term and makes the sentence true.

1. When your body is able to work at its best, you are <u>physically fit</u>.

2. A <u>warm-up</u> includes all the activities of one exercise session.

3. Tension caused by worrying is <u>fatigue</u>.

4. When you take in more <u>calories</u> than your body can use, the extra food is changed to body fat.

5. Your <u>blood pressure</u> is the force of blood against your artery walls.

6. A steady state is a pace you can keep up for <u>5</u> minutes.

7. If you can <u>talk</u> when you are doing aerobic exercise, you are not working hard enough.

8. Being unable to concentrate on a task may be a sign of <u>fatigue</u>.

9. <u>Sleep</u> is a refreshing quietness or a quiet change from other activities.

10. REM sleep is sleep with <u>dreams</u>.

11. If you are physically fit, your body is more <u>efficient</u>.

12. The first part of a workout is the <u>cardiorespiratory fitness</u>.

13. Good <u>posture</u> gives your inner organs more room.

14. You should jog on <u>hard</u> surfaces to prevent foot and leg injuries.

15. Physical exercise can sometimes reduce <u>mental fatigue</u>.

Short Answer

Write the numbers 16 to 23 on your paper. Write a complete sentence to answer each question.

16. What is the difference between flexibility and endurance?

17. What happens to calories that your body is unable to use?

18. Why is making your body efficient an important goal?

19. How can exercise improve your muscles and posture?

20. What is the value of having an exercise program?

21. Why should you cool down after exercising?

22. What are three causes of fatigue?

23. How can physical exercise help reduce mental fatigue?

Essay

Write the numbers 24 and 25 on your paper. Write paragraphs with complete sentences to answer each question.

24. Describe what would happen to someone who could not sleep.

25. What should a person do to get started on an exercise program?

ACTIVITIES FOR HOME OR SCHOOL

Projects to Do

1. List ten ways you can add to the amount of daily exercise you get. Walking or riding a bicycle instead of riding in a car or bus may be one way. Helping with active household chores may be another.

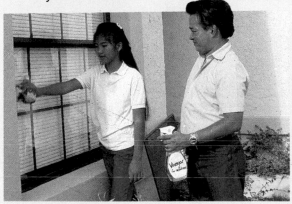

■ *Doing chores improves fitness.*

2. Plan an exercise program for yourself. Be sure your plan gives you at least 20 minutes of vigorous exercise three times a week. Discuss your program with your physician, your school nurse, or your physical education teacher before you begin it.

3. List the different kinds of aerobic exercise you do now. About how many minutes of aerobic exercise do you get each week? What different kinds of aerobic exercise might you add?

4. Keep a record of the amount of sleep you get each night for a week. Write down how you feel each morning, too. Do you think you are getting as much sleep as you need? How can you tell?

Information to Find

1. Some exercises that help strengthen muscles are described in this chapter. What other exercises help strengthen certain muscles? Which muscles do they help strengthen? Contact an exercise specialist, or look in the library for books that tell about different exercises.

2. Look in a telephone book for the local address of the American Heart Association. Call or write the Association. Or write to the national headquarters at 7320 Greenville Avenue, Dallas, TX 75231. Ask for information about ways that exercise helps strengthen the heart.

3. What are some effects of stress on the body? Is stress always harmful? Talk with a physician about stress. Ask about ways to cut down on the harmful effects of stress. Find out how exercise can help eliminate stress that can threaten your wellness.

Books to Read

Here are some books you can look for in your school library or the public library to find more information about exercise and physical fitness.

Bershad, Carol, and Deborah Bernick. *Bodyworks: The Kids' Guide to Food and Physical Fitness.* Random House.

Liptak, Karen. *Aerobics Basics.* Prentice-Hall.

CONTROLLING DISEASE

Some diseases are caused by conditions outside your body. Your body has natural defenses against many of those diseases. Other diseases arise from conditions inside your body. You can help your body prevent or control both kinds of diseases. First, you can find out what makes them begin. After learning more about diseases and about how your body responds to them, you can choose behaviors that will increase your chance of staying healthy. But knowledge alone will not keep you from getting diseases. Your responsibility is to use your knowledge to form health habits that will help you maintain wellness all your life.

GETTING READY TO LEARN

Key Questions

- Why is it important to learn about disease?
- Why is it important to know how you feel about avoiding disease?
- How can you take more responsibility for protecting yourself from disease?
- How can you take more responsibility for keeping disease from spreading?

Main Chapter Sections

1 Communicable Disease
2 Controlling Communicable Disease
3 Some Communicable Diseases
4 Noncommunicable Disease

1 Communicable Disease

At the time Christopher Columbus sailed to America, most people died before the age of 40. One hundred years ago, few people lived past the age of 50. Today, many people in the United States live to be more than 70 years old. People are living longer today for many reasons. One reason is that people are better able to control disease. A **disease** is any condition that damages or weakens a part of the body.

Physicians and scientists have been able to help people control many communicable diseases. A **communicable disease** is a disease that can spread from one person to another.

disease (dihz EEZ), any condition that damages or weakens a part of the body.

communicable disease (kuh MYOO nih kuh buhl • dihz EEZ), a disease that can spread from one person to another.

■ *Many people remain healthy throughout their lives.*

What Causes Communicable Disease?

Communicable disease is caused by tiny living creatures called **microbes**. Different kinds of microbes live in different places, but microbes are almost everywhere. Some microbes cause disease, but many of them are harmless. Some kinds of microbes are even helpful to people. For example, one kind turns milk into cheese. Another kind, yeast, causes bread to rise. Certain microbes are used to make medicines. Some microbes are necessary to help break down food inside your digestive system.

There are four main groups of microbes. **Viruses** are the smallest kind of microbe. Viruses are tiny pieces of living matter. They live in all kinds of cells. When a virus invades a living cell, it takes control. The virus uses parts of the cell in order to live and multiply. Each kind of virus can live in only certain kinds of cells.

microbes (MY krohbz), tiny living creatures; some cause communicable diseases.

viruses (VY ruhs uhz), smallest kind of microbe; multiply in living cells.

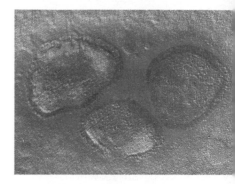

■ *Disease-causing virus*

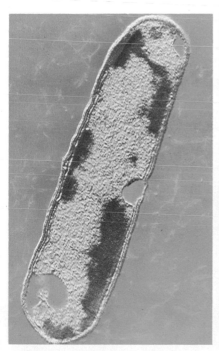

■ *Rod bacteria*

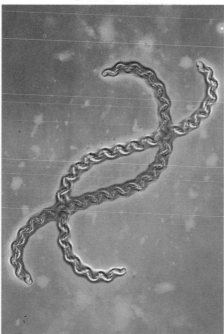

■ *Spiral bacteria*

■ *Round bacteria*

Another group of microbes is called **bacteria**. Each one is only one cell. Some bacteria can move on their own; others are carried by wind, water, or food.

bacteria (bak TIHR ee uh), one of the four main groups of microbes; each is only one cell.

207

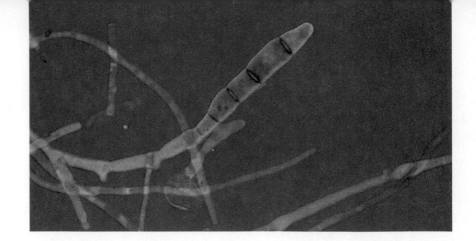

■ *Some fungi can grow on or inside the body and can cause disease.*

fungi (FUHN jy), one of the four main groups of microbes; cannot live and grow by themselves.

protozoa (proht uh ZOH uh), largest kind of microbes; single-celled creatures that can move on their own.

A third group of microbes is called **fungi.** Fungus cells cannot move on their own. Fungi cannot live and grow by themselves, so they grow where they can get food from other things. Some fungi grow on or inside people's bodies.

Protozoa are the largest of the microbes. Each protozoan is a single-celled creature that can move on its own. Protozoa most often live in ponds, streams, or other wet places.

Microbes can live only where they can get what they need to stay alive. All microbes need food and water to stay alive. Some microbes need air; others do not. Some microbes must live in warm places. Other microbes can live only in cold temperatures. Some microbes cannot live inside the body because there they cannot get what they need.

But many other kinds of microbes can live inside the body and cause harm. Each kind causes a different disease. Some kinds of disease microbes are not very common, while others are very common. Chicken pox, for example, is caused by a virus that is common in the United States. Smallpox is caused by a virus that is very rare. Scientists think the smallpox virus now exists only in the laboratory.

■ *Protozoa are single-cell microbes that move on their own. Many kinds of protozoa can cause disease.*

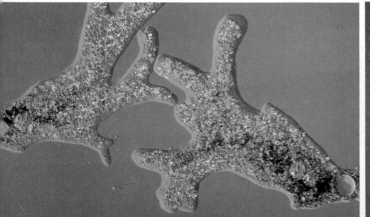
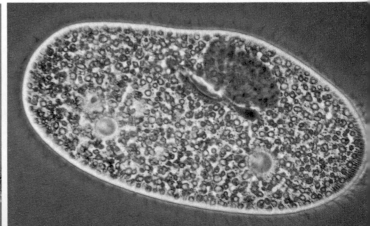

How Do Microbes Cause Disease?

Disease-causing microbes can harm people in two different ways. Some microbes make **toxins,** or harmful wastes. The toxins cause disease by interfering with the way the body works. Other microbes cause disease by directly attacking the body's cells. Many disease microbes can harm people in both ways at the same time.

toxins (TAHK suhnz), harmful wastes that can cause disease by changing the way the body works.

■ Some microbes produce toxins that cause diseases.

Having a small number of microbes inside your body often does not harm your health. The danger begins when the microbes multiply. The multiplying of microbes inside your body is an **infection.** If your body does not stop the microbes from multiplying, a few can become a million in a very short time.

Having a large number of harmful microbes in your body can make you ill. The microbes may make toxins in amounts that are harmful to your body. Or they may damage so many cells that some parts of your body cannot work properly.

infection (ihn FEHK shuhn), the multiplying of microbes inside your body.

How Does Your Body Fight Disease?

Very often your body can get rid of microbes before they make you ill. White blood cells in your body fight the microbes. The white blood cells surround and digest harmful microbes. As the microbes multiply, the white blood cells also grow in number until they have destroyed the microbes.

Certain kinds of white blood cells make substances called **antibodies,** which kill harmful microbes. Antibodies coat disease microbes and make them harmless. Each kind of antibody works against only one kind of disease microbe. To fight many different kinds of microbes, your body has to make many different kinds of antibodies.

Making antibodies takes time, however. You may remain ill until your white blood cells have made enough of the right antibodies to work against the harmful microbes in your body.

Some antibodies stay in your blood after you get better. They give you immunity to the disease you had. Having **immunity** means you are protected from the microbes that cause the disease. Some kinds of antibodies stay in your blood all the time. For that reason, you have certain diseases, such as chicken pox, only once. The chicken pox antibodies make you immune to, or safe from, the chicken pox virus for the rest of your life.

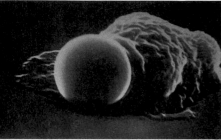
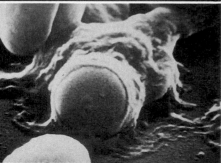
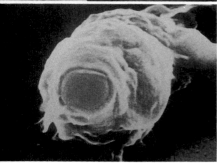

■ *White blood cells can destroy some microbes by surrounding them, above, or by producing antibodies, right.*

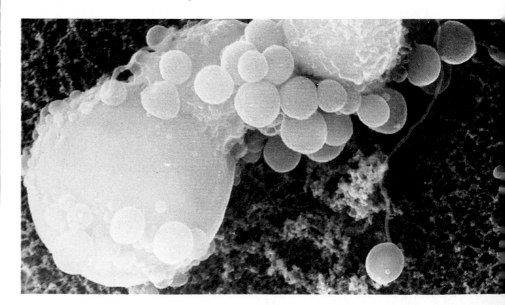

210

■ *Good nutrition, regular exercise, and plenty of sleep can help you resist communicable diseases.*

You can help your body fight harmful microbes by keeping your resistance strong. When you have **resistance,** your body is able to fight, or resist, microbes that cause disease. The best way to build resistance is to follow healthful habits. Such habits include eating a balanced diet, exercising, resting, and getting enough sleep. When your body has strong resistance, it can help fight against harmful microbes that are beginning to multiply.

resistance (rih ZIHS tuhns), the ability of your body to fight microbes that cause disease.

STOP REVIEW SECTION 1

REMEMBER?

1. Name four groups of microbes.
2. How do microbes cause disease?
3. How do antibodies give you immunity?

THINK!

4. How might each kind of microbe enter a person's body and cause an illness?
5. What would you include in a daily schedule to help yourself build resistance to disease?

2 Controlling Communicable Disease

In the past, many people died if they had a communicable disease. But scientists have learned how microbes cause disease and have found ways to fight most of these diseases. Most communicable disease can now be controlled.

Today, four main weapons are used to fight communicable disease. Substances called **vaccines** protect people from some diseases. A vaccine gives a person immunity to a certain disease. The person becomes immune without having been ill.

KEY WORDS

vaccines
antibiotics
sanitation
hygiene habits
injection
booster
penicillin
epidemic
sewage

vaccines (vak SEENZ), substances made to protect people from certain diseases.

■ *The use of antibiotics, left, and improved sanitation, right, are two weapons against communicable diseases.*

antibiotics (ant ih by AHT ihks), medicines developed to kill harmful bacteria.

sanitation (san uh TAY shuhn), the ways people keep their surroundings clean and free of disease microbes.

Medicines have been made that can kill harmful bacteria. Such medicines are called **antibiotics.** They can be used to cure many communicable diseases.

Methods of **sanitation,** the ways people keep their surroundings clean and free of disease microbes, have improved. Sanitation helps keep certain diseases from starting or spreading.

■ *Covering a sneeze, left, and then washing your hands, right, can help stop the spread of some diseases.*

People's own **hygiene habits,** or ways of keeping clean, also affect the spread of disease. Washing the hands has been found to help control the spread of certain common illnesses, such as colds. Covering coughs and sneezes can control the spread of microbes from the mouth and nose.

hygiene habits (HY jeen • HAB uhts), the ways people keep themselves clean.

How Do Vaccines Control Disease?

A vaccine has in it the kind of microbe that causes a particular disease. The microbes in the vaccine are weakened or dead, so they cannot multiply and cause an infection. But your body reacts to the microbes as if they were alive and strong. Your white blood cells make antibodies to fight them. The antibodies remain in your blood and give you immunity to the disease.

For example, when you were an infant, you were probably given a vaccine against measles. The measles vaccine is given as an **injection,** or shot. Some other vaccines can be swallowed. Nasal-spray vaccines are also being made.

Since you have been vaccinated, you will probably have immunity to measles for the rest of your life. Not all vaccines give you immunity all your life. Some give you immunity to a disease for only a few years. Then you need a **booster,** or more of the same vaccine, to keep your immunity. For example, all people need tetanus boosters every ten years.

injection (ihn JEHK shuhn), a shot; a method of giving a vaccine.

booster (BOO stuhr), a later dose of a vaccine received earlier; sometimes needed to maintain immunity to a disease.

213

RECOMMENDED VACCINES

Disease	Age(s) When Vaccine Is Given	Age When Booster Is Needed
Diphtheria	2, 4, 6, and 18 months	between 4 and 6 years; then every 10 years
Measles	15 months	6 years
Mumps	15 months	6 years
Pertussis (whooping cough)	2, 4, 6, and 18 months	between 4 and 6 years
Polio	2, 4, and 18 months	between 4 and 6 years
Rubella (German measles)	15 months	6 years
Tetanus	2, 4, 6, and 18 months	between 4 and 6 years; then every 10 years
HIB	2, 4, 6, and 15 months	no booster needed

Source: U.S. Public Health Service, Advisory Committee on Immunization Practices

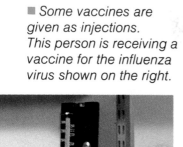

■ *Some vaccines are given as injections. This person is receiving a vaccine for the influenza virus shown on the right.*

There are many different vaccines for influenza because it is caused by many kinds of viruses. Each virus causes a different kind of influenza. That is why certain people must be given a vaccine against influenza every year. Each vaccine is for a certain kind of influenza virus.

Vaccines now protect people against many communicable diseases in the United States. The disease-causing microbes still exist, but vaccines have given people immunity to them. Some public health agencies give free or low-cost vaccines. Many people get their vaccines at their physicians' offices. The table lists recommended vaccines. Do you have a record of the vaccines you received as a young child? Is it time for you to have a booster?

How Do Antibiotics Control Disease?

In 1928 a British scientist named Alexander Fleming studied bacteria. He grew the bacteria in dishes. As the bacteria grew, they formed patches of color in the dishes. Each patch held millions of bacteria. The patches grew larger as the bacteria multiplied.

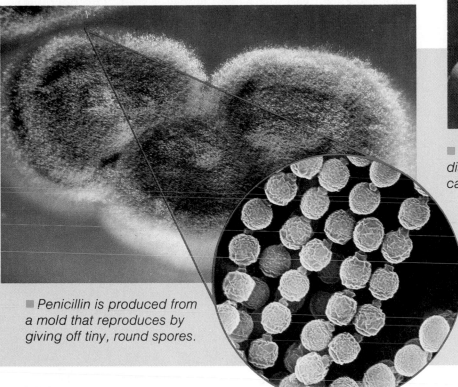

■ *Alexander Fleming discovered the antibiotic called penicillin.*

■ *Penicillin is produced from a mold that reproduces by giving off tiny, round spores.*

One day Fleming noticed fuzzy spots of mold in the dishes of bacteria. Fungi in the air had fallen into the dishes and had started to grow. As the spots of mold spread, the bacteria around them died. The fungi made a substance that killed the bacteria. Fleming called the substance **penicillin.** Penicillin was the world's first antibiotic.

During World War II, physicians gave penicillin to soldiers who had badly infected wounds. Many of the soldiers were weak, and their bodies could not fight the infections. Yet many of the soldiers recovered soon after receiving the antibiotic. The penicillin destroyed the harmful microbes that had caused the infections.

penicillin (pehn uh SIHL uhn), the world's first antibiotic.

215

Today there are many kinds of antibiotics. Antibiotics can work only against diseases caused by bacteria. Physicians select certain antibiotics for certain infections.

Antibiotics do not work against diseases that are caused by viruses such as colds or influenza. But scientists are working on medicines to fight viruses. A few illnesses caused by viruses can be shortened by new medicines if the medicines are used just as the illnesses start. The best way to fight diseases caused by viruses is to rest. Rest gives your body's own defenses a chance to work against the viruses.

How Does Sanitation Control Disease?

About 600 years ago, a disease called *bubonic plague* spread through Europe. The disease microbe was carried by rats. Fleas bit the rats and the microbes entered the fleas. When the fleas bit people, the microbes in the fleas infected the people.

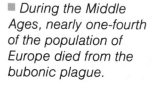

■ *During the Middle Ages, nearly one-fourth of the population of Europe died from the bubonic plague.*

Thousands of people died every day from the disease. An epidemic was happening. An **epidemic** is the quick spread of a disease to large numbers of people.

In the past, many communicable diseases could cause epidemics. The diseases spread quickly because people did not know enough about microbes and how diseases spread.

epidemic (ehp uh DEHM ihk), the rapid spread of a disease to large numbers of people.

216

The spread of many communicable diseases has been stopped by improved sanitation, including regular disposal of garbage.

They did not realize that their actions were making people become ill. Water and wastes from people's houses flowed into open ditches and then into the water that people drank. People often threw garbage into the streets. Such practices gave harmful microbes many places to grow. Microbes that caused disease were everywhere.

Modern sanitation helps people keep their surroundings clean and free of harmful microbes. However, people need to be responsible for their own actions in handling wastes so they do not defeat the purpose of their community's sanitation services.

Garbage Disposal. Nearly all communities have ways of disposing of garbage safely. Garbage is collected often so that it does not pile up. Some communities bury garbage and build over it. Other communities burn it to make energy. These methods keep microbes that grow in the garbage away from people.

217

Sewage Treatment. The waste from drains in people's homes and other buildings is called **sewage.** In most communities, sewage moves through underground pipes from buildings to a sewage treatment plant. In the plant, the sewage is treated to destroy harmful microbes. Once destroyed, these microbes can no longer add to the spread of disease.

Water Treatment. Most communities in the United States have a treated water supply. Rain, melted snow, and other kinds of fresh water are collected and stored, often in reservoirs. Dirt is removed, and chemicals are sometimes added to the water to kill harmful microbes. The water is then stored in a way that keeps it clean. Pipes carry the water from the storage place to buildings. Water that comes to homes and other buildings must be safe to drink.

Food Preparation. In the past, milk, meat, and other foods often carried harmful microbes. Now communities in the United States have laws that make food businesses prepare, handle, and sell food safely. Workers in restaurants and factories must prepare food in ways that keep it free from harmful microbes.

■ *Sanitary food preparation, left, stops the spread of certain communicable diseases. Pasteurization, right, kills most of the microbes in milk.*

In the past, milk carried microbes that caused a disease called *tuberculosis*. Many people died from drinking milk with the tuberculosis microbes in it. In the 1860s, a French scientist named Louis Pasteur found a way to make milk safe. Now milk is *pasteurized*, or heated to a temperature that kills harmful microbes without changing the taste or nutrients of the milk.

Washing your hands after using the rest room stops certain diseases from spreading.

How Do Hygiene Habits Control Disease?

Signs posted in rest rooms of food-handling businesses remind workers that they must wash their hands before returning to work. That is good advice for everyone: wash your hands after using the rest room. Several communicable diseases can be spread by the microbes on unwashed hands that touch food other people will eat or things other people will handle.

Colds and hepatitis are diseases spread by microbes on unwashed hands. Both diseases are caused by viruses.

Personal hygiene habits, such as hand washing, help keep those harmful microbes from spreading in your community. Together with vaccines, antibiotics, and sanitation, personal hygiene habits help control communicable disease.

STOP REVIEW SECTION 2

REMEMBER?

1. What are four ways of fighting communicable disease?
2. How do antibiotics control disease?
3. What are two ways communities can get rid of garbage safely?
4. Why are food and water treated?

THINK!

5. Could an epidemic of bubonic plague happen today? Why or why not?
6. What are some of your personal responsibilities for helping prevent the spread of microbes to or from your body?

Making Wellness Choices

Jenny has been selected as a cafeteria assistant. On her first day, the cafeteria manager explained to all the new assistants that being clean and neat is very important. The manager told them about wearing hair nets and gloves and washing their hands. The manager reminded the assistants that they would be handling food that other students would eat. Before lunch one day, Jenny noticed another cafeteria assistant covering a sneeze with her hands. The same girl went to the food-serving area without washing her hands.

 What could Jenny do? Explain your wellness choice.

Health Close-up

The World's First Successful Vaccine

The first vaccine was made less than 200 years ago in England. At that time, smallpox was a common and dangerous communicable disease. Many people died of it. Those who survived were often left with terrible scars.

Dr. Edward Jenner thought smallpox could be prevented. He had studied cowpox, a disease like smallpox, but less dangerous. Dr. Jenner noticed that a person never suffered from smallpox after having had cowpox. Dr. Jenner thought that if healthy people could get cowpox on purpose, they might be protected from smallpox.

In 1796 Dr. Jenner experimented. He took some matter from a cowpox sore. Then he scratched a healthy boy's arm and rubbed the matter into the scratch. The boy got cowpox, just as Dr. Jenner had expected.

Three months later, Dr. Jenner scratched the boy's arm again. This time, he rubbed matter from a smallpox sore into the scratch. The boy did not get smallpox. Having cowpox microbes in his system had given him immunity to smallpox. Dr. Jenner had given the world its first successful vaccine.

Since Dr. Jenner's time, scientists have learned how his vaccine worked. The matter from the cowpox sore had cowpox viruses in it. The viruses entered the boy's body through the scratch, causing the boy to become slightly ill. His white blood cells made antibodies to destroy the cowpox viruses. Some of those antibodies remained in his blood after he got better.

The smallpox virus is much like the cowpox virus. When smallpox viruses entered the boy's body, cowpox antibodies were already in his blood. The cowpox antibodies attacked the smallpox viruses at once. The smallpox viruses were destroyed before they could multiply and make the boy ill.

Since Dr. Jenner's discovery, scientists have made vaccines for many diseases. Through the efforts of many people, the vaccine against smallpox has eliminated that disease from the world.

■ *Edward Jenner produced the first successful smallpox vaccine.*

Thinking Beyond

1. Do you know of any diseases, other than smallpox, that have been eliminated from the world? What are they?
2. What would your community be like if there were no vaccines?

221

3 Some Communicable Diseases

Science has helped people by giving them tools such as vaccines, treatments, and sanitation methods to control many serious communicable diseases. People have also learned that their own actions and habits can keep many illnesses from spreading. However, some communicable diseases still exist. Even though science cannot get rid of those diseases, people can help control their spread.

■ *Scientific research has led to the development of many different kinds of medicines to fight communicable diseases.*

symptoms (SIHMP tuhmz), signs of a disease.

What Are Colds?

Colds are the most common communicable disease in the United States. The **symptoms,** or signs and feelings, of a cold can include a runny or stuffy nose, a sore throat, and coughing. Any one of more than 100 different viruses can cause an illness called a "cold." That is one reason there is no vaccine for colds.

People often "catch cold" by breathing in droplets of water coughed or sneezed into the air by someone who has a cold. Cold viruses are also spread by microbes when people with unwashed hands touch other people. For those reasons, it is a good idea to stay away from people who have colds. It is always a good idea to wash your hands after handling shared objects and before touching your face.

Most colds are not serious. However, they can cause people to miss school or work. If you get a cold, you should rest, cover your sneezes with disposable tissues, and drink plenty of water and juices.

What Is Hepatitis?

Hepatitis is an illness caused by several different viruses. The viruses infect the liver. One of these viruses, the hepatitis A virus, is most often spread from person to person by unwashed hands or by the sharing of food.

Preventing hepatitis is like preventing many other communicable diseases. Hand washing, particularly after using the rest room, is your best defense. As always, wash your hands before preparing food and serving it to yourself and others. Finally, avoid sharing the same food item or drinking container with other people. Saliva, which may contain the hepatitis A virus, can be shared that way.

Elderly people who get hepatitis become quite ill. They can have nausea, vomiting, yellow coloring of the skin, stomachache, and fever. The usual treatment is rest in order to help the liver heal.

■ *Hepatitis can be spread by sharing drinking containers.*

223

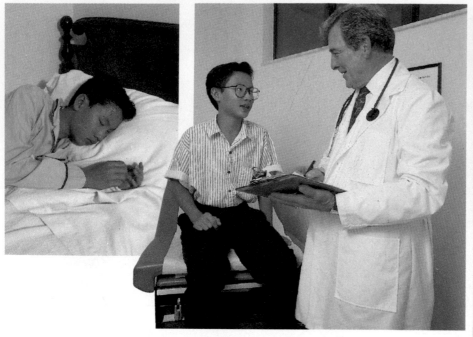

■ *A person with mononucleosis needs plenty of rest for recovery. To avoid spreading the disease, the person should not share food or drinks.*

What Is Mononucleosis?

Another communicable disease caused by a virus is *mononucleosis.* This illness starts suddenly with fever, swollen lymph glands, tiredness, and sore throat.

Mononucleosis is communicable. The virus is passed between people, or **transmitted,** by way of saliva or droplets from the mouth. Since the infection can be spread from mouth to mouth, prevention habits include not sharing bites of food and not sharing the same drinking container. Sometimes family members, friends, or sports team players forget that many illnesses can be spread by sharing drink containers.

Persons who have mononucleosis, or "mono," mainly need rest. Their own bodies will try to fight the infection. Any items that touch their mouths or noses, however, need to be cleaned with hot, soapy water and rinsed well. Cleaning these things will help prevent the spread of the illness.

transmitted (trans MIHT uhd), passed between people.

224

What Are Sexually Transmitted Diseases?

Diseases spread by intimate body contact are called **sexually transmitted diseases,** or STDs. Such diseases are a dangerous health problem. Two sexually transmitted diseases are chlamydia and gonorrhea. *Chlamydia* can cause swelling of and scars on the ovaries and testes. The chlamydia microbes are like bacteria and can be passed by mothers who have the infection to their babies during birth. *Gonorrhea* has no symptoms in females, but causes painful urination in males. It can damage the heart, the ovaries and testes, and the joints. Both gonorrhea and chlamydia can be treated with antibiotics. There are no vaccines against these sexually transmitted diseases.

sexually transmitted diseases (SEHKSH uh wuh lee • trans MIHT uhd • dihz EE zuhz), diseases spread by intimate body contact.

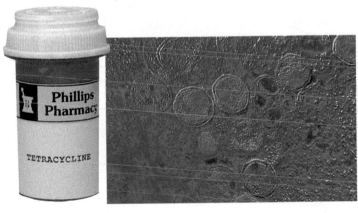

■ *Chlamydia, left, and gonorrhea, right, can both be treated with antibiotics.*

What Is AIDS?

A disease that has become a dangerous health problem in recent years is *acquired immunodeficiency syndrome,* or *AIDS.* AIDS is caused by a virus called *HIV.* HIV enters the body, multiplies, and then kills certain white blood cells called T lymphocytes, or helper T cells. Those T cells are most often the first to recognize harmful microbes in the body. They signal other white blood cells to destroy the microbes or other foreign cells. By destroying those T cells, HIV weakens the body's natural immunity to all diseases. People with HIV infection develop AIDS, which means that they cannot fight off disease. They often get diseases that healthy people do not get. People with AIDS can get pneumonia and a kind of cancer that is rare in healthy people. There is no vaccine for HIV infection. There are no medicines to cure AIDS.

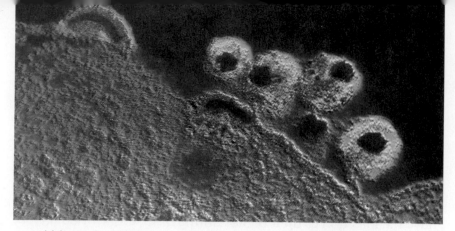

■ *After destroying a cell, AIDS viruses move on to other cells.*

Although AIDS is a deadly disease, it can be prevented. The AIDS virus, HIV, is almost always transmitted in one of three ways. The virus has to get into a person's blood. One way it can do so is through sexual contact between a healthy person and an infected person. A second way it can be transmitted is by the sharing of injection needles used by a person who has the infection. A third way HIV can be spread is from a mother who has the infection to her infant before or during birth.

Some people have also gotten HIV when they received blood containing the virus during a transfusion. Since all blood is now tested for HIV, this method of transmission is now unlikely.

HIV cannot be spread by touching an infected person. Healthy people can hold hands, play sports, and go to school with an infected person without getting HIV or AIDS.

STOP **REVIEW** **SECTION 3**

REMEMBER?

1. What are three communicable diseases caused by viruses?
2. What parts of the body can be damaged by STDs?
3. What are the three ways in which HIV is transmitted?

THINK!

4. Why is AIDS in the news so much?
5. Why is hand washing so important for stopping the spread of many illnesses?

SECTION 4 Noncommunicable Disease

In the past, communicable diseases were the leading cause of death. This is no longer true. Today in the United States, cancer and heart disease take more lives than any other diseases. Diseases such as high blood pressure and diabetes mellitus are also major health problems for many people.

Such diseases are more common today than they were in the past. But they have been affecting people for thousands of years. For example, physicians studied the 2,100-year-old mummy of a woman from China. They learned that the woman had died of heart disease. One scientist has found signs of arthritis in ancient mummies from Egypt.

Diseases such as cancer and heart disease are not communicable diseases. They are not caused by microbes. They cannot pass from one person to another. Instead, such diseases come from inside a person's body. A disease of that kind is a **noncommunicable disease.**

noncommunicable disease (nahn kuh MYOO nih kuh buhl • dihz EEZ), a disease that begins inside a person's body, is not passed from one person to another, and is not caused by microbes.

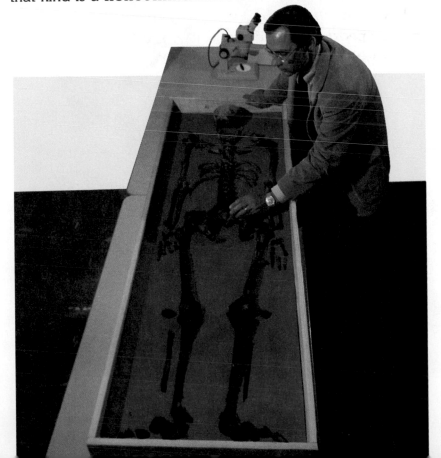

■ Noncommunicable diseases have been around a long time. The remains shown here are of a woman who died of heart disease over 2,000 years ago.

227

What Causes Noncommunicable Disease?

A noncommunicable disease may be caused by the way a person lives. For example, not eating a balanced diet and not getting enough exercise or sleep are poor habits. Over time, such habits may affect one or more parts of the body. When even one organ of the body does not work as it should, other parts of the body can no longer do their jobs properly. A person's whole body may be affected by a weak or damaged organ.

Many noncommunicable diseases are called **chronic** diseases because they last for a long time. A chronic disease may start when a person is young. It begins slowly, and the person may show no symptoms of disease for years. Some chronic diseases can be cured. Some can be stopped from

chronic (KRAHN ihk), lasting for a long time.

■ Poor health habits can lead to some noncommunicable diseases.

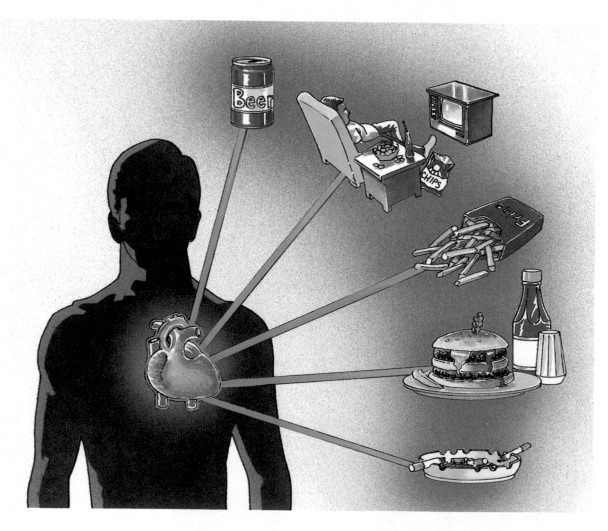

228

getting worse. People who have chronic diseases often need to make changes in their habits. Some people need treatment for the rest of their lives. With the correct treatment, many people with chronic diseases can lead satisfying lives. They may be physically ill in some ways, but they can maintain a state of wellness, too.

What Are Some Diseases of the Circulatory System?

The blood, the heart, and the blood vessels make up the circulatory system. Several noncommunicable diseases affect this body system, each in a different way.

Healthy blood vessels are smooth and open on the inside. Their walls can expand to let blood flow through them easily. The heart does not have to work extra hard to pump blood through healthy blood vessels.

One disease of the circulatory system begins when cholesterol or other fatty matter collects in the arteries and coats the walls. The fatty matter makes the arteries narrow. This condition is called *atherosclerosis*. When a person has this condition, blood cannot flow through the arteries as easily as it should. The heart must pump harder to keep the blood moving. Sometimes the arteries may become completely blocked. Blood cannot flow through them at all. Some tissues cannot receive the nutrients and oxygen they need. The cells in those tissues start to die.

■ *Some chronic diseases can be treated with physical therapy.*

■ *A clogged artery is a dangerous condition and can cause a heart attack.*

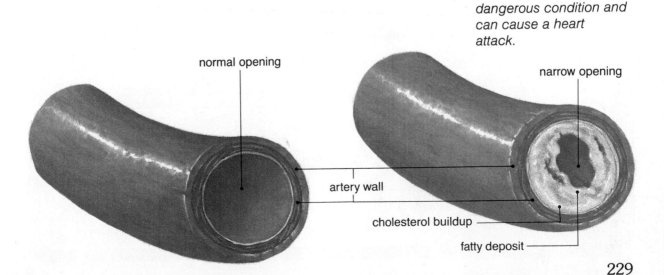

normal opening

narrow opening

artery wall

cholesterol buildup

fatty deposit

229

■ *People who have had heart attacks must follow certain diets and exercise plans. Exercise helps keep the heart healthy.*

If one of the arteries that sends blood to the heart itself becomes blocked, the result may be a *heart attack*. Without blood, that part of the heart begins to die and cannot help pump blood to the rest of body. A heart attack is very dangerous and needs immediate and proper care. Heart attacks take many lives every year. People who recover from heart attacks often have to follow a special diet and an exercise plan. They must not smoke cigarettes, because tobacco causes blood vessels to narrow.

People's health habits can make them likely to get diseases of the circulatory system. Eating lots of foods that are high in animal fats can put too much fatty matter in the arteries. Getting too little exercise or being overweight can make the heart muscle unable to pump blood very well.

WAYS TO PREVENT DISEASES OF THE CIRCULATORY SYSTEM

- Eat chicken, fish, and a variety of lean meats.
- Add no salt to foods.
- Get vigorous exercise at least every other day.
- Stay within a range of normal weight for your age and height.
- Do not use tobacco in any form.
- Learn how to control your life's stresses, or tensions.

What Is High Blood Pressure?

A person's blood pressure normally goes up and down. Blood pressure that stays high, however, is a serious health problem.

High blood pressure, or *hypertension,* is a serious disease of the circulatory system. In this disease, the blood pushes too hard against the artery walls. Sometimes there is no known reason for the disease. It is known that high blood pressure tends to be present in some families. Sometimes a person may have another health problem, such as kidney disease, that might contribute to high blood pressure.

Chronic high blood pressure makes artery walls hard and thick. When the arteries are less stretchy, the heart must work harder. Over time, high blood pressure can cause the heart to grow larger and weaker. High blood pressure also can cause a stroke. This happens when a blood vessel bursts in the brain.

What Is Cancer?

Another serious noncommunicable disease is *cancer.* There are many different kinds of cancer. Each kind of cancer changes specific kinds of cells in some part of a person's body. Cancer begins with a change in the way the cells grow. The cells start to multiply very quickly. They do not function as they should. They grow in an uncontrolled way and no longer fit together smoothly. After a while, they form a lump of cells called a **tumor.** Sometimes cells form a tumor that is not cancer. Many of these tumors are harmless.

As a cancer tumor grows, it crowds out normal cells. Finally, the tumor may stop one or more organs from working properly. Almost any cell in the body can become a cancer cell. Cancer that starts in one part of the body may also spread to other parts.

A person who has contact with certain substances is more likely to get cancer. Those substances are called **carcinogens.** Health habits may change the number of carcinogens with which a person comes in contact. For example, cigarette smoke has many different carcinogens.

SEVEN WARNING SIGNS OF CANCER IN ADULTS

1. **C**hange in bowel or bladder habits
2. **A**ny kind of sore that does not heal
3. **U**nusual bleeding
4. **T**hickening or lump in any part of the body
5. **I**ndigestion or difficulty in swallowing
6. **O**bvious change in a wart, mole, or birthmark
7. **N**agging cough or hoarseness in the throat

Source: American Cancer Society

tumor (TOO muhr), a lump of cells.

carcinogens (kahr SIHN uh juhnz), substances that can cause cancer.

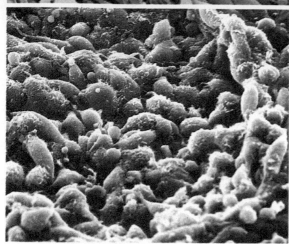

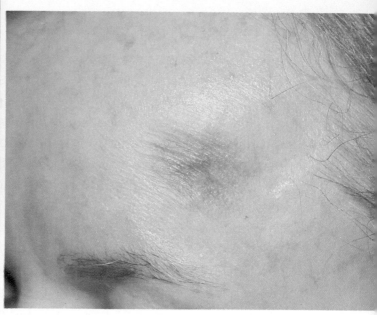

■ *Cancer begins with cells that grow and divide abnormally, top left. As they multiply, they form a tumor, bottom left. Skin cancer, right, consists of one or more tumors growing in the skin.*

They stay in a smoker's lungs. People who regularly smoke cigarettes increase their chance of getting lung cancer. Spending a lot of time in the sun without protection is another bad habit. It can cause skin cancer in some people. Sunlight contains many harmful rays that are carcinogens.

Some people die of cancer because they wait too long before they get a medical checkup. They even ignore warning signs of cancer. The list on page 231 shows the seven warning signs of cancer in adults. Share it with your family. A person who has any of these signs should see a physician immediately.

Having one or more of the signs does not mean a person has cancer. A physician can do tests to find out for sure. Then if the person does have cancer, the disease can be treated in its early stages. The cancer cells often can be destroyed before they spread and cause much damage. If a cancer tumor has formed, most often it can be removed. If cancer is found and treated soon enough, there is a much better chance of controlling it.

What Is Diabetes Mellitus?

The food that you eat contains fat, protein, and sugar. All three are absorbed in the intestines and carried into the blood. Sugar is carried to all your cells and is turned into the energy your body needs. To use sugar, your cells need a hormone called insulin. **Insulin** helps move sugar into your cells from your blood. There the cells turn the sugar into the energy your body needs. Any extra sugar is carried to your liver to be stored for later use.

A disease called *diabetes mellitus* develops in people whose bodies cannot make enough insulin. Without enough insulin, sugar stays in the blood and does not enter the cells. Therefore, the sugar level in the blood rises. High levels of blood sugar can cause blurred vision. When the blood sugar is high, the extra sugar goes into the kidneys and urine. When this happens people may have to urinate more often.

insulin (IHN suh luhn), a hormone that helps move the sugar in your blood into your cells.

■ *Diabetes mellitus cannot be cured, but it can be controlled with injections of insulin. Body cells need insulin to make energy from sugar in the blood.*

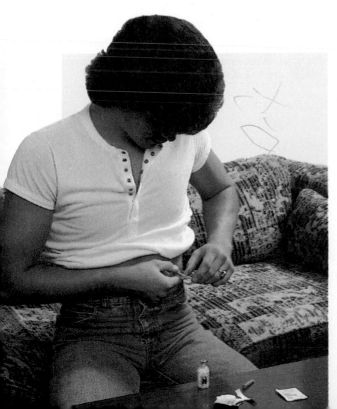

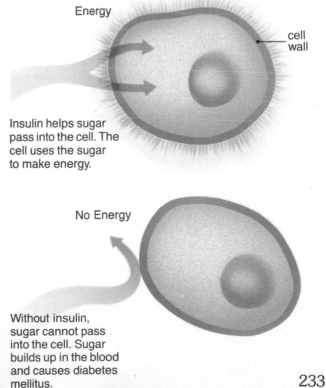

Energy

cell wall

Insulin helps sugar pass into the cell. The cell uses the sugar to make energy.

No Energy

Without insulin, sugar cannot pass into the cell. Sugar builds up in the blood and causes diabetes mellitus.

233

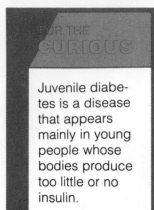

Juvenile diabetes is a disease that appears mainly in young people whose bodies produce too little or no insulin.

Diabetes cannot be cured. But healthful habits can often help control the condition. Most people with diabetes need to have well-balanced diets that are low in sugar and fat. They need to get regular exercise and to stay at a healthful weight. Excess body weight can cause the diabetes to become worse. Sometimes diet and exercise cannot control the disease. Then physicians order other treatments. Most young people with diabetes take injections of insulin at regular times to help their bodies use sugar properly.

How Can Noncommunicable Disease Be Controlled?

Scientists are studying noncommunicable diseases to learn about their causes. Scientists help physicians find ways to control or cure noncommunicable diseases. It is already known that through healthful living habits people can reduce their chance of getting some noncommunicable diseases. For example, regular exercise and a balanced diet that is low in fat and salt can help reduce a person's chance of developing diseases of the circulatory system. Avoiding tobacco and too much sunlight helps prevent some kinds of cancer. People can control their chance of getting some noncommunicable diseases.

REVIEW
SECTION 4

REMEMBER?

1. What causes cancer?
2. What happens in the body of a person with diabetes?
3. How can people control noncommunicable diseases?

THINK!

4. Why do noncommunicable diseases become chronic illnesses for some people?
5. How might high blood pressure affect a person's ability to be active?

Thinking About Your Health

Exploring Your Family Health History

Draw a family tree like the one shown here. Include your parents, your brothers and sisters, your aunts and uncles, and your grandparents. For each person, write in the names of any chronic or serious diseases that person has had.

Some diseases tend to occur often in certain families. Scientists are studying those diseases to learn which are inherited and which are due to the families' habits and environment.

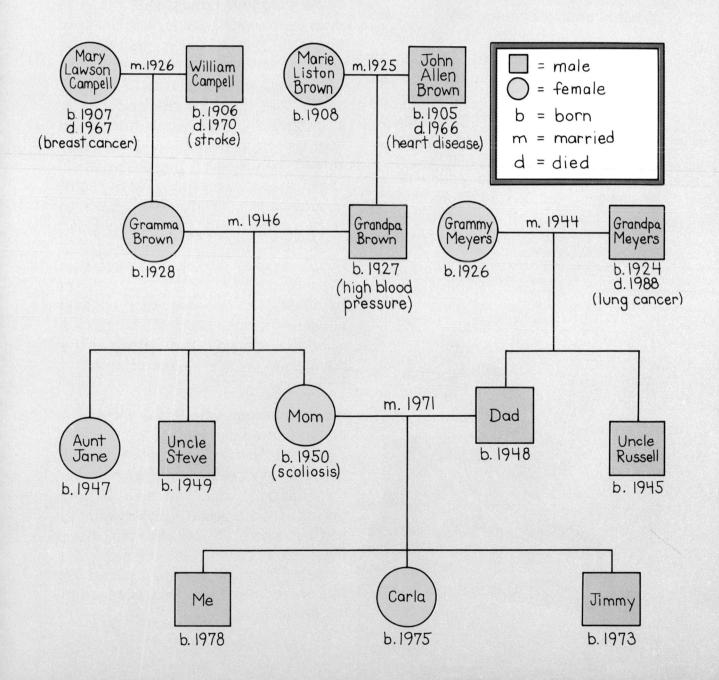

People in Health

An Interview with an Epidemiologist

John B. Waller, Jr., is concerned with preventing and controlling disease. He is an epidemiologist in Detroit, Michigan.

What is an epidemiologist?

An epidemiologist is a health detective. If a disease spreads all through a community and many people become ill, an epidemiologist tries to identify the disease. Then he or she tries to find out how the disease is spreading. An epidemiologist tries to find out what is causing the disease and what, if anything, can be done to control it. Many epidemiologists work in community health, a field that is concerned with the health of the total community.

■ *Dr. Waller studies the relationships between certain diseases and population centers.*

With what kinds of diseases are epidemiologists concerned?

Epidemiologists study all kinds of diseases, communicable as well as noncommunicable. When an epidemic occurs, epidemiologists try to find out certain facts about the disease. They try to discover if the disease is transmitted from person to person, by water or by air, or if the disease is transmitted at all. They also investigate why some noncommunicable diseases, such as some cancers and arthritis, are found more often among certain groups of people. Epidemiologists also try to gain information about problems that may not be considered diseases, such as child abuse. An epidemiologist is concerned with any situation that affects large numbers of people in a community.

Would a person who has a disease consult an epidemiologist?

Not usually. If a person gets a disease that might lead to an epidemic, an epidemiologist may go to see the person. The epidemiologist will want to find out where the person might have been exposed to the disease. The epidemiologist will also want to find out who else might have been exposed to the disease.

■ *Finding the causes of many new communicable diseases is difficult.*

Are epidemiologists physicians?

Not all epidemiologists are physicians. Some physicians study epidemiology after they become medical doctors. But many epidemiologists are not physicians. I am not a physician, but I am a doctor of public health. I received my doctor's degree from a school of public health rather than from a medical school.

How does someone become an epidemiologist?

A person who wants to become an epidemiologist must graduate from a four-year college and then continue his or her education for several more years. There are many subjects that an epidemiologist must study. First of all, he or she must study the sciences, such as chemistry, botany, and biology. An epidemiologist must also have a good background in the social sciences, computer science, and mathematics, including statistics. Statistics is the study of numbers to explain where and how often something occurs in a population.

What is the hardest part of your work?

The most difficult part of my work is finding the causes of noncommunicable diseases. For communicable diseases, there is usually a single cause—a particular microbe—that is possible to control. For most noncommunicable diseases, there are many causes or risk factors, including the environment and the ways people live, such as their eating habits. Noncommunicable diseases present difficult challenges. I enjoy meeting those challenges.

What do you like most about being an epidemiologist?

I like being a health detective. I like solving health puzzles.

Learn more about people who work as epidemiologists for your local health department. Interview an epidemiologist. Or write for information to the International Epidemiological Association, School of Public Health, Room 71-269CHS, University of California, Los Angeles, CA 90024.

Main Ideas

- Communicable diseases can be controlled by controlling microbes.
- Different microbes harm people in different ways.
- Vaccines, antibiotics, sanitation, and personal hygiene habits are four ways of controlling microbes.
- Today in the United States, cancer and various diseases of the circulatory system claim more lives than any other diseases.
- Scientists know that through healthful living habits people can reduce their chance of getting some noncommunicable diseases.

Key Words

Write the numbers 1 to 14 in your health notebook or on a separate sheet of paper. After each number, write the letter of the definition that best describes the term. Page numbers in ( ) tell you where to look in the chapter if you need help.

1. communicable disease (206)
2. bacteria (207)
3. fungi (208)
4. toxins (209)
5. antibodies (210)
6. resistance (211)
7. vaccines (212)
8. sanitation (212)
9. injection (213)
10. penicillin (215)
11. epidemic (216)
12. symptoms (222)
13. noncommuni-cable disease (227)
14. carcinogens (231)

a. a health problem that is not passed on to another person

b. a medicine developed to kill harmful bacteria

c. the spread of a disease to many people

d. harmful wastes made by microbes

e. the ability of the body to fight disease

f. a health problem that can be spread

g. signs of a disease

h. substances that make a person more likely to get cancer

i. the ways people keep their environment clean

j. a method of giving a vaccine

k. substances made by the body to fight disease

l. substances made to protect people from certain diseases

m. a group of microbes that cannot move by themselves

n. a group of microbes, some of which cause STDs

Write the numbers 15 to 29 on your paper. After each number, write a sentence that defines the term. Page numbers in ( ) tell you where to look in the chapter if you need help.

15. disease (206)
16. microbes (207)
17. viruses (207)
18. protozoa (208)
19. infection (209)
20. immunity (210)
21. antibiotics (212)
22. hygiene habits (213)
23. booster (213)
24. sewage (218)
25. transmitted (224)
26. sexually transmitted diseases (225)
27. chronic (228)
28. tumor (231)
29. insulin (233)

Remembering What You Learned

Page numbers in ( ) tell you where to look in the chapter if you need help.

1. What are some of the causes of communicable diseases? (207–208)

2. In what two ways do microbes harm people? (209)

3. What are two ways your white blood cells fight against harmful microbes? (210)

4. What can you do to build strong resistance? (211)

5. How are communicable diseases controlled? (212–213)

6. Against what kinds of diseases are antibiotics used? (215–216)

7. What happens to sewage in a sewage treatment plant? (218)

8. Why is milk pasteurized? (219)

9. What causes colds? (222)

10. What steps can be taken to prevent the spread of mononucleosis? (224)

11. What is an STD? (225)

12. How is HIV usually transmitted? (225–226)

13. How does cancer begin? (231)

14. Why does your body need insulin? (233)

Thinking About What You Learned

1. What are some ways in which physicians, scientists, and other people have worked together to control the spread of communicable diseases?

2. How is having immunity to certain diseases related to living a longer life?

3. Why is it important for health workers to know about certain kinds of communicable diseases that are spreading in a community?

4. Why is AIDS such a deadly disease?

5. How might a person's diet be related to some diseases of the circulatory system?

Writing About What You Learned

1. Suppose several people in your community have the same kind of communicable disease. These people became ill within 24 hours of each other. You are a community health worker. Write two or three paragraphs about your plan to help those who are ill and to prevent others from becoming ill.

2. Four main weapons are used to fight communicable disease today. See pages 212–213 if you need help in remembering them. Choose one of the weapons, and write a paragraph about how people would be affected if that weapon did not exist.

Applying What You Learned

ART

Design a colorful poster that illustrates the importance of having a personal plan for disease prevention.

Modified True or False

Write the numbers 1 to 15 in your health notebook or on a separate sheet of paper. After each number, write *true* or *false* to describe the sentence. If the sentence is false, also write a term that replaces the underlined term and makes the sentence true.

1. The best way to build <u>immunity</u> is to follow healthful habits.

2. Medicines that can kill <u>bacteria</u> are called antibiotics.

3. Penicillin was the world's first <u>vaccine</u>.

4. Many <u>noncommunicable</u> diseases can cause epidemics.

5. The milk you buy has been <u>pasteurized</u>.

6. Protozoa are the largest kind of <u>microbe</u>.

7. Chicken pox is caused by a kind of <u>fungus</u>.

8. White blood cells make <u>antibiotics</u>.

9. The way surroundings are kept clean is called <u>hygiene</u>.

10. Some vaccines require a <u>booster</u> after a few years.

11. The best way to fight diseases caused by <u>viruses</u> is to rest.

12. Wastes from the drains in a house are called <u>sanitation</u>.

13. A lump of cells is a <u>cancer</u>.

14. People with diabetes mellitus do not have enough <u>insulin</u>.

15. If an artery in the heart is blocked, you may have a <u>heart attack</u>.

Short Answer

Write the numbers 16 to 23 on your paper. Write a complete sentence to answer each question.

16. How are fungi different from viruses?

17. How do vaccines protect you from disease?

18. How do antibiotics control disease?

19. What are two diseases that are caused by viruses?

20. How can your diet affect the chance that you will get a noncommunicable disease?

21. What are the seven warning signs of cancer?

22. What health habits can help control diabetes?

23. How does sanitation help people control disease?

Essay

Write the numbers 24 and 25 on your paper. Write paragraphs with complete sentences to answer each question.

24. Why is it important to learn about disease?

25. What steps could you take if your community had an epidemic of a communicable disease?

ACTIVITIES FOR HOME OR SCHOOL

Projects to Do

1. With a small group of other students, think about solving some disease problem. Select one condition, and prepare a plan that describes how it might be controlled or treated in future years.

2. Write to the Food and Drug Administration, 5600 Fishers Lane, Rockville, MD 20857. Ask how foods and other materials are tested for carcinogens.

3. The chart on page 230 lists some ways to prevent diseases of the circulatory system. Talk with your family about those habits. How can families help each member practice healthful habits to control diseases?

■ *Limiting salt may help prevent some cases of hypertension.*

Information to Find

1. Pasteurization was one important process developed by the French scientist Louis Pasteur. Find out about his other discoveries. Your school library or public library may have books about the life and work of Louis Pasteur.

2. People who have had heart attacks sometimes need to make changes in their eating and exercise habits. What are some changes they might have to make? Interview a physician for this information. Or talk with someone from the local unit of the American Heart Association.

3. Many noncommunicable diseases are brought on by poor health habits. Select one noncommunicable disease. Find out how poor health habits contribute to that disease and affect a person's health in general. Determine what habit changes could reduce the risks. Present your findings to the class.

Books to Read

Here are some books you can look for in your school library or the public library to find more information about disease.

Fine, Judylaine. *Afraid to Ask: A Book for Families to Share About Cancer.* Lothrop, Lee & Shepard.

Hawkes, Nigel. *AIDS.* Franklin Watts.

Patent, Dorothy Hinshaw. *Germs!* Holiday House.

DRUGS CAN CHANGE THE BODY AND MIND

Every day, you take many different substances into your body. You swallow food and water and breathe air. Food, water, and air keep your body working as it should. However, some substances that you can swallow or breathe can change the way your body works. These substances are called drugs.

You can protect your health and even your life by learning more about drugs. Knowing the facts about drugs can help you make responsible decisions that will help you maintain wellness all your life.

GETTING READY TO LEARN

Key Questions

- Why is it important to know how you feel about the use of medicines and drugs?
- How can you learn to say no to illegal drugs?
- How can you learn to use medicines safely?
- How can you take more responsibility for your health where medicines and drugs are concerned?

Main Chapter Sections

1 Drugs That Can Help People Get Well
2 Dangers of Drug Abuse
3 Drugs That Are Abused
4 How People Can Avoid Drug Abuse

1 Drugs That Can Help People Get Well

medicine (MEHD uh suhn), a drug that people use to cure or treat certain health problems.

A drug that people use to cure or treat a certain health problem is a **medicine.** All medicines are also drugs. But some drugs are *not* medicines!

There are many different medicines. Some are injected into the body. Some are absorbed through the skin. Some come in the form of pills, capsules, powders, or liquids and are swallowed.

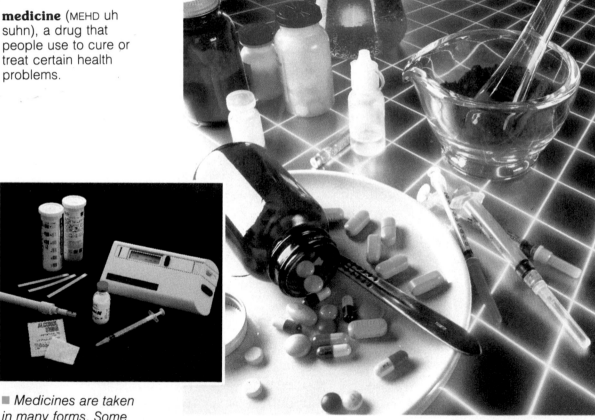

■ *Medicines are taken in many forms. Some medicines are swallowed as tablets, capsules, or liquids. Others, such as insulin, are injected beneath the skin.*

How Do Medicines Help People?

Some medicines cure diseases. Antibiotics, for example, cure certain diseases that are caused by bacteria. Antibiotics kill bacteria. Other medicines relieve the symptoms of an illness for a while. Insulin, for example, helps a person who has diabetes take care of the illness and its symptoms.

244

Each medicine makes some change in the body. Aspirin, for example, reduces fever and pain. Allergy injections and cough syrups also lead to specific changes in the body. But medicines may have more than one effect on the body. Some of the effects, called **side effects,** are unwanted. Some drugs cannot be used as medicines because their side effects are harmful.

side effects, unwanted and unneeded effects a medicine may have.

What Are Two Kinds of Medicines?

Some medicines are sold only by a special order, or **prescription.** Physicians and other qualified doctors are the only people who can order prescription medicines. They decide who should use these medicines and how much is needed. They also decide when and how the medicines should be used. Prescription medicines are prepared by health workers called *pharmacists.* Pharmacists work in hospitals and many stores where medicines are sold. They have been trained to prepare and package medicines.

prescription (prih SKRIHP shuhn), a special order given by a physician or another qualified doctor for a certain medicine.

■ *A physician can order a prescription medicine, which is prepared by a pharmacist.*

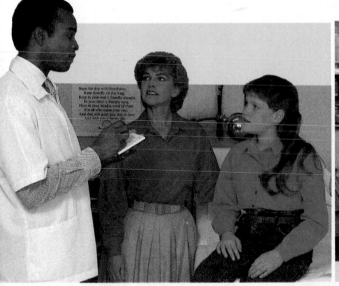

Some medicines can be bought without a prescription. These are called over-the-counter medicines, or **OTC medicines.** Most OTC medicines are used to treat minor health problems. Some cold pills, cough syrups, and pain relievers are OTC medicines. They are sold in pharmacies and in many kinds of stores.

OTC medicines, medicines that can be bought "over the counter," without a prescription.

245

How Can You Use Medicines Safely?

You should never take any kind of medicine unless a parent, guardian, or physician tells you to take it. Even then, you always need to take a medicine exactly as directed. Each medicine comes with directions that tell the proper way to use it.

Directions for using an OTC medicine are printed on its label. More directions are sometimes given on an extra sheet of paper inside the medicine package. Always look for the answers to the following questions as you read a set of directions: What symptoms does the medicine claim to relieve? What is the **dosage,** or correct amount of medicine to be taken at one time? How often can the medicine be taken? Over how many days can it be taken? What are the possible side effects of the medicine? Make sure you can answer all these questions before you take any medicine.

dosage (DOH sihj), the correct amount of a medicine to be taken at one time.

■ *OTC medicines should be taken only as directed by a parent or physician. Even then, read the label carefully before taking the medicine.*

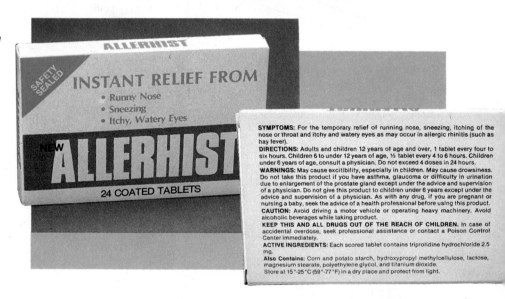

Prescription medicines also have labels that give directions for using them safely. The name of the physician and the date the prescription was ordered are printed on the label. The name of the person who should take the medicine is also on the label. If your name is not on the label, do not take the medicine. Prescription medicines are ordered for only one person. One person should not use another's prescription medicine.

MEDICINE SAFETY GUIDELINES

- Always check with a parent or the school nurse before taking any medicine.

- Do not use an OTC medicine unless the medicine is made to relieve your symptoms.

- Do not use any prescription medicine that was ordered for an earlier problem or for another person.

- Read the directions on the label each time you use a medicine.

- Always use medicines the way the directions tell you to use them. Report any side effects to a parent or guardian, your pharmacist, or your physician.

- Do not take two or more medicines unless your physician tells you to do so. Two medicines together can affect the body in ways that neither medicine does by itself.

- Do not use a medicine if you are not sure what it is.

- Read the expiration date on the label. Do not use or keep any medicine that is older than the expiration date. Throw out any medicines that are over one year old.

- Keep all medicines out of the reach of young children.

REAL-LIFE
SKILL

Updating Medicines in the Home

Take an inventory of the medicines found in your home. List each medicine and where it is found. Include the expiration date. Throw away any medicines whose expiration dates have passed.

medicine abuse (MEHD uh suhn • uh BYOOS), taking a medicine without following the directions and safety guidelines.

Be sure to ask your physician the purpose of the medicine when he or she gives you a prescription. The purpose may or may not be written on the medicine label. The label tells you the dosage. It also tells you when to take the medicine and how long to take it. Certain warnings and possible side effects are listed on the label. Take the prescription medicine exactly as directed.

If you notice any side effects after taking an OTC or prescription medicine, stop taking the medicine. Have an adult call your physician and describe what happened. The physician will tell you what to do.

Because there are ways that medicines can cause problems, the "Medicine Safety Guidelines" listed on the chart on page 247 are important. Taking a medicine without following the directions and safety guidelines is called **medicine abuse.** Sometimes a person abuses a medicine for a long time. This abuse can damage the body.

STOP **REVIEW SECTION 1**

REMEMBER?

1. What is the relationship between a drug and a medicine?
2. What is the difference between a prescription medicine and an OTC medicine?
3. Name three kinds of directions found on medicine labels.
4. Name five medicine safety guidelines.

THINK!

5. Why are there so many steps and guidelines for using medicines safely?
6. Why should the directions on medicine labels be read and followed carefully?

Health Close-up

What Is the FDA?

In the early 1900s, the United States government began to pass laws that set safety standards for foods and medicines. One of these laws is the Federal Food, Drug, and Cosmetic Act. This act makes it illegal for companies to sell impure foods and unsafe medicines and cosmetics. It also does not allow false or misleading labeling of any of these products. The Food and Drug Administration, or FDA, enforces this law. The FDA is part of the United States Department of Health and Human Services.

Another responsibility of the FDA is to approve all new medicines. Before a new medicine can be made for sale, the manufacturer must give the test reports on the medicine to the FDA. The tests must prove the medicine is safe to use

■ The FDA requires that all new medicines be tested extensively before they can be sold.

and that it works. The manufacturer must also describe how the medicine's strength and purity were tested. There must also be a list of all the ingredients in the medicine. Label directions and warnings for the medicine must be sent to the FDA. Plans for the making, packaging, and storing of the medicine must also be sent. If the medicine meets all FDA standards, the FDA gives the manufacturer approval to make the medicine.

After the FDA has given approval for a new medicine, it keeps on studying the medicine. FDA workers check reports of side effects caused by the medicine. They check factories and warehouses to make sure these places are clean. They also make sure that the medicine is being made and stored according to FDA requirements.

If FDA rules are not being followed, the FDA takes the manufacturer to federal court. The court may order that a harmful or impure medicine be destroyed. The court may also order that a medicine be removed from stores until the FDA can make sure the medicine is safe to use. In some cases, the FDA can order the manufacturer to stop making the medicine.

Thinking Beyond

1. How might people's health be affected if there were no FDA?
2. Why is it important to have information on medicine labels?

249

2 Dangers of Drug Abuse

Many people have been helped by medicines. But many people have been harmed by incorrect use of medicines and other drugs. **Drug abuse** is the repeated use of any drug for the wrong reasons.

What Are the Effects of Drug Abuse?

Drug abuse can be very harmful to a person's wellness. Drug abuse can often lead to drug dependence. **Drug dependence** is the physical or emotional need to take one or more drugs.

KEY WORDS

drug abuse
drug dependence
withdrawal
tolerance
overdose

drug abuse (DRUHG • uh BYOOS), the repeated use of any drug for the wrong reasons.

drug dependence (DRUHG • dih PEHN duhns), a harmful condition in which a person has a physical or an emotional need to take a drug (or drugs).

■ *The taking of some drugs can be very dangerous and can lead to drug dependence.*

withdrawal (wihth DRAW uhl), stopping the supply of a drug on which a person is physically dependent; usually causes painful physical symptoms.

With *physical dependence,* the person's body needs the drug. Each time the effects of the drug wear off, the person feels pain or becomes ill. These symptoms are caused by **withdrawal** of the drug. Taking more of the drug makes the symptoms go away for a while. To avoid the pain of withdrawal, the person keeps using the drug.

With *emotional dependence,* a person thinks he or she needs the drug. Taking the drug gives the person a false sense of well-being. A person with emotional dependence

250

cannot stop thinking about the drug. Each time the drug wears off, the person wants to feel its effects again.

Some drugs cause physical dependence. Others cause emotional dependence. Many drugs cause both kinds of dependence. Both kinds of drug dependence are harmful and can be very hard to break.

When people start smoking cigarettes, they think they can stop smoking any time they want. But many people find that they want cigarettes all the time. They feel this way because of a drug called *nicotine* in tobacco. This drug causes people to become physically dependent on cigarettes.

People's bodies can also build **tolerance** for, or get used to, certain drugs. When a person develops tolerance for a drug, larger and larger amounts of the drug are needed for the person to feel the original effects of the drug.

tolerance (TAHL uh ruhns), the body's ability to get used to amounts of certain drugs.

HOW TOLERANCE DEVELOPS

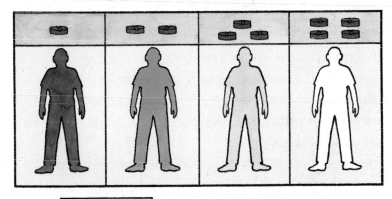

Decreasing effect of drug over time

■ *The danger from tolerance is taking a dosage of a drug that the body cannot handle. Death could result.*

As tolerance builds, a person is likely to take larger and larger doses of a drug to feel its effects. A person who continues to increase the dosage of a drug could take an overdose. An **overdose** is a dose large enough to cause serious harm to the body. An overdose can cause pain, loss of coordination, and even death. The effects of an overdose depend on the drug and on the person's tolerance for that drug. The same amount of a drug used by one person may be an overdose for another person. Even for the same person, a certain amount of a drug can cause mild effects at one time and deadly effects at another time.

overdose (OH vuhr dohs), a drug dose large enough to cause serious harm to the body.

251

Why Do Some People Abuse Drugs?

People start to abuse drugs for different reasons. Some people use medicines for the wrong reasons. They may try to get rid of a symptom, such as a headache, rather than deal with its cause, such as being tired or sad. They may take medicines without following the directions. They may take too much medicine or take it too often. They may use a medicine without checking with a physician.

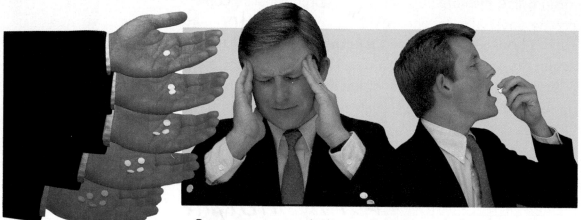

■ Some people abuse medicines. They take medicines to treat the symptoms of a problem rather than deal with the cause of the problem.

Sometimes people know that they are harming themselves by the way they use drugs. They may try to stop taking them. But they may find they cannot stop because they have become dependent on drugs. They have become drug abusers.

Some other people use drugs on purpose. But they do not accept the fact that this is abuse. They may start taking drugs because of peer pressure. Friends may try to pressure them into trying drugs. They may be told that drug abuse is fun, harmless, or exciting, or that other people will admire them for taking drugs.

Many people who abuse drugs believe that they will do so only for a short time. They may not know about drug tolerance and how it can lead to drug dependence. They ignore the consequences of breaking laws or causing safety risks to others on highways and elsewhere. They may think that the dangerous effects of drugs cannot happen to them. These people may take a drug every day and think they can stop whenever they wish. When they finally try to stop taking the drug, they find they cannot.

252

When a person uses drugs, the people who care about him or her are also affected.

Drugs cost a lot of money. Many people must borrow or steal to get enough money to satisfy their drug abuse.

How Does Drug Abuse Affect People Other Than the Drug Abuser?

Drug abuse affects more people than just the person abusing drugs. It affects the person's family members and friends. Some young people who are having trouble getting along at home or school may think they can take drugs to get away from their problems. But drug abuse only worsens relationships with family and friends.

In many cases, a drug abuser borrows or steals from family and friends in order to get the money needed to buy drugs. The cost of all drugs, especially illegal drugs, is high. Many drug abusers spend more than $100 on drugs each day.

People who abuse drugs have an effect on all the people where they live. Communities spend millions of dollars each year to arrest drug abusers, put them on trial, and put them in prison for drug-related crimes. Most of this money comes from the taxes community members pay for public safety.

REVIEW SECTION 2

REMEMBER?

1. What is the difference between physical and emotional drug dependence?
2. How does a person build tolerance to a drug?
3. How does peer pressure cause drug abuse?

THINK!

4. How can trying a harmful drug, even once, lead to drug abuse?
5. How can drug abuse worsen a person's problems at home or school?

Thinking About Your Health

What Are Your Attitudes About Taking Medicines?

Read the following statements. Think about each one.

1. When Leon has a headache, the first thing he does is ask a parent for medicine.
2. When Anne has a headache, she takes a pain medicine without telling her parents.
3. When Carl has a headache, he talks with a parent or the school nurse to figure out the cause of the pain.
4. Larson refuses to take any medicine at all.

Ask yourself questions about each statement. Do you feel something is not right with the statement? Do you agree with the action taken? Does it bother you that someone might agree with the statement? Why do you suppose some people depend too much on medicines when they have health problems?

3 Drugs That Are Abused

Some drugs change the way people think, act, and feel. These drugs, legal and illegal, are the ones most often abused. They can be divided into six groups according to their major effects.

What Are Stimulants?

Stimulants are drugs that speed up the circulatory and nervous systems. These drugs make a person feel more active and awake. Stimulants make a person's heart beat faster than normal. They also make the blood vessels smaller. Then it is not as easy for blood to flow through them. This condition causes a person's blood pressure to rise. Some stimulants make people restless, tense, and irritable. Repeated use of any stimulant may cause physical and emotional dependence. Use of a stimulant almost always raises a person's tolerance for that stimulant.

Caffeine is a mild stimulant found in coffee, tea, cocoa, chocolate, and many soft drinks. People who drink one of these beverages in the morning say it helps them feel wide awake. *Nicotine,* a drug in tobacco, is a much stronger stimulant. Use of caffeine or nicotine causes physical dependence, or addiction.

KEY WORDS

stimulants
depressants
narcotics
hallucinogens
flashback
inhalants
fumes

stimulants (STIHM yuh luhnts), drugs that speed up the circulatory and nervous systems.

■ *Stimulants, such as the caffeine in cola, coffee, chocolate, and tea, speed up the functions of the nervous system.*

255

■ *A cocaine "high" is quickly followed by depression.*

FOR THE
CURIOUS

Crack is one of the most dangerous illegal drugs. It harms the body and the personality. It quickly causes drug dependence. Punishment for selling, using, or having crack is most often a jail sentence.

Amphetamines are stimulants that are very strong. Amphetamines legally prescribed for people by physicians are carefully made. Some illegal amphetamines, however, are made with dangerous chemicals. Signs of amphetamine abuse are enlarged pupils, trembling, nervousness, and loss of appetite. People who take amphetamines over a long time may become violent. Large doses of amphetamines can make a person's heart rate dangerously high. An overdose often causes death.

Cocaine is one of the most dangerous illegal stimulants. It causes a pattern of very strong feelings. It is easy for people to develop an emotional dependence on cocaine. They feel a false sense of self-confidence. As that effect of the drug wears off, however, they are likely to feel very sad or depressed. To escape this frightening "down" following a cocaine "high," the person uses more of the drug. Once this up-and-down pattern is set, it is hard for the person to stop using the drug. There is strong physical and emotional dependence. The drug causes a user to develop higher and higher tolerance. Because of this, people who use cocaine can easily overdose. An overdose of cocaine, especially of the form called "crack," can result in death. Death is due to heart muscle damage.

What Are Depressants?

Drugs that slow down the body's systems are called **depressants.** These drugs affect a person's brain and nervous system. They can cloud a person's thinking. Depressants also slow down the heart and make other muscles relax. Some allergy medicines contain mild depressants. These medicines may make people sleepy as a side effect. Most strong depressants are sold only by prescription. They are used to calm patients who are very upset and to treat certain disorders of the nervous system. These drugs often make people fall asleep.

Some strong depressants include *alcohol, tranquilizers,* and *barbiturates.* It is illegal for alcohol to be sold to young people. Without a prescription, tranquilizers and barbiturates are illegal for anyone to have.

A person can become both physically and emotionally dependent on strong depressants. The body builds tolerance for these drugs very quickly. Because of this, it is easy for a person to take an overdose. If someone who is dependent on depressants stops taking the drugs, the withdrawal can be very dangerous. Withdrawal from strong depressants may even cause death. Withdrawal should be guided by a physician.

depressants (dih PREHS uhnts), drugs that slow down the body's systems.

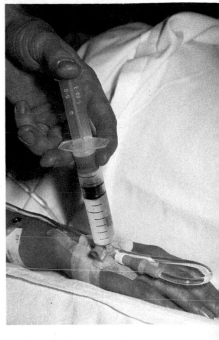

■ *Some depressants are used by physicians to calm patients before surgery.*

■ *Alcohol is a strong depressant on which people can become both physically and emotionally dependent.*

What Are Narcotics?

Narcotics are strong drugs that slow down the heart, the brain, and the nervous system. Narcotics also stop the brain from sensing pain.

Physicians write prescriptions for some narcotics. *Codeine* is a narcotic used in medicines to relieve strong pain or hard-to-control coughs. One of the strongest narcotics, *morphine,* is used as a pain reliever for people recovering from surgery.

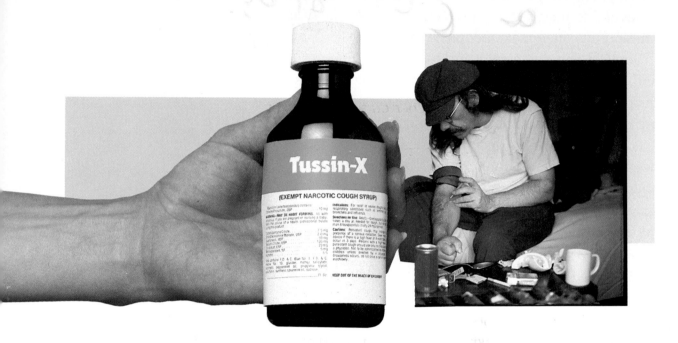

■ *Codeine is a narcotic that is used in many helpful medicines. Heroin, however, is an illegal drug and is an extremely dangerous narcotic.*

The most dangerous and life-threatening narcotic is *heroin.* Heroin has no medical use. It is an illegal drug. People who sell heroin often add things to it to make the amount look greater. Because of this, people who use heroin can never be sure how strong the drug is. They are always in danger of death from an overdose. Also, the virus that causes AIDS can spread among heroin abusers. This is because they often share the needles they use to inject the drug.

The use of any narcotic can cause a person to have strong physical and emotional dependence and high tolerance. Because of these dangers, narcotics cannot be bought legally in the United States without a prescription.

■ *Hallucinogens are illegal and dangerous drugs that change the way a person sees and hears things.*

What Are Hallucinogens?

Drugs that can change the way a person senses the world are called **hallucinogens.** These drugs change the way messages are carried by the nerves to the brain. Hallucinogens, such as *LSD* and *PCP,* can change the way a person sees or hear things. They may cause a person to see things that are not really there. Some people who have taken LSD have killed themselves. They have jumped from buildings because they believed they could fly. Others have walked in front of moving cars because they thought they could not be injured.

The effects of a hallucinogen may come back long after the person has stopped taking the drug. This is called a **flashback.** It can be very frightening and is not something a person can control. Because hallucinogens are so dangerous, it is illegal to make, sell, have, or use them.

hallucinogens (huh LOOS uhn uh juhnz), drugs that change the way a person senses the world.

flashback (FLASH bak), effects of a hallucinogen that come back long after the person has stopped taking the drug.

What Are Cannabis Drugs?

Two illegal drugs that you often hear about in the United States are *marijuana* and *hashish.* Both drugs are made from the hemp plant, also known as *Cannabis sativa.* The stem of the hemp plant has strong fibers used to make rope or cloth. Illegal drug dealers crush or chop the dried leaves and flowers of the plant to sell as marijuana. They make hashish from the sticky juice that comes from the plant's flower.

■ *Marijuana and hashish come from the hemp plant, Cannabis sativa.*

259

DRUGS AND THEIR EFFECTS

	Drugs	Possible Immediate Effects	Possible Long-Term Effects/Overdose
Stimulants	Amphetamines Cocaine Crack	increased alertness, increased heart rate and blood pressure, loss of appetite, sleeplessness, dry mouth, irritability, talkativeness, muscle twitching, extreme nervousness, chest pain, anorexia, marked psychological dependence	agitation, increase in body temperature, tremors, delusions, violent behavior, hallucinations, delirium, convulsions, death
Depressants	Alcohol Tranquilizers Barbiturates	slurred speech, flushing, headache, slowed heart rate and breathing, increased reaction time, drunken behavior, impaired coordination, confusion, narrow attention span, faulty judgment, poor memory, nausea, vomiting, respiratory depression, delirium	shallow breathing, cold and clammy skin, dilated pupils, weak and rapid pulse, anxiety and depression, emotional instability, respiratory depression, coma, death
Narcotics	Codeine Morphine Heroin	drowsiness, watery eyes, constricted pupils, itching, breathing difficulties, nausea, vomiting	slow and shallow breathing, flushing, clammy skin, decreased body temperature, spasticity, hypotension, increased chance of hepatitis, convulsions, coma, death
Hallucinogens	LSD PCP	lack of coordination, poor perception of time and distance, anxiety, withdrawn state, panic states, extreme apprehensiveness, hallucinations	persistent psychotic effects, flashbacks, permanent brain damage, death
Cannabis	Marijuana Hashish	disoriented behavior, laziness, poor concentration, increased appetite, distortion of spatial perception, difficulty with depth perception, altered sense of timing, lowered testosterone levels, increased heart rate, panic attack	fatigue, paranoia, lung damage, pulmonary system damage, reproductive cell damage, decrease in growth hormones, hallucinations, psychosis, brain damage, cancer
Inhalants	Paint thinner Model glue Gasoline Nail polish remover Freon Aerosol sprays	sneezing, coughing, nosebleeds, fatigue, lack of coordination, loss of appetite, headaches, disorientation, confusion, memory loss, nausea, decreased heart and respiratory rates, involuntary passing of urine and feces	bronchial irritation; decreased respirations; drunkenness; stupor; pulmonary congestion and edema; violent behavior; hallucinations; dyspnea; ketosis; hepatitis; permanent damage to brain, kidneys, liver, and bone marrow; death

Kinds of Drugs

Like most drugs, marijuana and hashish can affect different people in different ways. These drugs can also affect the same person in different ways at different times. Sometimes, the drugs work like stimulants and then like depressants. At other times, they act like hallucinogens. The effects are never certain.

Marijuana usually is rolled into cigarettes and smoked. It contains more than 400 substances, most of them harmful. One of the most harmful is a drug known as THC. Because marijuana is taken into the body as smoke, it also harms the lungs. Hashish is even more powerful and dangerous than marijuana. Marijuana and hashish can make a person feel confused. A user may not be able to concentrate. The developing brain and reproductive cells of young people can be greatly harmed.

■ *Marijuana and hashish can harm brain cells and can interfere with a person's ability to concentrate.*

What Are Inhalants?

Inhalants are chemicals that people breathe. Some inhalants affect people as some drugs do. Repeated sniffing can cause forgetfulness, dizziness, and headaches. Inhalants quickly damage the lungs, heart, brain, and liver. These damaged organs may never recover. In addition to causing permanent organ damage faster than most other abused substances, inhalants produce dependence sooner. People who abuse inhalants can die because they stop breathing or have heart attacks.

inhalants (ihn HAY luhnts), chemicals that have a druglike effect when they are breathed.

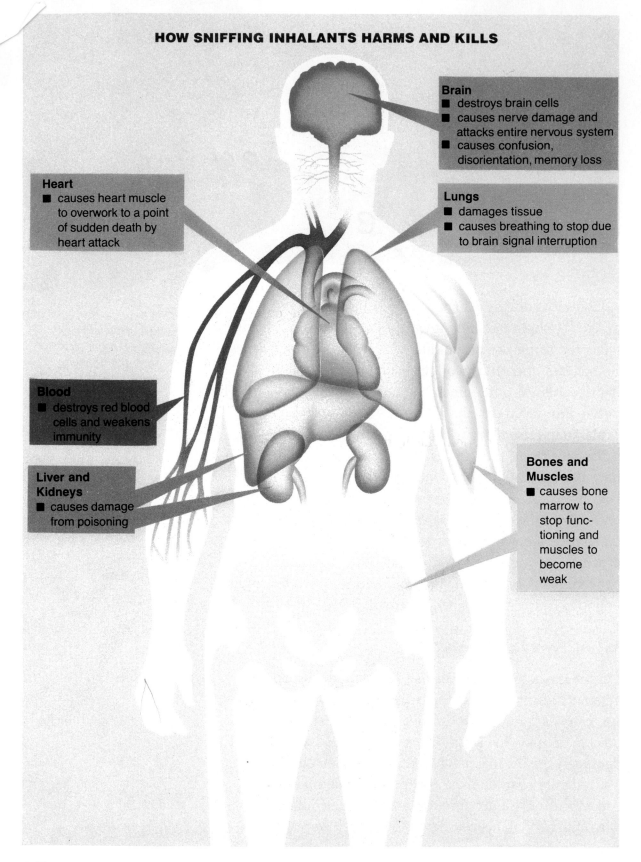

HOW SNIFFING INHALANTS HARMS AND KILLS

Brain
- destroys brain cells
- causes nerve damage and attacks entire nervous system
- causes confusion, disorientation, memory loss

Heart
- causes heart muscle to overwork to a point of sudden death by heart attack

Lungs
- damages tissue
- causes breathing to stop due to brain signal interruption

Blood
- destroys red blood cells and weakens immunity

Liver and Kidneys
- causes damage from poisoning

Bones and Muscles
- causes bone marrow to stop functioning and muscles to become weak

Inhalants such as freon and aerosol sprays are gases. Other inhalants called *solvents* are liquids that give off **fumes,** or gases. Paint thinner, model glue, gasoline, nail polish remover, and correction fluid are solvents.

Sometimes a person may breathe an inhalant by mistake. This may happen if a person is painting indoors with no windows open. The chemicals in the fumes pass from the person's lungs into the blood. The chemicals may change the way the person feels. The person may become dizzy or ill. To feel better, the person should go outdoors or open a window to breathe fresh air right away.

■ *Many common products contain dangerous inhalants that should be used with care.*

fumes (FYOOMZ), gases.

FOR THE
CURIOUS

To help make people aware that typewriter correction fluid is a dangerous inhalant, some manufacturers have put warning notices on the labels.

"Warning: Intentional misuse by deliberately concentrating and inhaling the contents can be harmful or fatal."

STOP REVIEW
SECTION 3

REMEMBER?

1. What are six kinds of drugs that are abused?
2. What are some harmful effects of using nonprescription stimulants?
3. What are the effects of sniffing inhalants?

THINK!

4. Why are the changes caused by hallucinogens so dangerous?
5. Why is marijuana especially harmful to young people?

4 How People Can Avoid Drug Abuse

People choose not to abuse drugs for many reasons. They know that drug abuse can damage their health. They do not want to form a dependence on any drug. They want to stay in control of their feelings and actions. They know that drug abuse might stop them from meeting their goals. They may not be able to enjoy their favorite activities. They know that abusing certain drugs is illegal.

■ *Most people do not abuse drugs. They know that drug abuse can prevent people from enjoying their favorite activities.*

Many people will never abuse drugs because they are prepared to resist pressures. They know what to say to someone who tries to tell them that taking drugs is fun and harmless.

How Can You Refuse an Offer to Abuse Drugs?

You have a right and a responsibility to refuse to do anything that can harm you. By refusing to abuse drugs, you show you have chosen to stay healthy and safe. Your decision may make the person who offers you drugs uncomfortable or angry at first. But when you refuse drugs, whether from someone you know or someone you do not

know, you do not have to worry about his or her feelings. Your concern is for your own health and your life.

Here are some ways to refuse when someone offers you a drug. These are also ways to refuse to take any other risks that can harm you.

1. If someone asks you to try a drug, say, "No, thank you." Always try to be polite. If the person keeps asking you, you can say, "No way!" in a convincing manner.
2. Another way to say no is to tell the person you have something better to do. You can tell the person you are going to ride your bicycle, play with your friends, or work on your hobby.
3. Knowing the facts about illegal drugs can help you say no. If someone asks you to try an illegal drug, you can say, "No, thanks. I know that drugs can kill a person."
4. Another way to say no to drugs is to change the subject. For example, if a friend offers you drugs, you might say, "No, thanks. Let's go skateboarding."
5. Sometimes the pressure from peers to try drugs can become heavy. When this happens, you can walk away.

Refusing something that can harm you is a positive health choice. It shows that you are self-confident and are taking responsibility for yourself. Knowing that you are able to refuse drugs can make you feel good about yourself. People will respect you for taking charge of your own health.

■ *Refusing to abuse drugs shows self-confidence and self-esteem. Saying no to drugs is a positive health decision.*

MYTH AND **FACT**

Myth: There is no harm in using a drug just once.

Fact: Each person responds differently to drugs. If a drug is not prescribed for you, you never know what your reaction will be. People have died from trying a drug just once.

Who Can Help You Decide to Refuse Drugs?

The pressure to abuse drugs is great in many schools and neighborhoods in the United States. Peer pressure often makes refusing drugs hard to do. Who can help you when the pressure is great?

■ *Talking with parents or other adults you trust can help you handle the pressure to take drugs.*

One choice is talking to your parents about what is happening. Ask them how they handled pressures when they were your age. Parents can help you recognize your feelings, such as sadness, emotional hurt, or anger. The best thing you can do is talk about the pressure with a family member or another person you trust. Talking with a good listener helps you understand your feelings and find ways to act that will not harm you.

Sometimes you see messages about refusing drugs on television or in magazines. These messages are designed to make people think about how dangerous drugs are.

You may have heard that if you make good choices, good things will happen as a result. This is very true for people who refuse to take unnecessary risks. One of the greatest risks that any person can take is to try drugs. Trying drugs even once is a risk. You never know how a drug might affect you. When you decide ahead of time that good things will happen to you because you will not take drugs, then you are more likely to enjoy life and be in control of it.

STOP **REVIEW SECTION 4**

REMEMBER?

1. What are three ways to avoid drugs?
2. What kind of trouble can a person get into by taking drugs?
3. How is refusing something that can harm you a positive health choice?

THINK!

4. Suppose a good friend offered you some drugs and your friend became angry because you refused. Is this person really your friend? Explain.
5. Why is making a plan to refuse illegal drugs a responsible choice?

Making Wellness Choices

Jill is walking through the park when two older girls approach her. Jill has seen the girls before at school. The girls ask Jill if she wants to be part of their group. Jill eagerly says yes and follows the girls to another part of the park. Six other girls are smoking marijuana there.

Jill suddenly feels very uneasy. She has learned at home and at school that marijuana is illegal. She knows that it is harmful to her health.

 What should Jill do? Explain your wellness choice.

267

People in Health

An Interview with a Pharmacologist

> *Sandra E. Burke works for a pharmaceutical company. She is a pharmacologist in North Chicago, Illinois.*

When did you decide to become a pharmacologist?

I became interested in science when I went to college. I took a class in which I studied the human body systems. I discovered I was interested in the circulatory system. I decided to keep studying the circulatory system even after I graduated from college. I took a job in a pharmacology lab doing research. For about ten years, I worked as a technician in different labs. Then I returned to school for my doctoral degree.

Is a pharmacologist a kind of pharmacist?

A pharmacologist is not a pharmacist. A pharmacologist does not sell medicines to people. That is what a pharmacist does. A pharmacologist tests and studies the drugs that pharmacists sell. A pharmacologist studies medicines to make sure they are effective and safe.

How does a person become a pharmacologist?

Someone who wants to become a pharmacologist often begins in high school by taking science classes. Then the person may enter a life-science program in college. The person needs to get a doctoral degree in science. A person who has received any kind of doctoral degree is called "doctor." Most pharmacologists are doctors of pharmacology (the study of drugs). Some are doctors in a related field of science. Some pharmacologists are also medical doctors, or physicians.

■ *Dr. Burke works for a company that manufactures medicines.*

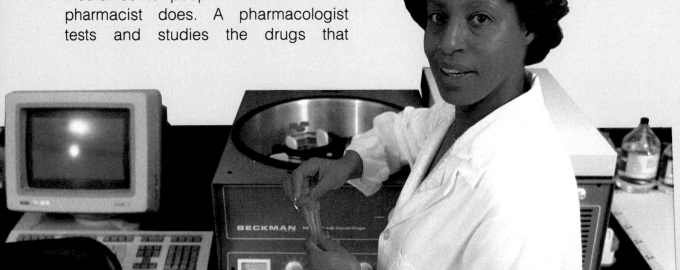

■ *A pharmacologist tests medicines.*

Does that mean that everyone who works in a pharmacology laboratory has to be a doctor?

Some laboratory workers are not doctors. They are technicians or research associates.

For what kind of company do you work?

I work for a company that researches, develops, and manufactures drugs and related products. Some of the products are sold as over-the-counter medicines. Some are sold only by prescription. Many of my company's other products are used by physicians, hospitals, and medical laboratories. For example, kits that we make are used to test for illnesses, such as liver diseases and AIDS.

What do you like most about your work?

I like the daily challenges that come with testing the effects of drugs. It is like being a detective. For example, I might try to find out why different dosages of some drugs cause blood to flow differently. There are so many different kinds of reactions to drugs. I always question what the reaction will be and how I can make the drug better.

What would you tell young people about becoming a pharmacologist?

Scientific investigation can be very exciting. I would ask them if they thought playing detective in the area of science would be exciting. If they said yes, I would tell them to think about going into the field of pharmacology.

> *Learn more about people who work as pharmacologists for pharmaceutical companies, universities, or the government. Interview a pharmacologist. Or write for information to the American Pharmaceutical Association, 2215 Constitution Ave., N.W., Washington, DC 20037.*

Main Ideas

- When you use medicines wisely, they can help treat or cure health problems.
- Drug abuse can threaten a person's wellness.
- People who abuse drugs not only harm their own bodies but also risk harming their relationships with family members and friends.
- Drugs that are most often abused can be divided into six groups according to their major effects on the body.
- Learning why and how to refuse drugs can help you be in control of your health and your life.
- You can talk with a parent or another person you trust when the pressure to use drugs becomes very great.

Key Words

Write the numbers 1 to 9 in your health notebook or on a separate sheet of paper. After each number, copy the sentence and fill in the missing term. Page numbers in ( ) tell you where to look in the chapter if you need help.

medicine (244)
prescription (245)
dosage (246)
medicine abuse (248)

withdrawal (250)
overdose (251)
depressants (257)
narcotics (258)
flashback (259)

1. Drugs that slow down the body are called ___?___ .

2. Taking a medicine without following directions is ___?___ .

3. A special order, or ___?___ , is given by a physician or another qualified doctor for certain medicines.

4. A ___?___ is an effect of a hallucinogen that comes back long after the person has stopped taking the drug.

5. A drug that people use to cure or treat a certain health problem is a ___?___ .

6. The ___?___ is the correct amount of a medicine.

7. Strong drugs that slow down the heart, the brain, and the nervous system and also stop the brain from sensing pain are called ___?___ .

8. During ___?___ , a person feels pain or is ill as the physical effects of a drug wear off.

9. An amount of any drug large enough to cause serious harm to the body is an ___?___ .

Write the numbers 10 to 18 on your paper. After each number, write a sentence that defines the term. Page numbers in ( ) tell you where to look in the chapter if you need help.

10. side effects (245)
11. OTC medicines (245)
12. drug abuse (250)
13. drug dependence (250)
14. tolerance (251)
15. stimulants (255)
16. hallucinogens (259)
17. inhalants (261)
18. fumes (263)

Remembering What You Learned

Page numbers in ( ) tell you where to look in the chapter if you need help.

1. How do medicines enter the body? (244)

2. Who prepares the medicine for a prescription? (245)

3. What do the directions on a medicine label tell you? (246, 248)

4. What should you do if you have side effects after taking medicine? (248)

5. How can drug abuse lead to drug dependence? (250–251)

6. How does a person's body build tolerance to a drug? (251)

7. How do people misuse drugs? (252)

8. How do stimulants affect a person's body? (255)

9. Name four kinds of stimulants. (255–256)

10. Name three kinds of depressants. (257)

11. What danger exists when a person builds tolerance to depressants? (257)

12. Name two inhalants. (263)

13. How can sniffing inhalants harm a person? (261–263)

14. What are some ways to refuse drugs? (264–265)

15. What can you do when peer pressure to use drugs becomes very great? (266–267)

Thinking About What You Learned

1. How can a medicine that is designed to help you feel better harm your health?

2. How can you take medicine safely when a parent or other adult is not at home to help you?

3. How can misuse or abuse of an OTC medicine be avoided?

4. Why is it dangerous for a person to believe that he or she can use illegal drugs a few times without being harmed?

5. Why do most people choose not to misuse or abuse drugs?

Writing About What You Learned

Write a short skit or oral report to present to the rest of the class. Give a presentation that will persuade the class to refuse or avoid drugs. Encourage your classmates to ask questions or make comments about refusing or avoiding drugs.

Applying What You Learned

MUSIC

Write a song that tells of the dangers of drugs. You need to make up your own words, tune, and perhaps sound effects. You may wish to work with two or three other students. Present your song to the rest of the class or to other classes.

CHAPTER
TEST

Modified True or False

Write the numbers 1 to 15 in your health notebook or on a separate sheet of paper. After each number, write *true* or *false* to describe the sentence. If the sentence is false, also write a term that replaces the underlined term and makes the sentence true.

1. Cocaine is a <u>stimulant</u>.

2. <u>Codeine</u> is a medicine.

3. If you need more and more of a drug to get the same physical effect, you are developing <u>withdrawal</u>.

4. If you take an aspirin for a headache and develop a rash, you are having a <u>side effect</u>.

5. <u>Caffeine</u> is a legal stimulant.

6. You can legally obtain <u>amphetamines</u> only if you have a <u>prescription</u>.

7. Taking a medicine without following the directions and safety guidelines is <u>dosage</u>.

8. A person with an <u>emotional</u> drug dependence will be physically sick without the drug.

9. Because <u>cigarettes</u> contain nicotine, people can become physically dependent on them.

10. Amphetamines are <u>depressants</u>.

11. The most dangerous narcotic is <u>heroin</u>.

12. Marijuana and <u>cocaine</u> are both made from the plant *Cannabis sativa*.

13. Paint thinner gives off <u>fumes</u>.

14. <u>Drug abuse</u> is the repeated use of any drug for the wrong reasons.

15. Alcohol is a <u>stimulant</u>.

Short Answer

Write the numbers 16 to 23 on your paper. Write a complete sentence to answer each question.

16. For what problems might a physician prescribe a depressant?

17. What is the difference between a depressant and a stimulant?

18. What drugs can cause flashbacks?

19. Who can help you decide to refuse drugs?

20. How can knowing the facts help you make a responsible decision about drugs?

21. What is a side effect?

22. What is the difference between an OTC medicine and a prescription medicine?

23. How can tolerance lead to an overdose?

Essay

Write the numbers 24 and 25 on your paper. Write paragraphs with complete sentences to answer each question.

24. Why is it important to decide how you feel about drugs before someone offers them to you?

25. Why do people abuse drugs?

272

ACTIVITIES FOR HOME OR SCHOOL

Projects to Do

1. Ask a parent to help you check how medicines are stored in your home. Are the medicines stored properly? Are they in a cool, dry place? Are they out of the reach of young children? Post a list of the medicines and their expiration dates on the inside of the storage cabinet for quick reference.

■ *Do you know what is in your family medicine cabinet?*

2. Write a sentence that explains your reasons for saying no to using illegal drugs. Combine your sentence with those of the others in your class to make an essay. Read the essay to other classes.

3. Form a "Just Say No Club." Ask a parent or teacher to help you.

Information to Find

1. Many drugs are illegal in the United States. Learn about your state's laws for four or five illegal drugs. What can happen to a person who is found with these drugs? You might ask your librarian for help in finding information. It may also be helpful to speak with a local police officer.

2. Find out how some of the illegal drugs were given their nicknames, such as "angel dust" and "pot."

Books to Read

Here are some books you can look for in your school library or the public library to find more information about medicines and illegal drugs.

Ardley, Neil. *Health and Medicine*. Franklin Watts.

Browne, David. *Crack and Cocaine*. Franklin Watts.

Woods, Geraldine. *Drug Use and Drug Abuse*. Franklin Watts.

273

IS ALCOHOL A PROBLEM IN YOUR FAMILY?
ALATEEN
For Young People Affected by Someone Else's Drinking
IN ALATEEN YOU CAN:
Meet others who share your problems
Learn about alcoholism as an illness
Share your experience
Build your self-confidence
CALL:
OR WRITE FOR CONFIDENTIAL INFORMATION TO:
Thank you for not smoking
American Cancer Society
NEW YORK CITY DIVISION, INC.
AMERICAN CANCER SOCIETY
19 West 56th Street, New York 10019
BEST TIP YET:
DON'T START!
DANGER
The Decision is Yours
QUITTER'S GUIDE

CHAPTER 9

TOBACCO AND ALCOHOL

Millions of adults use alcohol, tobacco, or both in their daily lives. Many adults did not know about the long-term risks when they began using these substances. Some people do not even know that alcohol and tobacco contain drugs.

You can protect your health and even your life by learning more about alcohol and tobacco. As you grow older, you will have the legal right to try alcohol and tobacco. But with that right comes a responsibility. Knowing the facts about alcohol and tobacco can help you decide not to use these substances, and you can protect your wellness.

GETTING READY TO LEARN

Key Questions

- Why is it important to learn about the harmful effects of alcohol and tobacco?
- Why is it important to know how you and your family feel about the use of alcohol and tobacco?
- How can you learn to refuse alcohol and tobacco?
- What can you do to become responsible for your health when it comes to alcohol and tobacco use?

Main Chapter Sections

1 Dangers of Tobacco Use

Fewer people in the United States are using tobacco now than ten years ago. This decrease in use is because the dangers are better known now. People who use tobacco most often burn it in cigarettes, pipes, or cigars, and inhale the smoke. Others use tobacco in the form of chewing tobacco or snuff. Tobacco that is not smoked is called smokeless tobacco. Some people use both forms. Both smoking and using smokeless tobacco have immediate and long-term dangers.

■ *Both smoking and using smokeless tobacco can harm your health.*

What Substances Are in Cigarette Smoke?

Cigarette smoke has more than 3,000 different substances in it. Over 200 of them have been identified as poisons. At least 16 of the substances in tobacco are known to cause cancer.

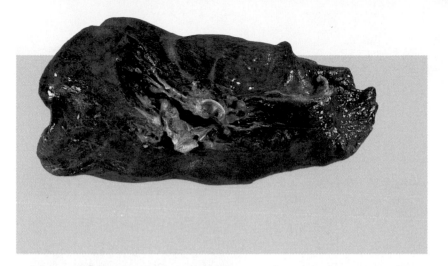

Tar can destroy the ability of the lungs to exchange gases. This lung is from a person who smoked tobacco for several years.

Most of the cancer-causing chemicals in cigarette smoke are found in tar. **Tar** is a sticky, brown substance. Filter-tipped cigarettes are designed to remove tar from smoke that is inhaled. However, some tar is left in cigarette smoke even after the smoke has passed through a filter.

Think about this example. A person who smokes two packages of cigarettes each day takes about 400 puffs. With each puff, the person inhales about 2.5 milligrams of tar. This means with those 400 puffs, a smoker inhales as much as 1,000 milligrams of tar each day. (As a comparison, a small paper clip has a mass of 1,000 milligrams.)

The lungs can rid themselves of small amounts of foreign substances. But they cannot rid themselves of 1,000 milligrams of tar each day, so tar builds up in the lungs. It coats the bronchial tubes and blocks many of the alveoli. The blocking prevents oxygen from passing through the walls of the alveoli into the blood. The smoker may need to take many extra breaths to get enough oxygen. Thus, in addition to risking cancer, a smoker may feel tired all the time.

All tobacco products contain a stimulant drug called **nicotine.** Nicotine speeds up the heart rate. It also raises blood pressure by making blood vessels narrower. Nicotine speeds up the working of the nervous and endocrine systems. That is why some smokers say smoking gives them energy or makes them feel relaxed.

However, nicotine is a poison. It is often used as an insecticide. An insecticide is a substance used for killing insects.

tar, a cancer-causing, sticky, brown substance found in cigarette smoke.

nicotine (NIHK uh teen), a stimulant drug in all tobacco products.

277

There are many organizations and many methods that can help a person stop smoking.

carbon monoxide (KAHR buhn • muh NAHK syd), a poisonous gas in cigarette smoke.

Nicotine is the drug in tobacco that causes physical and emotional dependence. Nicotine makes people want to keep smoking. In 1988 the United States surgeon general reported that nicotine dependence is very hard to break. More than half of the smokers in the United States say they have tried to stop smoking at one time or another. Some smokers have tried many times. Communities, hospitals, and health groups give help to people who want to stop smoking.

Another harmful substance in cigarette smoke is a poisonous gas called **carbon monoxide.** When a smoker inhales, carbon monoxide enters the blood instead of oxygen. Thus, carbon monoxide keeps the cells from getting the oxygen they need to use energy to do their jobs.

What Are the Immediate Effects of Smoking?

The use of tobacco has been linked with many health problems. For example, all the different substances in cigarettes play a role in allergies of smokers and the people around them. Asthma is a serious allergy of the respiratory system. A person having an asthma attack has great trouble breathing. Asthma is often triggered by tobacco smoke.

Tobacco use affects the smoker's digestive system, too. Substances in tobacco keep the body from getting certain vitamins from food, particularly vitamins B and C. Without these vitamins, smokers have less resistance to certain infections.

Tobacco is known to harm the unborn babies of mothers who smoke. Because of the carbon monoxide in tobacco, the mother's body may be unable to send enough oxygen to a developing baby. Nicotine also affects nutrients received by the unborn baby. Often the baby of a mother who smokes is smaller at birth than it should be.

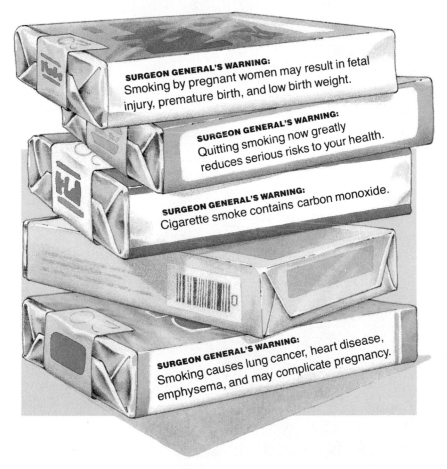

SURGEON GENERAL'S WARNING: Smoking by pregnant women may result in fetal injury, premature birth, and low birth weight.

SURGEON GENERAL'S WARNING: Quitting smoking now greatly reduces serious risks to your health.

SURGEON GENERAL'S WARNING: Cigarette smoke contains carbon monoxide.

SURGEON GENERAL'S WARNING: Smoking causes lung cancer, heart disease, emphysema, and may complicate pregnancy.

■ Every pack of cigarettes must carry one of these warnings from the surgeon general.

MYTH AND **FACT**

Myth: Low-tar, low-nicotine cigarettes are safer cigarettes.

Fact: Smokers who are used to brands with more tar and nicotine tend to inhale low-tar, low-nicotine cigarettes more deeply. They get more tar and nicotine from each cigarette. These cigarettes are just as unhealthful as any other kind.

Two other immediate results of tobacco smoking have to do with money. First, the dollar cost of tobacco is high. Many people spend a lot of money for tobacco. Only a small amount of this cost pays for the ingredients in tobacco products. Much more of the money is for taxes and the heavy advertising of tobacco products.

The second cost from smoking is for fire and burn damage. When smokers are careless with cigarettes, they can burn themselves and nearby objects. Clothing and furniture are damaged by dropped ashes.

Tobacco smoking has social effects for smokers. These include an unattractive smell and appearance. Stale smoke stays in the clothes and hair of smokers. Although the smoker cannot smell it, other people can. Smokers also get a yellow stain on their teeth and often on their fingers.

■ *Fire is another danger of smoking tobacco. Many people die in fires that are caused by careless smokers.*

What Are the Long-term Health Risks of Smoking?

Smoking damages many organs of the body. Smoking is linked to lung damage, cancer, heart disease, and other health problems.

Lung Damage. Cigarette smoke causes changes in the lungs. Tar buildup blocks small air passages in the lungs. Tar also contributes to the rupture of the alveoli in the lungs. Once ruptured, alveoli cannot be repaired. They cannot release carbon dioxide or take in oxygen. This results in a lung disease called *emphysema*.

Tar in cigarette smoke can also destroy the cilia and add mucus in the bronchial tubes. This damage causes dust and tar to stay in the tubes and make them swell. This causes a disease called *chronic bronchitis*. People who have chronic bronchitis cough a lot. The disease can be cured, but only after a person stops smoking. Some of the damage to the lungs may remain.

Cancer. The surgeon general of the United States has linked cigarette smoking to lung cancer. This disease happens when the tar in cigarette smoke irritates cells in the lungs and changes them. They become cancer cells. When cancer cells multiply, they replace healthy lung tissue. The cancerous tissue keeps the person from getting the oxygen he or she needs. Lung cancer often is not detected until it has reached a late stage. By this time, treatment does not help very much. Most people who get lung cancer die from the disease.

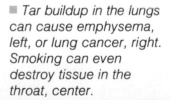

■ *Tar buildup in the lungs can cause emphysema, left, or lung cancer, right. Smoking can even destroy tissue in the throat, center.*

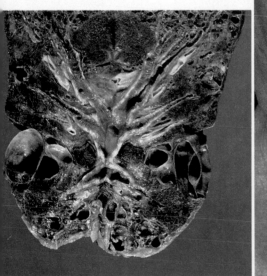

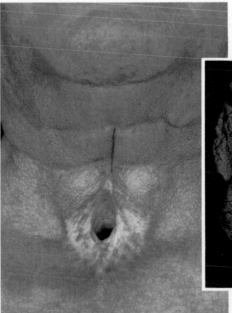

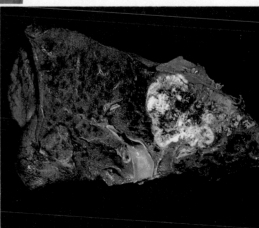

Smoking increases the risk of getting other cancers, too. Because it irritates tissues, smoking is tied to cancers of the mouth, esophagus, and organs of the digestive system. The American Cancer Society reports that nearly one-third of all cancer deaths are caused by smoking cigarettes.

Heart Disease. Heart disease is one of the major health risks for smokers. Nicotine and carbon monoxide together are the main cause of heart disease in smokers. Nicotine causes the heart to beat fast and blood vessels to narrow. It is not easy for blood to flow through narrowed blood vessels. This narrowing causes the heart to work harder than it should. When the heart works harder, it needs more oxygen than it did before. But at the very time the heart needs more oxygen, the smoker inhales carbon monoxide instead. Once again, less oxygen is getting to the heart. Over time, the heart muscle weakens, which often leads to heart disease.

A person who smokes is more likely to have more health problems than a nonsmoker. In fact, the average life span of a smoker is about eight years shorter than that of a nonsmoker.

Making Wellness Choices

Jessica has invited Valerie to spend a Saturday evening at her house. The same night, Jessica's older brother is having a party. Shortly after Valerie arrives, Jessica's parents leave the house. Jessica and Valerie go outside and sit on the back porch. During the evening, some of the people at the party come to the back porch to smoke cigarettes. One of the guests asks Jessica and Valerie if they would like to smoke a cigarette. Valerie accepts the offer.

? What might Jessica say to avoid smoking? Explain your wellness choice.

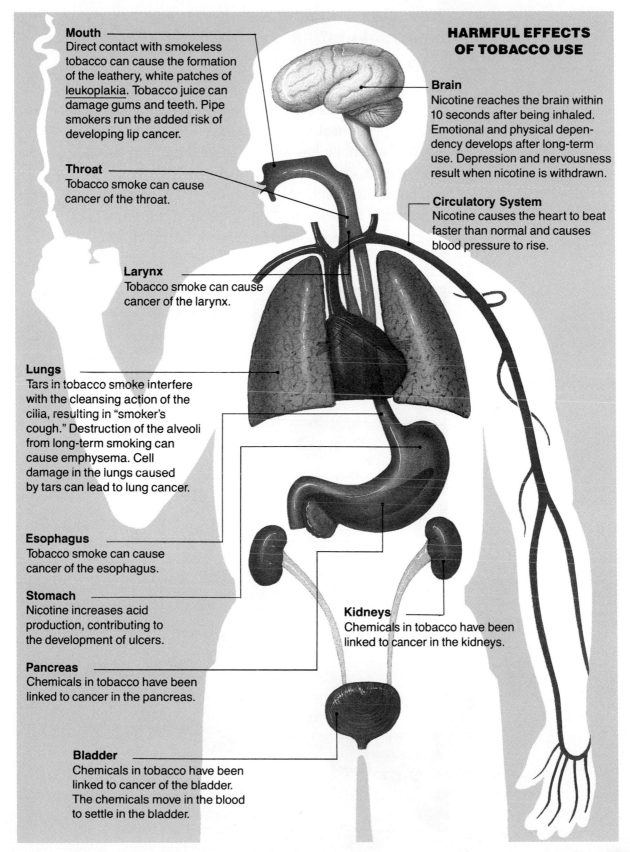

HARMFUL EFFECTS OF TOBACCO USE

Mouth
Direct contact with smokeless tobacco can cause the formation of the leathery, white patches of leukoplakia. Tobacco juice can damage gums and teeth. Pipe smokers run the added risk of developing lip cancer.

Throat
Tobacco smoke can cause cancer of the throat.

Larynx
Tobacco smoke can cause cancer of the larynx.

Lungs
Tars in tobacco smoke interfere with the cleansing action of the cilia, resulting in "smoker's cough." Destruction of the alveoli from long-term smoking can cause emphysema. Cell damage in the lungs caused by tars can lead to lung cancer.

Esophagus
Tobacco smoke can cause cancer of the esophagus.

Stomach
Nicotine increases acid production, contributing to the development of ulcers.

Pancreas
Chemicals in tobacco have been linked to cancer in the pancreas.

Bladder
Chemicals in tobacco have been linked to cancer of the bladder. The chemicals move in the blood to settle in the bladder.

Brain
Nicotine reaches the brain within 10 seconds after being inhaled. Emotional and physical dependency develops after long-term use. Depression and nervousness result when nicotine is withdrawn.

Circulatory System
Nicotine causes the heart to beat faster than normal and causes blood pressure to rise.

Kidneys
Chemicals in tobacco have been linked to cancer in the kidneys.

283

How Can Tobacco Smoke Harm Nonsmokers?

Tobacco smoke is known to be very harmful to smokers. It is also known that tobacco smoke harms nonsmokers. Smoke that leaves the lighted end of a cigarette is called **sidestream smoke.** Some studies have shown that sidestream smoke has more of certain harmful substances than what a smoker inhales. Therefore sidestream smoke can harm the health of nonsmokers.

Scientists have found that a person in a room where other people are smoking breathes in as much of certain cancer-causing chemicals in one hour as a person who

sidestream smoke (SYD streem • SMOHK), smoke that leaves the lighted end of a cigarette.

■ Sidestream smoke contains cancer-causing chemicals that can harm the health of nonsmokers.

smokes 25 filter-tipped cigarettes. Many other tobacco chemicals also enter the air in sidestream smoke. These chemicals can cause many health problems in nonsmokers as well as in smokers. For example, children whose parents smoke may have lung problems. Babies of parents who smoke are much more likely to get respiratory diseases. Sidestream smoke also irritates the eyes, nose, and throat.

People who have chosen not to smoke want to maintain their wellness. Many people are trying to have laws passed against smoking in public places. They want no sidestream smoke in schools, restaurants, and offices. There are now "clean indoor air laws," which either do not allow smoking or limit smoking areas in many public places.

What Are the Dangers of Smokeless Tobacco?

Chewing tobacco and snuff are two kinds of smokeless tobacco. Chewing tobacco is made of low-quality tobacco leaves. It is placed between the gum and cheek and is chewed. Snuff, which is powdered tobacco, is placed between the lower lip and gum or is sniffed through the nose.

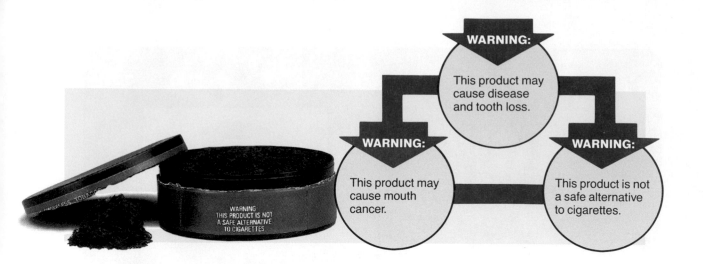

WARNING: This product may cause disease and tooth loss.

WARNING: This product may cause mouth cancer.

WARNING: This product is not a safe alternative to cigarettes.

■ *As with cigarettes, smokeless tobacco packages show a warning from the surgeon general.*

■ *Smokeless tobacco damages the tissues inside the mouth as well as the lips and teeth.*

Because smokeless tobacco produces no smoke, many people think that using it is safer than smoking cigarettes. This is not true. People who use smokeless tobacco risk the same harmful effects. All tobacco products contain nicotine and other harmful substances. When a person places smokeless tobacco in the mouth or nose, these substances are absorbed. Nicotine and other chemicals enter the blood through the lining of the mouth, stomach, or nose. The person who uses smokeless tobacco feels the same effects of nicotine as a person who smokes tobacco does. The heart beats faster than it should. The blood vessels become narrower. The person may form a physical dependence on nicotine. He or she will find this dependence hard to break.

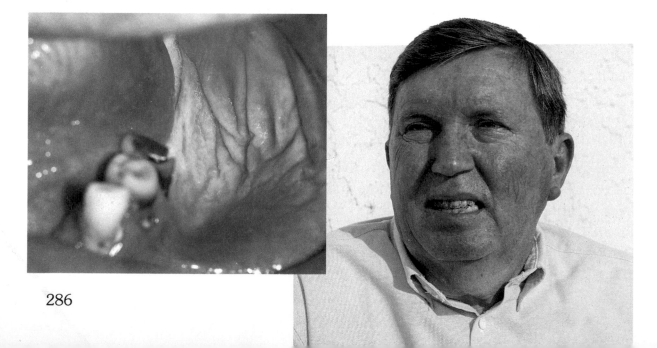

There are other health risks to people who use smokeless tobacco. For example, many kinds of chewing tobacco have sugar in them. They cause tooth decay. Smokeless tobacco may cause bad breath and discolored teeth. It reduces a person's sense of taste and smell. Using smokeless tobacco over a long time can cause the gums to shrink away from the teeth. This shrinking can result in serious gum disease and tooth loss. When tobacco juices irritate tissues, sores may form in the mouth, throat, and stomach. These sores sometimes become cancerous. People who use tobacco products are taking chances with their health and well-being.

REVIEW SECTION 1

REMEMBER?

1. Name three harmful substances in cigarettes.
2. What stimulant in tobacco causes physical and emotional dependence?
3. Name four organs that can be damaged by cigarette smoking. How are these organs affected?
4. How does smokeless tobacco affect the mouth, teeth, and gums?

THINK!

5. In what public places could sidestream smoke be especially harmful?
6. What kinds of people suffer the most from sidestream smoke?

2 Dangers of Alcohol Use

KEY WORDS

ethanol
intoxicated
hangover
alcoholism
alcoholic
malnutrition
ulcers

Some adults drink alcohol to relax. Beer, wine, and liquor are sometimes served at adult parties. Some family customs include drinking a little alcohol with meals. Other adults drink alcohol to celebrate important times. However, they do not drink very much, and they do not drink often enough to have problems with alcohol. They are called *social drinkers.* But many people cannot or do not control their drinking. They drink too much alcohol too often. Alcohol causes problems for them. They abuse this drug. By abusing it, they harm themselves and other people. They are called *problem drinkers.*

■ *When a person drinks too much alcohol, he or she can cause problems for other people.*

What Are the Immediate Effects of Alcohol on the Body?

Alcohol causes changes in all people who drink it. These changes happen in stages.

At first, a person's moods and feelings change. Alcohol is a depressant. It slows down the parts of the brain that control the way a person feels and acts. Alcohol often makes a person act in ways that would normally be embarrassing. The person may talk loudly or start a fight.

As a person drinks more alcohol, more parts of his or her brain slow down. The person's vision may become blurred. He or she may lose some control over muscles and have trouble talking and walking. Alcohol also may irritate the stomach so much that the person vomits. Finally, the person may have so much alcohol in the body that he or she passes out.

How Does Alcohol Change the Body?

The chemical name for the alcohol found in beer, wine, and liquor is **ethanol.** When ethanol is swallowed, it passes from the stomach and small intestine into the blood. The blood carries the ethanol to all parts of the body, which are changed by the drug. The *blood alcohol level* is the percentage of alcohol in the blood.

ethanol (EHTH uh nawl), the chemical name for the alcohol found in beer, wine, and liquor.

■ *Different amounts of alcohol in the bloodstream produce certain effects. Special equipment is used to measure blood alcohol level.*

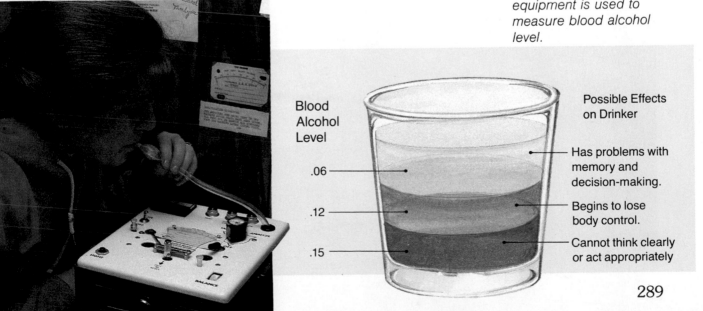

Blood Alcohol Level

Possible Effects on Drinker

.06 —— Has problems with memory and decision-making.

.12 —— Begins to lose body control.

.15 —— Cannot think clearly or act appropriately

289

As a rule, the more alcohol a person drinks during a given period, the higher the person's blood alcohol level. However, the person's size also affects blood alcohol level. A large person has more blood to thin out the alcohol. Thus it takes more alcohol to produce a certain blood alcohol level in a large person than a small person. Young people usually have smaller bodies than adults. For this reason, drinking even a small amount of alcohol can cause a young person to feel rapid and severe changes.

Even a low blood alcohol level affects a person's ability to make wise decisions. With a little higher level, the person loses control over his or her actions and is no longer able to think clearly. When someone has reached this blood alcohol level, he or she is said to be **intoxicated.**

The liver is the organ that removes ethanol from the blood. But even after all the ethanol is removed from the blood, the person may still feel ill, or have a **hangover.** A hangover may last for several hours or even one or two days.

What Are the Immediate Effects of Alcohol on Safety?

A person affected by alcohol risks having accidents. He or she may fall or bump into things while walking. The person is not in control of his or her body and mind. A person who is out of control cannot make good decisions or do things safely. Almost anything the person tries to do while or after drinking alcohol may cause an accident.

Accidents involving alcohol cause more deaths than do some major diseases. In traffic accidents alone, half of all deaths involve someone who has been drinking. Alcohol is also involved in a high number of deaths from other kinds of accidents. The charts show what percentage of the total number of accidents and accident deaths in recent years were alcohol-related.

REAL-LIFE
SKILL

Learning More About Alcohol and Accidents

Contact a group called Students Against Driving Drunk (SADD) at P.O. Box 800, Marlboro, MA 01752, (508) 481-3568 for more information.

ACCIDENTS INVOLVING ALCOHOL

Kind of Accident	Percentage Involving Alcohol
Home accidents	25% (1 out of 4)
Falls	75% (3 out of 4)
Traffic accidents	50% (1 out of 2)

ACCIDENT DEATHS INVOLVING ALCOHOL

Kind of Death	Percentage Involving Alcohol
In a fire	80% (4 out of 5)
In a car	50% (1 out of 2)
By drowning	66% (2 out of 3)

Scientists also say that half of the people who abuse, or physically hurt, their wives or husbands have been drinking at the time. One-third of the parents who abuse their children have been drinking. When people drink, they lose control of their emotions so much that they can harm the people to whom they are closest.

What Is Alcoholism?

A problem drinker may form a physical and emotional dependence on alcohol. Dependence on alcohol is called **alcoholism.** Alcoholism is considered a disease. A person with this disease is an **alcoholic.**

People who are alcoholics cannot control their drinking. Every day they feel a need for alcohol. They cannot stop after one drink. They keep drinking alcohol until they become intoxicated. Getting intoxicated day after day can lead to all the health problems caused by alcohol.

Alcoholism can harm a person's life in other ways. People who are intoxicated cannot work, play, study, or do anything else well. Young people who are alcoholics often drop out of school. Adults who are alcoholics often lose their jobs.

alcoholism (AL kuh haw lihz uhm), dependence on alcohol; considered to be a disease.

alcoholic (al kuh HAWL ihk), a person with a physical and emotional dependence on alcohol.

■ An alcoholic may even risk losing his or her job in order to have a drink.

■ *Family members are often affected when a person drinks too much alcohol.*

The only help for alcoholism is to stop drinking. When a person who is an alcoholic first stops drinking, he or she usually goes through painful withdrawal. The person may shake and twitch. He or she may see frightening things that are not really there. The person often needs the help of a treatment program in order to end the dependence on alcohol.

People who are alcoholics must recover for the rest of their lives. They stay in control of their drinking behavior by never drinking. If they have one drink, they may lose control and have many more. Soon they would become dependent on alcohol again.

There are warning signs of alcoholism. Often other people see these signs long before the drinker accepts that he or she has a problem. People who are alcoholics drink alcohol often. They may say they drink to "feel better." Alcoholics may fight with everyone, even friends and family.

They may get intoxicated and act recklessly. They may hide alcohol and sneak drinks when they think no one is watching. There may be periods when alcoholics cannot remember where they were or what happened to them. These periods without memory are called *blackouts*.

What Are the Effects of Alcohol on Health?

Alcohol keeps a person from feeling hungry. A person who drinks a lot of alcohol often has a very poor diet. The person may drink instead of eating. He or she soon becomes unhealthy and weak because the body does not get all the nutrients it needs. The lack of nutrients leads to a health problem called **malnutrition.** Malnutrition makes the body less fit and less able to prevent illness.

malnutrition (mal noo TRIHSH uhn), a health problem caused by a lack of nutrients.

Alcohol has many calories. But it has no proteins, vitamins, or minerals. For this reason, the calories in alcohol are said to be "empty calories." They give energy, but not the nutrients needed for staying healthy. Alcohol also keeps the body from using certain vitamins from food. So even if a person who drinks a lot of alcohol eats a balanced diet, the person may show signs of malnutrition.

Heavy, repeated use of alcohol harms body systems. Alcohol can damage nerve cells in the brain and other parts of the nervous system. Alcohol may cause **ulcers,** or painful sores in the stomach and other organs of the digestive system. Alcohol may also harm the liver, which is an important organ in the digestive and excretory systems.

ulcers (UHL suhrz), painful sores on tissues in the digestive system.

This damage to the liver is called *cirrhosis* of the liver. It prevents the liver from getting rid of body wastes and from doing its other jobs. Cirrhosis cannot be cured unless drinking stops in the early stages of the disease.

■ *A person who drinks a lot of alcohol may not get the nutrients he or she needs to be healthy.*

WHAT HAPPENS WHEN ALCOHOL REACHES PARTS OF THE BODY

Brain
Alcohol reaches the brain soon after it is swallowed. The circulatory system carries it there. Alcohol continues to reach the brain until the liver has had time to filter and change all the alcohol.

Circulatory System
The blood carries the alcohol to all parts of the body, including the brain, heart, and liver.

Liver
The liver changes the alcohol to water, carbon dioxide, and energy. The liver can change only about 0.5 ounce (14.7 milliliters) of alcohol an hour. Until the liver has had time to remove all the alcohol from the blood, the alcohol continues to pass through all parts of the body, including the brain.

Stomach
Alcohol reaches the stomach; some is absorbed through the stomach walls into the circulatory system.

Small Intestine
Most alcohol enters the small intestine from the stomach. It is absorbed through the walls of the small intestine and enters the circulatory system.

REMEMBER?

1. Why is alcohol called a depressant?
2. Explain the term *blood alcohol level.*
3. Explain the connection between alcohol abuse and malnutrition.
4. What are some behaviors that may signal alcoholism?

THINK!

5. Why do you think a person would become dependent on alcohol?
6. Why is it not safe to travel in a boat or car with someone who has been drinking alcohol?

Thinking About Your Health

What Is Your Attitude About Alcohol Abuse?

Seven situations are described below. Each one has to do with abusing alcohol in some way. Read about each situation. How would each one make you feel? Think of a word or phrase to describe your attitude.

1. You hear a stranger who was drinking alcohol sing loudly in a public place.
2. You see a neighbor who was drinking alcohol hurt one of his or her children.
3. In the newspaper, you read about a high school student who died in a boating accident. The accident was caused by a driver who had been drinking alcohol.
4. You know of someone who was killed by an intoxicated driver.
5. While at a public park, you see someone you know intoxicated.
6. You see a classmate sneak a drink of alcohol at school.
7. Someone you care about is drinking too much alcohol.

Health Close-up

AA and Al-Anon

There are an estimated 18 million people in the United States who are problem drinkers. Many may be alcoholics. Alcoholics Anonymous (AA) was founded in 1935 to help people with alcohol problems stop drinking.

AA is now a worldwide organization of both men and women who share their experiences and hopes with each other to solve their common problem—drinking alcohol. Through AA, alcoholics and problem drinkers learn how to live without alcohol one day at a time. There are no dues or fees for AA membership. The only requirement for membership is a desire to stop drinking.

AA members believe that alcohol affects the lives of four to five people other than the problem drinker. These are usually family members. That is why AA formed Al-Anon in 1954. Al-Anon gives families of problem drinkers an

■ *Alateen members help one another deal with alcohol-related problems.*

opportunity to share their experiences. Al-Anon members learn what they can do to help someone with an alcohol problem. They also learn to deal with family members or friends who are still actively drinking.

In 1957 a young person whose parent was an alcoholic and whose other parent belonged to Al-Anon formed Alateen. The members of this group are 12 to 20 years old. Alateen serves the same purpose as Al-Anon, but it is for young people. In some places, there are groups for young people under 12 years old. These groups are called Pre-Alateen. The goal of all the Al-Anon groups is to help people affected by an alcohol problem.

■ *AA provides educational programs for alcoholics who want to help themselves.*

Thinking Beyond

1. What are some ways that a person's life could be affected by the alcohol dependence of a family member?
2. What special problems might face a young person whose parent or guardian is an alcoholic?

297

3 How Alcohol and Tobacco Use Begin

Many young people who start using alcohol or tobacco do so because they see some adults around them using these drugs. They see happy- and healthy-looking people in alcohol and tobacco advertising. Some young people may think that using these drugs will make them look grown-up. Pressures like these make some young people want to try alcohol and tobacco.

How Does Peer Pressure Contribute to Alcohol and Tobacco Abuse?

"Going along with the crowd" is a saying often used to explain how peer pressure works. Peer pressure can affect how people dress, where they go, what they do, and who their friends are. There are many positive behaviors that can come from the influence of peers. For example, a young person may be influenced by members of a sports team to join the team. However, peer pressure is often given as a reason for a person's decision to abuse drugs.

■ *Advertising sometimes makes drinking and smoking seem glamorous.*

■ Peer pressure can cause people to do things that may be harmful. However, peers can also help one another make healthful decisions.

All people need to be liked and accepted. Sometimes this need will win out over knowledge and common sense when a young person must make a decision about using drugs. If friends pressure a person to take drugs, the person's need to "be a part of the group" may make it hard to say no. However, there are some things you can do to help lessen the pressure on you to use drugs.

■ Remind peers that refusing to use a drug—tobacco, alcohol, or any other drug—is a personal choice.

■ Simply say, "No, thanks."

■ Make a statement about how drugs don't interest you. This may help keep you from having to explain all your reasons.

■ Suggest a different activity, or walk away.

■ Avoid situations in which drug use may be expected.

■ Associate with people who do not take drugs.

No matter how you handle peer pressure, you should realize that your choices need to be based on what is best for you. Having high self-esteem and a positive self-concept makes it easier to say no to people who offer you drugs. Knowing clearly the values and rules of your family will help you remember what is expected of you. Knowing that peer friendships and social groups can change and be outgrown is a step toward gaining self-esteem.

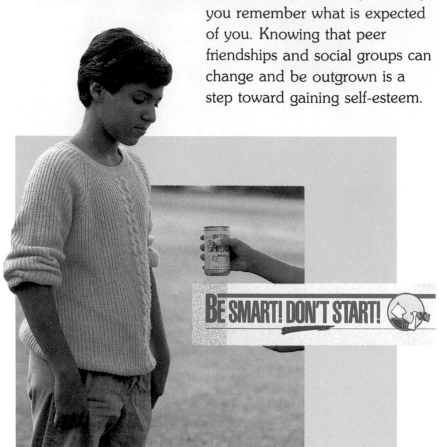

BE SMART! DON'T START!

■ Someone who wants you to drink alcohol is not concerned about your health and well-being.

What Causes Alcoholism Among Young People?

There are many reasons that some young people may start drinking alcohol. Peer pressure, family influences and problems, and advertising may lead some young people to try alcohol. Later, some young people may drink more to try to escape feelings caused by emotional problems such as loneliness or an unhappy family life. But by escaping in this way, these young people do not learn how to handle tough situations in healthful ways.

■ *Young alcoholics take many of the same kinds of risks that older alcoholics do. Some young drinkers also try to hide their problem.*

About one out of seven teenagers who drink forms a dependence on alcohol. The early signs of alcoholism in young people are hard to see. A young alcoholic is not likely to think that he or she drinks to cover up a problem. In most cases, young people who are alcoholics want to believe they drink "to feel good" or "to be social." People who are alcoholics most often deny to themselves and to others that they have a dependence on alcohol.

STOP REVIEW
SECTION 3

REMEMBER?

1. How does peer pressure contribute to alcohol and tobacco use?
2. What are three causes of alcoholism in young people?

THINK!

3. How might a mix of the drugs nicotine and alcohol affect a person?
4. Where might a young person who is an alcoholic go for help?

4 Choosing Not to Use Alcohol and Tobacco

KEY WORD

abstain

abstain (ab STAYN), to choose to do without.

Many people use or abuse alcohol and tobacco, but many others do not. They **abstain** from, or do without, alcohol and tobacco. They know that abstaining from what can harm them helps them enjoy wellness.

Some people do not drink alcohol because

- they know that alcohol could make them unhealthy.
- they know they might become dependent on alcohol.
- they want to stay in control of their behavior.
- they do not like the way people act when they drink.
- they know that drunk drivers cause accidents.
- they believe that alcohol might stop them from reaching their goals in life.
- they know that it is against the law for young people to drink alcohol.

For what other reasons might someone decide not to use alcohol?

■ People who choose not to smoke or drink find better ways to have fun.

SMOKING IS VERY DEBONAIR

SMOKING IS VERY GLAMOROUS

SMOKING IS VERY SOPHISTICATED

Some people do not use tobacco because

- they believe tobacco will make them less attractive.
- they believe tobacco will cause serious diseases.
- they believe smoke, ashes, and cigarette butts bother people.
- they believe cigarettes and smokeless tobacco are a waste of money.
- they believe cigarettes are a fire hazard.
- they believe they do not have to "go along with the crowd." Instead, they make their own choices.
- they know that it is against the law for young people to smoke cigarettes.

For what other reasons might someone decide not to use tobacco?

 *Many people do not smoke because they know it will make them less attractive.*

STOP | **REVIEW**
SECTION 4

REMEMBER?

1. Give three reasons why people do not drink alcohol.
2. Give three reasons why people do not use tobacco.

THINK!

3. How might your friendship with someone change if that person kept trying to get you to drink alcohol?
4. What might you do if someone offered you a cigarette?

303

People in Health

An Interview with a Director of an Alcohol and Drug Treatment Center

Jeffrey R. Olson understands the dangers of alcohol and other drugs. He directs an alcohol and drug treatment center in Bismarck, North Dakota.

How do you help people who have alcohol problems or other drug problems?

I treat people with alcohol or drug dependence by counseling, or advising, them. I help them handle their feelings so that they do not think they need to use drugs to feel all right. I work with individuals, families, and other groups.

Do people come to you on their own for help?

Some do. Others are under an outside pressure that makes them come. Some

■ *Mr. Olson tries to find out why certain people drink alcohol or use other drugs.*

people have been ordered by a judge to get help. These people have been arrested for using alcohol or other drugs. There are times when people come for treatment because of pressure from a family member. There are also people who have been warned by their employers that if they do not get help for their alcohol or other drug problems, they will lose their jobs.

Do you work with many young people?

I treat many young people. In most cases, juvenile court or their parents have them come to the treatment center. Some of these young people have been caught with alcohol or an illegal drug. They have broken the law.

Why do some young people drink or take drugs?

There are many reasons. One reason is anger. A young person might be angry with his or her parents because of rules at home. The most common reason, however, is a person's low self-esteem. A young person who has low self-esteem is more easily influenced by peer pressure. A young person might drink or take other drugs just because he or she wants to belong to a group and the group uses drugs. Sadly, alcohol or other drug use only makes that person's low self-esteem still lower.

■ *Few people with alcohol or other drug problems ask for help.*

How does alcohol use make self-esteem worse?

I use the "WART" definition to explain the effects of drug dependence on self-concept. The term WART stands for *with alcohol, repeated trouble.* This means that people who drink or take other drugs cause many problems for themselves. Knowing that they brought on these problems, the people feel guilty and sad. They feel less and less important. In other words, they lose self-esteem. They get worse.

How do you help them raise their self-esteem?

First, they must totally stop using alcohol or any other drugs. For me to help them, they must be drug-free. The people who can stay drug-free have fewer problems. They feel better about themselves. Their self-esteem rises.

I call this time of recovery ROSE. That stands for *return of self-esteem.* A person who goes through treatment changes from a WART to a ROSE.

What are the chances of recovery for people who get help?

For those who get help, there is a good chance of recovery. This does not mean that a person will recover after being treated once. The person might need to go through treatment two or three times over many months to recover. Just walking in the door of a treatment center in the first place gives that person a good chance of recovery.

What advice do you give young people about alcohol?

They must keep away from all harmful substances. My advice is to not underestimate the harm that alcohol can do. A lot of young people think that only marijuana and cocaine are dangerous drugs. Alcohol can be just as deadly. It can destroy their health just as any other drug can.

Learn more about counselors or directors who work in substance abuse centers. Interview one of these people or write for information to the National Association of Substance Abuse Trainers and Educators, Southern University at New Orleans, 1521 Hillary Street, New Orleans, LA 70118.

Main Ideas

- Both smoking and using smokeless tobacco are forms of drug abuse.
- Heart disease is a major health risk for smokers.
- Accidents involving alcohol cause more deaths than do some major diseases.
- A person who often uses alcohol may have a physical and emotional dependence on alcohol.
- Some young people start using alcohol and tobacco because they see adults around them using these drugs.
- High self-esteem makes it easier to say no to people who may offer you drugs.
- Alcoholism, if untreated, can cause many serious physical, emotional, and social health problems.

Key Words

Write the numbers 1 to 12 in your health notebook or on a separate sheet of paper. After each number, copy the sentence and fill in the missing term. Page numbers in ( ) tell you where to look in the chapter if you need help.

tar (277)
nicotine (277)
carbon monoxide (278)
sidestream smoke (284)
ethanol (289)

intoxicated (290)
hangover (290)
alcoholism (292)
alcoholic (292)
malnutrition (294)
ulcers (294)
abstain (302)

1. A person with an alcohol dependence may be an ___?___ .

2. A ___?___ is the illness someone might have after drinking too much alcohol.

3. If you ___?___ from doing something, you choose not to do it.

4. The chemical name for the drug found in alcohol drinks is ___?___ .

5. A gas found in cigarette smoke that is a poison is ___?___ .

6. ___?___ is a dependence on alcohol and is considered to be a disease.

7. A stimulant drug found in all tobacco products is ___?___ .

8. People are said to be ___?___ when they have a high blood alcohol level.

9. A health problem caused by a lack of nutrients is ___?___ .

10. Alcohol may cause ___?___ , painful sores in the stomach or other organs.

11. When tobacco burns, it forms a sticky, brown substance called ___?___ .

12. Smoke that leaves the lighted end of a cigarette is ___?___ .

Remembering What You Learned

Page numbers in ( ) tell you where to look in the chapter if you need help.

1. What are two ways that nicotine can affect your circulatory system? (277)

2. What harmful substances other than nicotine are in tobacco? (277–278)

3. What diseases can be caused by cigarette smoking? By using smokeless tobacco? (280–282, 286–287)

4. How can smoking cigarettes cause lung cancer? (281)

5. In what ways does tobacco harm nonsmokers? (284–285)

6. How does alcohol affect a person's brain? (289)

7. How does alcohol change a person's moods or feelings? (289)

8. Why might a person who has been drinking have an accident? (291)

9. How can a person who has alcoholism be helped? (293)

10. In what ways does heavy, repeated use of alcohol harm a person's body systems? (294–295)

11. How can peer pressure be linked to drinking or smoking? (298–299)

Thinking About What You Learned

1. How might it feel to become dependent on eating or drinking something?

2. Why is learning about the dangers of alcohol and tobacco important for young people?

3. How might experimenting with alcohol and tobacco at a young age be a risk to a lifetime of good health?

4. Why do some people drink so much and smoke so often even though both activities are so harmful to their health?

5. What might you and your friends do to stay away from alcohol and tobacco? Name activities you can do instead of using either drug.

Writing About What You Learned

1. Many people who drink give the following reason for drinking. They say, "Millions of people drink alcohol. It must not be very bad for them." Write a paragraph that responds to this statement.

2. Suppose a smoker's lungs could speak. Write a short story that tells what the lungs would say to persuade the smoker to stop smoking.

Applying What You Learned

ART

Create a counter-advertising message on a poster or for a T-shirt. Select a picture and slogan for an alcohol or tobacco product. Design your poster to make fun of the product or warn others about it.

Modified True or False

Write the numbers 1 to 15 in your health notebook or on a separate sheet of paper. After each number, write *true* or *false* to describe the sentence. If the sentence is false, also write a term that replaces the underlined term and makes the sentence true.

1. Filter-tipped cigarettes remove <u>nicotine</u> from smoke that is inhaled.

2. Alcohol is a <u>stimulant</u>.

3. Smoking can keep the body from getting certain <u>vitamins</u> from food.

4. Some alcoholics have <u>blackouts</u>.

5. <u>Chronic bronchitis</u> occurs when too many alveoli in the lungs rupture.

6. Chewing tobacco contains <u>sugar</u>.

7. A <u>social drinker</u> drinks too much alcohol too often.

8. <u>Carbon dioxide</u> is a poisonous gas.

9. Some teenagers begin drinking alcohol because of <u>peer pressure</u>.

10. If you <u>abstain</u> from alcohol, you never drink it.

11. It takes <u>less</u> alcohol to make a large person intoxicated than a small person.

12. Nicotine <u>increases</u> the heart rate.

13. Smoke from the lighted end of a cigarette is <u>sidestream smoke</u>.

14. Drinking too much alcohol can cause a <u>hangover</u>.

15. <u>One-fourth</u> of all traffic-accident deaths involve alcohol.

Short Answer

Write the numbers 16 to 23 on your paper. Write a complete sentence to answer each question.

16. Why does cigarette smoke make a person cough?

17. How does nicotine in smokeless tobacco get into the body?

18. What are the three categories of drinking?

19. What are some physical signs that a person is intoxicated?

20. How does a person's size affect blood alcohol level?

21. Why do one-half of all car accidents involve people who are drinking alcohol?

22. How can malnutrition result from drinking alcohol?

23. What are three long-term health risks of smoking cigarettes?

Essay

Write the numbers 24 and 25 on your paper. Write paragraphs with complete sentences to answer each question.

24. Think of a situation in which someone your age has a chance to drink alcohol. Describe the situation, and tell how the person should deal with it.

25. Describe the path of tobacco smoke through the human body. Include how the substances in the smoke affect various parts of the body.

ACTIVITIES FOR HOME OR SCHOOL

Projects to Do

1. Interview older people who do not smoke. They might include older brothers and sisters, parents, and friends of your family. Ask them the following questions:
   - What are your reasons for not smoking?
   - What healthful effects has not smoking had on your life?
   - How do you feel when people around you smoke?
   - What advice would you give to people who want to stop smoking? To people who have started?

   Do different people give similar answers? Which questions do different people answer in similar ways?

2. With some of your classmates, write a skit in which a young person tries to persuade a friend or classmate to begin smoking cigarettes. Have the friend refuse politely. Have him or her give reasons for saying no.

Information to Find

1. Look in a telephone book for the address of the local office of the American Lung Association. Call or write to the Association and ask for material for young people that explains why smoking is dangerous. Share the information with your classmates.

2. What warnings must appear on all tobacco packages and in all tobacco advertisements? The warnings are required by law. Find out when the law was passed. Why was it passed? Your librarian can tell you where to find this information.

3. Prepare a bibliography of books written for young people about teenage alcoholism or drug abuse. Read one of the books, and present a report about the book to your class. Your school library or public library may have the information you need.

Books to Read

Here are some books you can look for in your school library or the public library to find more information about alcohol and tobacco.

A Little More About Alcohol. Alcohol Research Information Service.

Stepney, Rob. *Tobacco.* Franklin Watts.

■ *Practice handling peer pressure.*

SAFETY AND FIRST AID

Many kinds of accidents and emergencies can happen in or near your home. Knowing how accidents happen can often help you prevent them. If you cannot prevent an accident or emergency, you can reduce the chance of injury by being prepared and knowing what to do.

Sometimes an accident or emergency leaves you or someone else seriously ill or injured. By knowing how to help, you can keep the illness or injury from getting worse. When you are able to act safely and help in an emergency, you show others how responsible you can be.

GETTING READY TO LEARN

Key Questions

- Why is it important to learn about safety and first aid?
- Why is it important to show your feelings about safety in your actions?
- How can you learn to make choices that will help keep you safe?
- What can you do to become more responsible for your actions in an emergency?

Main Chapter Sections

1 Preventing Home Accidents
2 Handling Emergencies
3 Giving First Aid for Some Common Emergencies
4 Giving First Aid to Save a Life

1 Preventing Home Accidents

An **accident** is an unexpected happening that can cause someone to be hurt or property to be damaged. It is important for all family members to work at preventing accidents at home. Each family member needs to know the different kinds of accidents that are likely to happen in a home. Knowing how and where accidents can happen can help you take control to prevent injury. You can take steps to keep accidents from hurting you and others.

KEY WORDS

accident
electric shock
flammable
poison

accident (AK suh duhnt), an unexpected happening that can cause someone to be hurt or property to be damaged.

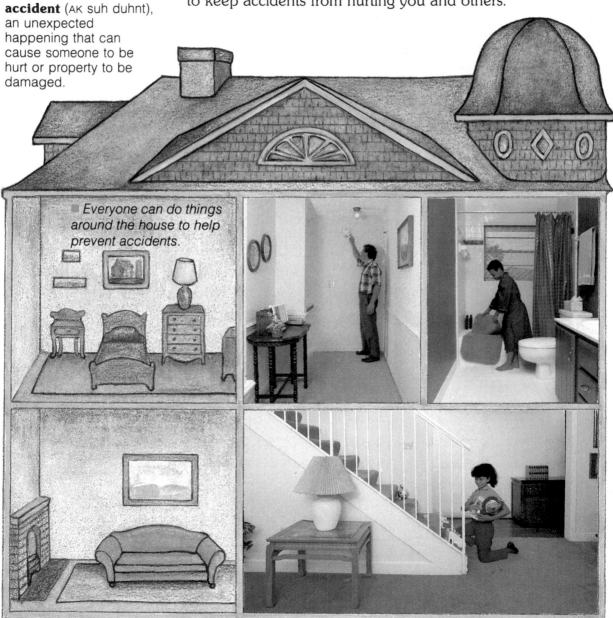

■ Everyone can do things around the house to help prevent accidents.

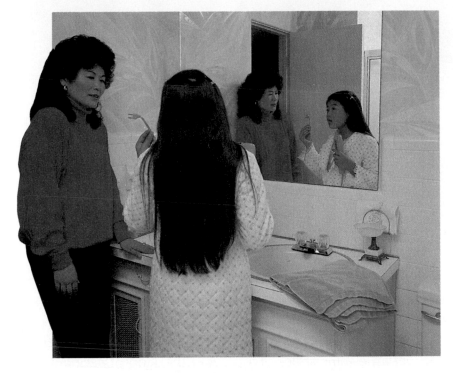

Finding and replacing damaged wires can prevent fires and electric shocks.

How Can You Prevent Electric Shocks?

The lights, the television, and many other things in your house use electricity. Electricity is a form of energy that flows through thin wires made of metal. Touching the metal while electricity is flowing through it is very dangerous. It can give a person a painful jolt called an **electric shock.** A strong electric shock can burn tissue or even kill a person. Electrical wires are covered with plastic or rubber to prevent people from getting a shock. Electricity cannot flow through these covers.

An accident may happen if the cover of an electrical wire is damaged. Tell an adult at once if you see an electrical wire with a cracked, worn, or frayed covering. The wire should be replaced.

Electrical wires should be placed where they will not be damaged or trip people. Lamp cords or extension cords should be placed along a wall or under furniture.

Electricity is wired to outlets. To make an electrical appliance work, you have to insert its plug into an outlet. Be careful not to touch the metal part of the plug as you put it into the outlet. If the plug looks damaged in any way, do not use it. Tell an adult so that the plug can be replaced.

electric shock (ih LEHK trihk • SHAHK), a painful jolt caused by direct contact with electricity.

313

■ *Name three electrical hazards in this kitchen.*

Do not plug too many appliances into one outlet. If one of the appliances or wires were to spark, an electric shock or fire could result.

Young children sometimes insert small objects into outlets and get an electric shock. To prevent this kind of accident, put tape or safety plugs over outlets that are not being used.

Electricity flows through water very easily. Never handle the plug or any other part of an electrical item with wet hands. Never stand in water while you are using an electrical appliance or tool. Keep all electrical wires and appliances away from water. For example, do not put a lamp or radio near the bathtub. Make sure the area around the bathroom sink is dry before you use a hair dryer or other electrical appliance.

■ *Name three fire hazards in this room.*

flammable (FLAM uh buhl), able to burn easily.

How Can You Prevent Fires?

Two things are needed to start a fire: heat and something that can burn. You can prevent fires by keeping these two things away from each other.

Paper, cotton cloth, and nylon burn easily. Materials that are able to burn easily are called **flammable.** Do not leave flammable objects near a heat source. For example, never pile newspapers or laundry near a stove, heater, or furnace. Do not place a couch or chair close to a heater or fireplace. Always use a screen in front of a fireplace fire to prevent sparks from hitting the carpet or furniture.

Always be careful near fire or heat. Stand or sit at a safe distance from a campfire. Your clothes could start to burn from a sudden spark or flame. Watch the campfire to see how far it shoots sparks.

Liquids made from oil, such as gasoline or paint thinner, are very flammable. Flammable liquids give off gases that you can smell. These gases, called fumes, are also flammable. The fumes are so flammable that a spark can make them explode. Keep flammable liquids away from sparks and heat. Store them in their original containers or in containers that are labeled FLAMMABLE. These containers should have tight lids and should be made of metal. Never store flammable liquids in glass jars or other containers that could leak or break.

■ Flammable liquids should be safely stored in metal containers.

Oily rags are very flammable. A pile of oily rags gets very warm. The pile may catch fire by itself, without any outside heat source. To prevent such fires, put oily rags in a metal container with a tight lid. Dispose of the container safely as soon as possible.

Many accidents with fire can happen in a kitchen. A kitchen has heat sources, flammable objects, electrical wires, and grease that can catch fire. To prevent accidents, keep pot holders, aprons, and other flammable objects away from the stove burners. Turn pot handles toward the middle of the stove. Then you are less likely to knock over a pot or spill something on a burner. If grease splashes on the stove or wall, wipe it off immediately but carefully.

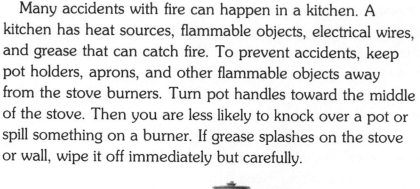

■ *Special care should be taken in the kitchen to prevent accidents.*

How Can You Prevent Poisoning Accidents?

poison (POYZ uhn), anything that makes a person sick when it gets inside the body.

A **poison** is anything that makes a person sick when it gets inside the body. Common substances may become poisons if swallowed or breathed in. Many poisonous substances are found in most homes. For example, paint thinner, rubbing alcohol, and ammonia are all poisons. When used in the wrong way, common household products, such as cleaning fluids, bleaches, and detergents, can also be poisons. Medicines can be poisonous if they are not used properly.

To help prevent someone from being accidentally poisoned, keep all substances in their original containers. The label on a container warns that the substance inside is poisonous. The label also gives special directions for using the substance. For example, the label on a can of paint

316

thinner may say, "Avoid breathing fumes. Do not use indoors." If paint thinner or another poison is kept in an unlabeled can, someone may use the poison in the wrong way.

Accidents with poisons can happen if young children eat or drink them. You can help keep your family safe by being alert for harmful substances. To prevent poisoning accidents, your family should store all household cleaners and chemicals where young children cannot reach them. Keep the containers on high shelves or in locked cupboards. Store all poisons in "child-proof" containers, if possible. Use medicine bottles with caps that young children cannot pull off. Never swallow any substance if you are not sure it is a safe beverage or food. Do not swallow any pills or liquids from unmarked bottles. By following these safety habits, you can help prevent common poisoning accidents in your home.

■ *Household cleaners and chemicals need to be stored on a high shelf or in a locked cabinet so that poisoning accidents can be prevented.*

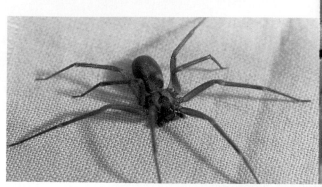

■ *The bites of a black widow spider, right, and a brown recluse spider, left, are poisonous and require immediate medical attention.*

Chemicals and other substances are not the only poisonous things that can cause harm. Some spiders are poisonous. A bite from a poisonous spider can be very dangerous. The female *black widow spider* is poisonous. This kind of spider is often found in woodpiles, sheds, and basements. Another poisonous spider is the *brown recluse spider*. It is often found under rocks and in dark corners inside buildings. If you are bitten by a poisonous spider, see a physician immediately.

Like certain spiders, certain snakes are poisonous. Snakes often lie under bushes, fallen branches, and rocks. If they are surprised, they may strike at your feet or legs. To avoid snakebites, you can follow a few simple rules. If you are hiking, stay on the trail. Keep checking the ground in front of you. Wearing thick boots and long pants in areas where snakes are found will also keep you safe.

 **REVIEW**
SECTION 1

REMEMBER?

1. What causes an electric shock?
2. What two things are needed to start a fire?
3. Name three flammable materials.
4. What makes a substance a poison?

THINK!

5. What are three actions you can take at home to show that you care about your family's safety?
6. How can you make a kitchen safe for young children?

Health Close-up

Safety Around Firearms

Guns and rifles are among the ten most common causes of accidental death in the United States. Many firearm accidents take place when people handle guns at home. These accidents most often happen because someone does not know about firearm safety or is handling a firearm carelessly.

No one should handle a gun at any time unless he or she has been trained in firearm safety. Before handling a gun, a person should learn from a qualified person the correct ways to handle firearms. The local police department can help a person find a qualified teacher. Many police departments also offer firearm safety classes.

Millions of people each year use firearms safely for hunting. But risky habits with guns can cause deadly hunting accidents. Each year at least 2,000 people die accidentally while hunting. However, people who know how to handle firearms safely usually have fewer accidents.

■ *Firearms need to be kept in a locked cabinet.*

People who hunt safely know to keep a gun's safety lock on until they are ready to shoot. A safe hunter always carries his or her gun in a way to control the direction of the muzzle. This way, the muzzle is pointed away from the hunter even if he or she stumbles. Before pulling the trigger, a safe hunter always checks the target to be sure he or she knows what it is.

A safe hunter always unloads a gun before leaving it unattended. Loaded guns should never be left leaning against walls, fences, or trees. Finally, a safe hunter never climbs while carrying a loaded firearm.

Everyone who handles a gun needs to follow these basic safety guidelines for firearms:

■ Assume that every firearm is loaded. Treat it that way!
■ Never point a firearm at yourself or anyone else.
■ Keep firearms away from children.
■ Store firearms and bullets apart from each other in separate locked cabinets.
■ Never clean a firearm without first making sure it is not loaded.

Thinking Beyond

1. Why should you assume every firearm is loaded?
2. Why should firearms and bullets be stored separately?

2 Handling Emergencies

An **emergency** is an unexpected situation that calls for quick action. Some emergencies are caused by accidents. For example, if someone knocks over a candle, it might set a tablecloth on fire. You must act quickly to smother the flames or throw water on them. A sudden illness may also cause an emergency. Then you would need to find medical help immediately. Sometimes weather, such as a severe storm, causes an emergency. You might need to act quickly to protect yourself or others.

KEY WORDS

emergency
fire extinguisher
disaster
hurricane
tornado
electrical storm
blizzard
earthquake

emergency (ih MUR juhn see), an unexpected situation that calls for quick action.

■ There are many things that you can do to prepare for an emergency such as a hurricane. These people are boarding up windows to keep flying objects from breaking the glass.

In an emergency, unprepared people panic or feel confused. They are not ready or able to act quickly to help themselves or other people. But if you stay calm in an emergency and know what to do, you can help keep yourself and others safe. You can take pride in yourself when you can stay calm and perhaps help others.

What Can You Do to Prepare for Emergencies?

Being prepared for emergencies helps you act quickly and safely. Preparation helps you feel in control of yourself and helps others feel calm. One way to prepare is to put emergency telephone numbers where you can find them quickly. Write numbers for your family physician, the fire department, police department, and Poison Control Center on a card. Help your family by putting a card on or near each telephone in your home. If these numbers are not printed inside the front cover of your telephone book, list them there as well. Keep the telephone book by the telephone so that you can find the numbers quickly.

If an emergency happens and you do not have an emergency telephone number, you can call the operator by dialing 0 (zero) for help. In some communities, you can call 911 for help in an emergency. Check to see if 911 is an emergency number in your community.

■ *Post emergency telephone numbers on or near the telephone so you can find them quickly in an emergency.*

Call emergency numbers only in an emergency. If you call them at other times, you may keep someone who really needs help from getting a call through. If you do make an emergency phone call, tell the person who answers exactly what is wrong and where help is needed. Let the person you call hang up before you do. That way you know that he or she has all the needed information.

Another way to prepare for emergencies is to store important supplies in your home. In a severe storm, the electricity could go out, or you might not be able to leave your home to buy food. You can help your family put together an emergency kit of supplies to keep all of you safe, clean, and nourished at home for a few days.

■ Many communities have a control center where 911 emergency calls are directed to the proper agency.

■ One way to be prepared for an emergency is to have an emergency kit in your home.

322

■ *Not all fire extinguishers can be used on all kinds of fires.*

fire extinguisher (FYR · ihk STIHNG gwihsh uhr), a metal tank filled with water or chemicals for putting out a fire.

To be prepared for a fire at home, keep a fire extinguisher handy. And make sure that everyone knows how to use it. A **fire extinguisher** is a metal tank filled with water or chemicals that can be used to put out a fire. Different kinds of fire extinguishers are used to put out different kinds of fires. Fire extinguishers have codes:

A — flammable solids

B — flammable liquids

C — electrical

One kind of fire extinguisher, marked A, is often filled with water or another nonflammable liquid. This kind of extinguisher is used when wood, cloth, or some other solid material is burning. A fire extinguisher that has water in it should never be used for an electrical or a grease fire.

Another kind of fire extinguisher, marked B, holds a detergent foam or carbon dioxide. The foam or the carbon dioxide smothers the fire when it is sprayed. This kind of fire extinguisher is used for fires involving gasoline, grease, or other flammable liquids.

A third kind of fire extinguisher, marked C, holds a chemical powder. The powder releases carbon dioxide when it is sprayed on a fire. This kind of extinguisher is used for electrical fires or burning flammable liquids. Some fire extinguishers with chemical powder may also be used when a solid material is burning.

■ *Families should plan ahead for safe action during emergencies.*

You and your family can prepare for emergencies by planning what to do in certain situations. Your family should plan several ways to get out of your home in case of fire or any other disaster. Be sure to agree on a place outside where everyone should meet if you have to leave your home in an emergency. Then each person should practice using all the escape routes. Also, whenever you go into a friend's home or any other building, always notice where the doors or fire exits are.

What Can You Do in a Fire?

A fire cannot burn without oxygen from the air. This means that cutting off the air supply is the best way to put out a small fire. If your clothes catch fire, drop to the ground and roll. You can also smother the flames by wrapping yourself in a rug or blanket. Do not run. Running gives the fire more air and makes it burn more. If you baby-sit young children, teach them this way to remember what to do: STOP, DROP, ROLL.

To smother a small fire, throw a heavy rug on it or dump dirt over it. If the fire is in a can or container, put the lid on tightly. The lid keeps air from reaching the fire, and the fire will go out.

If you cannot put out a fire inside a building, get out immediately. Close all doors behind you to slow the spread of the fire. As you go, warn other people by shouting "Fire!" or by setting off the fire alarm. Do not stop to call the fire department. After you are outside, use the nearest fire box or telephone to call the fire department. Once you are out of a burning building, do not go back inside.

If you wake up at night and smell smoke or hear a fire alarm or smoke alarm, get out of bed immediately. Crawl to stay low, because smoke, most gases, and heat rise. In a fire, some dangerous gases may settle on the floor. You can breathe most safely about 1 foot (30 centimeters) off the floor. Crawl to the door and touch it as high as you can reach. If the door feels cool, open it just a little and check for smoke or flames outside. If the way is clear, leave quickly. Be sure to close all doors behind you.

If the door feels hot to your touch, the fire is just outside. Do not open the door. Find another way to leave the room. If you are on the ground floor, climb out through a window.

If you are too far above the ground to jump or climb down safely, you should wait for help near the window.

■ *If your clothing catches fire, remember: STOP, DROP, ROLL.*

■ *Do not open an interior door that is hot to the touch.*

Keep the window open just a little so that you can breathe fresh air. Shout or signal for help. If you can, put a fabric flag on the window. This is a signal to fire fighters that someone needs help. While you wait, block all the cracks under the doors with towels, blankets, sheets, or clothing. Wet the cloths if you can. Blocking the cracks helps keep outside air from fanning the fire. It also helps keep smoke from reaching you.

If you cannot wait safely for help and you must escape through a smoke-filled hall, crawl out and keep your head low. To keep from breathing smoke, cover your mouth and nose with a cloth, such as a handkerchief. Wet the cloth if possible. The water will help keep smoke and gas out of your lungs. The water will also cool the smoke and gas. These actions will help keep hot smoke from harming your respiratory system.

What Can You Do to Be Safe in a Disaster?

A **disaster** is an emergency situation sometimes caused by forces in nature. Families cannot control these forces. But they can make plans to limit injury caused by disasters. Some injuries are caused by not knowing what to do or by lack of emergency supplies.

Ask for a family meeting to plan for the disasters that are most likely to happen where you live or where you travel on vacations. Planning is not meant to make you worry. Instead, plans help you be confident and not too afraid if something does happen. If you do not know what kinds of weather problems to plan for, call a weather forecaster in your community or the city emergency office. People there can tell you about the most likely problems and how to prepare.

disaster (dih ZAS tuhr), an emergency situation sometimes caused by forces in nature.

■ *Planning ahead can save time, and maybe your life, in the event of a disaster.*

Hurricanes. A **hurricane** is a violent storm with high winds and heavy rains. Hurricanes most often start at sea and move toward land. A hurricane may cause flooding, blow trees over, or destroy buildings. Weather forecasters can track a hurricane and give warnings several days before the storm moves over land.

hurricane (HUR uh kayn), a violent storm with high winds and heavy rains.

327

■ *A hurricane is a huge, swirling storm that forms over tropical waters. Hurricanes can bring strong winds, heavy rains, and floods to coastal areas.*

When a hurricane moves in the direction of your community, radio and television stations give a hurricane warning. The warning tells when the hurricane is expected to reach your area. Your family will most often have several days to prepare for it. In this time, you can do a number of things. Bring loose items from your yard inside or tie them down so they will not blow away or hit people. Make sure your home emergency kit is ready. Shut all doors and windows tightly, and board them up if possible. Some families even leave the community for a safer area.

During a hurricane, stay in the most protected part of your home. Go to the basement if your home has one. If it does not, stay on the lowest level of the building. Stay in a closet or a shower. These two places have strong frames of wood or pipe, which help keep them secure. Keep away from windows in case the storm shatters the glass. Keep a battery-powered radio and flashlight with you. If the wind and rain suddenly stop, do not leave the building. The storm is probably not over. In the center of each hurricane is a large, quiet part, called the "eye." A calm time during the storm means that the eye of the hurricane is passing over you. Then the rest of the storm follows shortly.

Do not leave your home until you hear an announcement that the storm has left the area. Be very careful when you go outside. The heavy rains may have caused a flood. The wind may have blown down power lines. The water on the ground and damaged electrical wires create a danger of electric shock.

Tornadoes. A **tornado** is a tall funnel of wind that whirls at very high speed. The wind funnel moves with the narrowest part near the ground. The bottom of the funnel, however, may be as wide as 1 mile (1.6 kilometers). When a tornado touches the ground, it can destroy everything in its path. It can blow apart houses and overturn trucks and cars.

Radio and television stations give a tornado warning when a tornado is sighted in the area. If you hear a tornado warning, go to a safe place right away. Even with new ways of forecasting weather, people usually have only 20 to 30 minutes' warning at most. Take a flashlight and a battery-powered radio with you. If possible, go underground into a tornado shelter or basement. If you live in a building that has no basement, go to an inner hall or a closet in the interior of the ground floor. An interior location is the safest place during a tornado because you are away from windows. You will not be hit by flying glass or other objects in these places.

If you are outdoors when a tornado approaches, lie in a low area, such as a ditch. Lie flat against the ground until the tornado passes. Cover your face with a cloth to protect your eyes and nose from dust. If you are in a camper, mobile home, or motor vehicle when a tornado approaches, do the same thing. Do not stay inside. Stay in a protected place until you hear an all-clear bulletin.

tornado (tawr NAY doh), a tall funnel of wind that whirls at very high speed.

■ *If you hear a tornado warning, go to a storm shelter, a basement, or an inside wall or closet of your home. Stay away from all windows.*

Tornadoes can happen almost anywhere. However, most tornadoes are seen in the Midwest of the United States. They can happen at any time, but most occur during the hottest part of the day. Most tornadoes occur between the months of March and June.

Electrical Storms. A storm that has strong winds and rain with lightning is called an **electrical storm.** Lightning is a flash of electricity in the sky. Most lightning happens during rainstorms. Lightning may cause severe electric shock and burns if it strikes someone. It can also cause death. Lightning is more likely to strike people who are outdoors than those indoors during electrical storms.

When a storm with lightning begins, go indoors and stay away from windows. Do not touch wires, telephones, electrical appliances, or water faucets. Electricity from the lightning could flow through any of these things. Some families unplug appliances, including home computers and televisions, during electrical storms.

electrical storm (ih LEHK trih kuhl • STAWRM), a storm that has strong winds and rain with lightning.

■ *Tall objects are often hit by lightning. However, many buildings are protected by lightning rods that channel the charge safely to the ground.*

THE DANGERS OF LIGHTNING

States Where Deaths Attributed to Lightning Occur Most Frequently	Places Where People Are Killed by Lightning Most Often
1. Florida 2. North Carolina 3. Texas 4. Tennessee 5. New York 6. Maryland 7. Louisiana 8. Arkansas 9. Ohio 10. Pennsylvania	1. in open fields 2. under trees 3. on or near water 4. near tractors or other heavy equipment 5. on golf courses 6. at telephones

Source: National Oceanic and Atmospheric Administration

If you cannot get indoors during an electrical storm, protect yourself by staying low. Lightning strikes the tallest object in an area, so stay out of open fields. If you are on a hill, move to lower ground. Do not stand near trees or telephone poles. Since electricity flows through water, you should also stay away from water. If you are boating or swimming when an electrical storm begins, get out of the water right away.

■ *Many people are killed each year in states where lightning frequently occurs.*

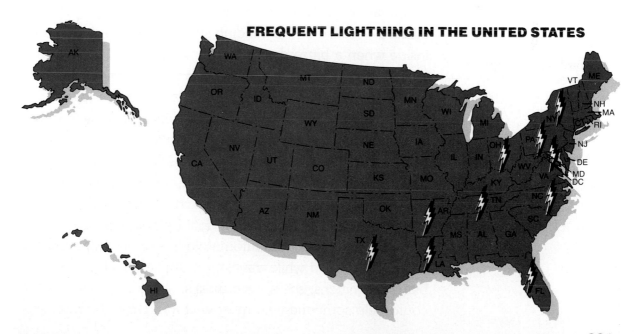

FREQUENT LIGHTNING IN THE UNITED STATES

■ You can prepare for a winter emergency by packing the right supplies—warm clothing, food, and water.

blizzard (BLIHZ uhrd), a dangerous snowstorm with strong winds, heavy snowfall, and very cold temperatures.

Blizzards. A **blizzard** is a dangerous, violent snowstorm with strong winds, heavy snowfall, and very cold temperatures. It is nearly impossible to see anything in a blizzard because of the blinding snow and wind. If you are inside when a blizzard starts, do not leave the building. You could get lost, even trying to walk a short, familiar distance.

If you are caught outdoors in a blizzard, try to follow something you can touch, such as a fence or a ditch. If you cannot get to a building, crouch in a place that gives you shelter from the wind. Keep your muscles moving so that you keep blood flowing through the blood vessels to your legs, face, and feet. Slap your legs, rub your face, and stamp your feet. Keep moving until help arrives.

A family can pack an automobile in winter to prepare for a sudden blizzard while traveling. Supplies, such as blankets, mittens, socks, face masks, snack food, and water, could help someone who must wait in a car to be rescued.

Earthquakes. Some natural disasters are not caused by storms. An **earthquake** is a strong shaking or sliding of the ground. An earthquake is caused by underground volcanic action or shifting rock layers. It most often lasts for only a minute or less. In that short time, however, it can crack roads, destroy buildings, and snap power lines.

If you are indoors when an earthquake begins, stay calm. You need to avoid being hit by falling things. If you can, stay with an adult. Quickly find a place where you will be protected from falling objects. Crawl under a piece of sturdy furniture or stand in a doorway between two rooms. Stay away from windows, mirrors, and tall bookcases or cabinets. Do not go outdoors, because the chances that falling objects will hit you are greater there.

If you are outdoors when an earthquake happens, try to move to a yard, a field, or another open area. Stay away from buildings, walls, poles, power lines, or anything else that may fall on you.

earthquake (URTH kwayk), a strong shaking or sliding of the ground.

■ *Earthquakes can damage and destroy buildings.*

An earthquake creates the danger of fire and explosion from broken gas lines. Do not light a match indoors during or immediately after an earthquake. If a gas line has broken, any spark or flame may cause an explosion. Find a way to get out if the building is damaged. Then meet your family at the place you decided on during your disaster drill. Stay away from broken power lines or damaged buildings. Follow instructions from police, fire fighters, or public safety workers. Listen to the radio or television for safety announcements and instructions.

In any disaster or emergency, remember to stay calm. If you have your supplies ready and can act quickly and safely, you will be able to help yourself and others.

REVIEW
SECTION 2

REMEMBER?

1. Name three ways to prepare for emergencies at home.
2. Why should you stay near the floor during a fire?
3. What are five kinds of disasters caused by nature?

THINK!

4. Why should young people think about preparing for disasters?
5. How can being prepared for emergencies help you feel confident?

Thinking About Your Health

Are You Prepared for a Natural Disaster Emergency?

Even though an emergency is unexpected, you can be prepared for acting quickly in a disaster. How do you know if you are prepared? If you answer yes to all the following questions, you are likely to be ready if a natural disaster should happen.

- Do you have emergency telephone numbers near each phone in your home?
- Have you and your family put together an emergency kit of supplies that will help you stay safe, clean, and nourished for a few days if needed?
- Has your family planned at least two escape routes from your home in case of an emergency?
- Have you and your family planned a place to meet if you should have to leave your home in an emergency?
- Do you think you can remain calm in the event of a natural disaster or other emergency?

334

3 Giving First Aid for Some Common Emergencies

An accident or other emergency may leave a person injured or ill. In the few minutes before medical help arrives, you can do certain things to help the person. The immediate care given to someone who is injured or suddenly ill is called **first aid.** First aid that is properly given can keep a person's injury or illness from getting worse. It may even save someone's life.

What Can You Do About Broken Bones?

A broken or cracked bone is called a **fracture.** The flesh around a fracture may hurt, swell, or change color. The broken part may also be bent at a strange angle. Often a person cannot tell the difference between a bad sprain and a fracture. Always treat the injury as a fracture just to be safe. If you suspect a fracture, call 911 or your local emergency number.

A broken bone may tear through the skin and cause bleeding. If there is bleeding, try to stop it at once by pressing a clean cloth on top of the wound. Do not try to push the broken bone back under the skin. You might tear more tissue if you push the bone.

Do not allow the person to move the broken bone or try to straighten out the fracture. If necessary, use a soft support, such as a pillow or rolled-up towel to hold the injured part still. Apply ice wrapped in a cloth to help ease the pain and swelling. Try to keep the injured person calm and quiet until medical help arrives. Put a coat or blanket around the person to keep him or her warm.

If the victim must be moved, use a splint to hold the broken bone still. A **splint** is something straight, such as rolled-up newspaper, used to keep a broken bone and joints at both ends from moving. Tie the splint against the fractured area with four wide strips of cloth. Tie one strip at each end of the splint. Then tie a strip on each side of the break. Do not tie the bands too tightly. You might stop the flow of blood and cause more tissue damage.

first aid, immediate care given to someone who is injured or suddenly ill.

fracture (FRAK chuhr), a broken or cracked bone.

splint (SPLIHNT), something straight and stiff used to hold a broken bone still.

■ *If it is necessary to move the victim, a forearm splint can be used to hold a broken bone still.*

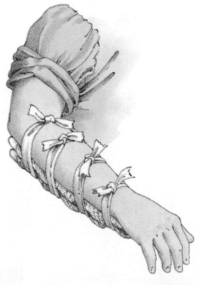

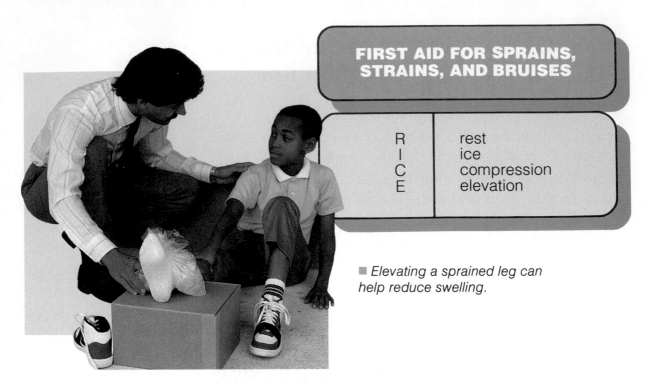

R I C E	rest ice compression elevation

■ *Elevating a sprained leg can help reduce swelling.*

What Can You Do About Burns?

An accident involving heat or fire may cause a burn. A slight, or *superficial,* burn turns the skin red. A worse kind of burn, or *partial-thickness* burn, causes the skin to swell in blisters. The very worst kind of burn, or a *full-thickness* burn, makes the flesh look charred or white.

■ *Minor burns need to be treated with cold water to stop the burning and to reduce pain.*

336

Burn care requires three kinds of action. First, stop the burning of skin. Second, cool the burned area with cool water. Third, keep the skin from getting infected. These actions help the skin heal quickly.

Do not put any kind of grease or ointment on a burn. Grease traps the burn's heat in the skin and makes the burn worse. Treat a minor or blistered burn with cold water first. The cold water stops the burning and reduces the pain. Gently pat the area dry to avoid rubbing painful skin or breaking blisters. Blisters help keep microbes on the skin from infecting injured tissue. Cover the burn with a dry, clean cloth.

If someone has a burn that looks charred or white, call for medical help immediately. Do not touch the burned area. Never try to pull pieces of clothing away from the burn. Cool and cover the burned area. Keep the burned person quiet while you wait for help.

When you give first aid for a burn on an arm or leg, try to keep the burned part raised above the level of the heart to slow down the flow of blood. This keeps down swelling and pain.

What Can You Do About Frostbite and Cold Exposure?

A person who is outdoors during very cold weather may get frostbite. **Frostbite** is a condition in which certain tissues of the body freeze. Frostbite most often affects the ears, nose, cheeks, fingers, and toes. An early sign of frostbite is a stinging or tingling feeling. The flesh may look red at first. This is a sign of cold. Then it becomes gray or white and feels stiff and numb. It feels cold to the touch.

If you think that you or someone else has frostbite, gently cover the frozen part with clothing. Then go indoors and begin to warm the frozen part at once. Never use direct heat to treat frostbite. The victim should not stand near a hot stove or fire. The frozen part should not be dipped in hot water, but you may place it in lukewarm water until it is red and feels warm. Do not rub the frozen area, and do not let anything brush or scrape it. Frostbitten flesh is stiff and can easily be damaged.

frostbite (FRAWST byt), a condition in which certain tissues of the body freeze.

■ *Frostbite needs to be treated by gently warming the frozen area.*

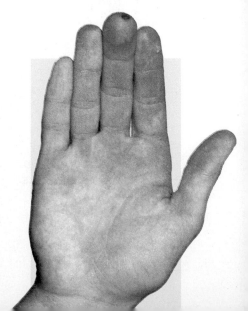

hypothermia (hy poh THUR mee uh), a condition in which the body temperature becomes too low.

Hypothermia, or cold exposure, can happen when the body's temperature becomes too low. Early signs of hypothermia are confusion, shivering, sleepiness, and numbness. If the body's temperature keeps dropping, the person's breathing and heartbeat rate will keep getting slower until they stop. Without emergency treatment, the person will die. First aid for a person with hypothermia involves keeping the person warm and dry, and taking him or her to the hospital immediately or calling 911 for help.

What Can You Do About Heat Exposure?

The body has a complex system that helps it adapt to many different temperatures. However, this system can fail during long exposure to very high or very low temperatures. Health problems can then happen.

Hyperthermia, or heatstroke, can happen when the body's temperature becomes too high and the person is unable to sweat. A person with heatstroke has a rapid but strong pulse, has hot, dry skin, and may have a stomachache.

hyperthermia (hy puhr THUR mee uh), a condition in which the body temperature becomes too high and the body is unable to sweat.

■ *A person suffering from heat exhaustion should be moved to a cool place, made to lie down, and given drinks of cool water.*

He or she may also have a headache and may have trouble seeing. Heatstroke is a life-threatening emergency. A person with heatstroke should receive first aid immediately. Someone should also call an ambulance because the person will need to be taken to a hospital. The part of the nervous system that controls body temperature cannot function without medical care. The person's body must be cooled as quickly as possible with cloths soaked in cold water. The person should be given 4 ounces of cool water every 15 minutes unless the person vomits or becomes unconscious.

People with mild hyperthermia, or heat exhaustion, have cold, sweaty skin and a rapid, weak pulse. They may feel faint. Heat exhaustion is often caused by too much sweating. First aid for such people means taking them to a cool place, having them lie down, putting cool, wet cloths on them, and giving them drinks of cool water.

Heat exhaustion can be prevented by drinking plenty of water or juice before and during activity in hot weather. People can also avoid staying in very hot places and dress in light clothes to limit sweating.

How Can You Help During a Seizure?

A person with epilepsy, a head injury, or a high fever may possibly have a seizure. A **seizure** is a sudden uncontrollable attack caused by some unusual nerve cell activity in the brain. The exact cause of epilepsy seizures is often unknown.

If you think someone is having a seizure, lower the person to the floor. Clear away any nearby objects to keep the person from being injured. Do not put anything into the person's mouth. Do not try to stop the person from shaking or moving. When the seizure action ends, turn the person onto his or her side. This prevents choking on saliva. When the person awakens, be reassuring and let the person rest awhile. Call for medical help if the person becomes unconscious.

People who have diabetes may become ill when they have too little sugar in their blood. This is called an *insulin reaction.*

REAL-LIFE
SKILL

Moving an Unconscious Person

If an unconscious person must be moved, you should carefully roll the person onto a blanket. Then pull the blanket to move the person out of danger.

seizure (SEE zhuhr), a sudden uncontrollable attack caused by unusual nerve activity in the brain.

339

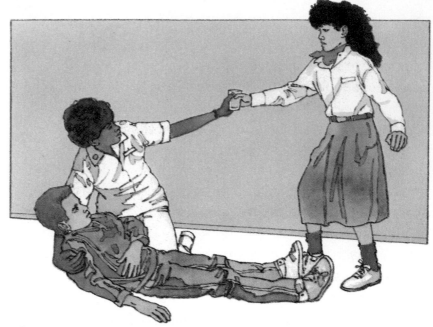

■ *If a person with diabetes has an insulin reaction and is conscious, give the person a sweet drink, such as orange juice. If the person is unconscious, get medical help immediately.*

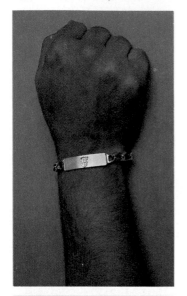

■ *Medical bracelets alert health workers about special medical conditions.*

Symptoms may be headaches, dizziness, hunger, and shakiness. They need to get necessary sugar quickly to avoid a seizure.

 **REVIEW
SECTION 3**

REMEMBER?

1. What can you do to help someone who breaks a bone?
2. How can you treat a burn that is not charred or white?
3. What is the difference between hypothermia and hyperthermia?
4. What can you do to help a person having a seizure?

THINK!

5. Why should a person not move someone who might have a fracture?
6. Why is it best to do so little when someone has a seizure?

4 Giving First Aid to Save a Life

There are several emergencies that can threaten a person's life. These are situations in which a person cannot breathe or has been seriously injured. These situations require immediate first aid.

Each life-threatening emergency requires its own kind of first aid. The first aid should be given only by a person who has had training. The American Red Cross gives classes in first aid. Other groups, such as the Scouts, the YMCA, and the YWCA, may also have classes.

■ *Many community organizations offer classes in first aid.*

Even without training, you can help in emergencies. If you find a person injured or unconscious, call 911 or your local emergency number or send someone for medical help. Try to keep the injured person comfortable and calm until trained help arrives.

What Can You Do About Choking?

A person begins to choke when something blocks the flow of air into the lungs. Food may go down a person's trachea instead of the esophagus, for example. Or a young child may swallow an object that gets caught in the throat. When something partly blocks the throat, the choking person starts coughing. Do not interfere if the person can still speak, cough, or breathe. Do not hit the person on the back. This could make the choking worse. He or she can probably cough up the object without help.

If the person keeps choking and cannot speak, cough, or breathe, you must help at once. Begin the steps for first aid listed below. The first aid for choking is called **abdominal thrusts.** This involves the sudden, upward thrust of a fist against the diaphragm. The thrust forces out air trapped in the lungs, pushing out the trapped object.

abdominal thrusts (ab DAHM uhn uhl • THRUHSTS), first aid for choking.

HOW TO HELP SOMEONE WHO IS CHOKING

1. Check to see if the person cannot speak, cough, or breathe. If the person cannot do any of these, go to step 2.

2. After the person is standing, stand behind the person, slide your arms under the person's arms, and put your arms around his or her waist.

3. Close one hand into a fist, and hold it with the other hand. Place your hands so the thumbs are next to the person's body just above his or her navel.

4. With an upward and inward motion, press your fist quickly and forcefully into the person's abdomen. Keep doing this movement until the object is forced out of the throat.

Source: American Red Cross

If the person keeps choking, repeat the steps as shown. Do not give up until the person stops choking or until medical help arrives.

Choking is preventable. The most common object on which people choke is food. Cutting food into small pieces, chewing well, and not running or trying to talk while eating can all help prevent choking.

■ *Abdominal thrusts force air out of the lungs, pushing out any stuck objects.*

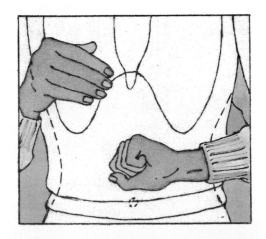

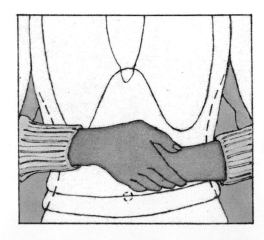

What Can You Do About Stopped Breathing?

Many situations may cause slowed or stopped breathing. A person's breathing may slow down or stop because he or she has had a heart attack, inhaled smoke in a fire, swallowed certain poisons, or nearly drowned. If you see someone who appears to be unconscious, shake the

RESCUE BREATHING

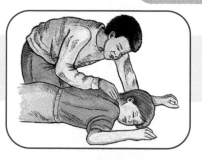

1. Tap the person and shout to see whether he or she responds.

2. If the person does not react in any way, look, listen, and feel for breathing for about 5 seconds.

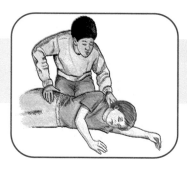

3. If the person is not breathing or you can't tell, roll the person onto his or her back, supporting the head and neck while you do so.

4. Tilt the person's head back and lift the chin. Recheck breathing.

5. If the person is not breathing, keep the head tilted back and the chin lifted. Pinch the nose shut, using the thumb and index finger of your hand that is on the person's forehead.

person's shoulder and shout, "Are you OK?" If the person tries to move, speak, or react in any way, his or her breathing has not stopped. If the person is not breathing, you should first make sure the air passage is open. It may be necessary then to begin rescue breathing at once.

Rescue breathing is a way of getting air into the lungs of someone who has stopped breathing. See the following steps for rescue breathing from the American Red Cross.

rescue breathing (REHS kyoo • BREETH ihng), first aid for stopped breathing.

6. Blow air into the victim's mouth. Give two slow breaths. Blow in until the chest gently rises.

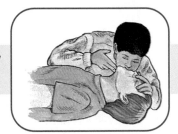

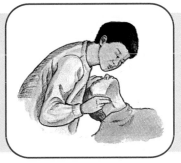

7. Check for a pulse. Put your fingers on the top of the person's neck just below the chin. Then slide your fingers into the grooves on the side of the neck. If the heart is beating, you will feel the pulse of the blood in one of the large blood vessels in the side of the neck. (If the victim does not have a pulse, you will need to give CPR.) Feel for the pulse for 5 to 10 seconds.

8. If the person has a pulse, give one slow breath about every 5 seconds. Do this for about 1 minute (12 breaths).

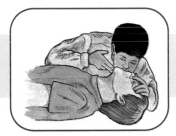

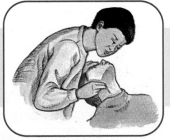

9. Recheck pulse and breathing about every minute. Continue breathing until the person starts to breathe on his or her own or until someone who has medical training arrives.

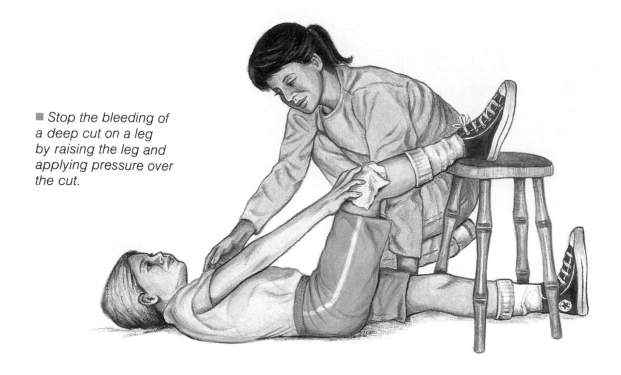

■ *Stop the bleeding of a deep cut on a leg by raising the leg and applying pressure over the cut.*

What Can You Do About Bleeding?

Any cut or wound in the skin may cause some bleeding. If the cut is small, the blood may clot and form a scab over the cut in a short time. The scab seals the cut. But the cut could still become infected. To prevent infection, wash a small cut with soap and warm water. You may then cover it with a sterile bandage to protect it while a scab forms.

If a cut or wound is large or deep, the blood may flow too quickly to clot. First, make the person sit or lie quietly to slow the heartbeat rate. Then, stop the bleeding as quickly as you can. Use the person's hand under yours to press a clean towel or cloth directly on top of the wound. If the blood soaks through, put another cloth over the first one and keep pressing. Do not lift the first cloth. That would keep blood from clotting over the wound. Call for emergency help as soon as possible.

If the bleeding comes from a wounded arm or leg, raise the arm or leg above the level of the heart. Raising the arm or leg makes the blood flow upward. This helps slow the bleeding. Keep applying pressure on the cut or wound until the bleeding stops.

What Can You Do About Poisoning?

An illness that comes on suddenly may be a sign of poisoning. If you think someone has swallowed a poison, quickly try to find out what poison was swallowed. Call 911 or the Poison Control Center for help. The telephone number is listed in the front of the telephone book. Tell the person at the center what poison you think was swallowed. That person can tell you what first aid to give until medical help arrives. Continue to watch the person's breathing. If it slows down or stops, begin rescue breathing immediately.

What Can You Do About Shock?

Shock is a condition in which the circulatory system slows down. Shock may come from any serious injury. It is most common in life-threatening accidents, such as severe burns.

The signs of shock include pale, clammy skin, weakness, and fast, irregular breathing. To help someone in shock, keep the person lying down on his or her back. If the person vomits, place him or her on one side. This position allows saliva to drain from the mouth, keeping the air passage clear. Help keep the person warm by placing blankets or extra clothing over and under the person.

shock (SHAHK), a condition in which the circulatory system slows down.

■ *A person in shock, who has vomited, needs to be kept lying down on one side.*

What Can You Do About Electric Shock?

A person receives an electric shock from contact with a source of electricity. People can receive electric shocks from lightning, damaged appliances, or broken power lines. Often a person cannot pull away from the electrical source once the electricity has begun to flow into the body.

347

To help someone who is being shocked, you must first stop the electricity. Turn off the electric power at the circuit breaker or fuse box. If the electricity is coming from an appliance, unplug the cord. If you touch someone who is receiving an electric shock, you will be shocked also. Do not touch the person until you are sure the flow of electricity has stopped. Then check the person's breathing. Electric shock may cause breathing to weaken or stop. Get medical help right away. Wrap the person with a blanket or clothing to prevent loss of body heat.

■ *Never touch a person who is being shocked by electricity. Stop the source of electricity as soon as possible. Use a stick or newspaper to remove an electrical plug.*

HELPING OTHERS STAY CALM

Touch	Keep a hand on the person so he or she knows you are close.
Talk	Speak slowly in a low and confident voice. Talk about anything that holds the person's attention.
Tell	Tell the person what you are going to do before you do it. This will make the person less afraid.

STOP **REVIEW**
SECTION 4

REMEMBER?

1. Name four life-threatening emergencies.
2. What should you do if you suspect someone's breathing may have stopped?
3. If you are alone with a person who is cut or wounded, what can you do before calling for medical help?

THINK!

4. Suppose you are with a friend. Suddenly she grabs at her throat and starts coughing. What should you do?
5. How could someone who is in shock suffocate?

■ *Keeping an injured person calm is an important first-aid step.*

Making Wellness Choices

Bob and John are hiking. Suddenly John calls for help. Bob finds John lying on the ground, holding his leg. John explains that he has tripped over a root and has landed on a branch. Bob can see blood starting to soak through John's clothes.

 What should Bob do? Explain your wellness choice.

People in Health

An Interview with a Paramedic

Rosy Vaughn understands how important it is to know first aid. She is a paramedic in Phoenix, Arizona.

What is a paramedic?

A paramedic is a person trained to give first aid and emergency care. A paramedic is usually called to help at fires, drownings, and other accidents. Paramedics are also called to help when people become very ill. Once on the scene, a paramedic gives first aid or other emergency care and then takes the person to a hospital.

■ *Paramedics, such as Ms. Vaughn, are trained to give first aid and emergency care.*

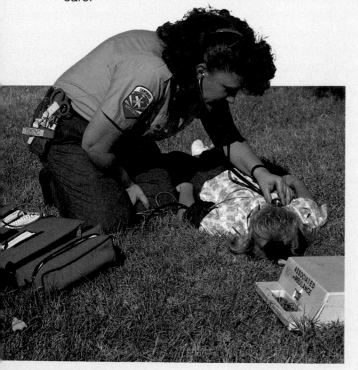

What kind of equipment does a paramedic use?

Paramedics use splints for broken bones and oxygen tanks to help people with breathing problems. Some other equipment includes a heart monitor and a defibrillator. A *defibrillator* is a machine used to shock a stopped heart into beating again. Paramedics also use something called a MAST suit.

What is a MAST suit?

MAST stands for *m*ilitary *a*nti-*s*hock *t*rouser. The suit looks like a pair of pants with hoses connected to it. Paramedics put the suit on someone who is bleeding severely. Air is pumped into the suit. The air pressure in the suit helps the person's blood pressure return to normal after a lot of blood has been lost.

How does a person become a paramedic?

A person who wants to become a paramedic must first complete a training course. After that, he or she starts as an emergency medical technician (EMT). An EMT learns first-aid skills such as rescue breathing, bandaging, and splinting. If a person does well as an EMT, he or she can take additional training to become an EMT-intermediate. After about a year's experience, an EMT-intermediate can advance to become a paramedic. A paramedic is trained to do more first-aid procedures than an EMT or an EMT-intermediate.

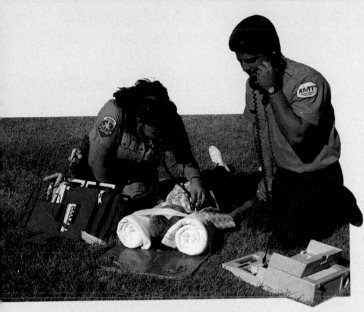
■ *Knowing what to do in an emergency can save lives.*

What has been the most rewarding part of being a paramedic?

One day, someone called me on the telephone to thank me for saving his life. A few weeks before that, I had given him CPR. [CPR stands for *cardiopulmonary resuscitation*. It is a life-saving technique that combines rescue breathing and chest compression.] The man's heart had stopped beating. He had stopped breathing. I used CPR to save his life.

What is the hardest part of your job?

The hardest part is when you never get the *chance* to save someone. The hardest part is seeing someone, particularly a young person, who has been killed in a traffic accident or is dead from a drug overdose.

How can young people help paramedics do their jobs better?

Young people can learn the emergency medical number for their community. They can learn what information is important to tell the operator in an emergency. Most of all, they can learn what to do to help someone until the paramedics arrive at an accident.

What first aid should young people know?

They should know basic first aid. They should know what to do if someone falls, gets burned, or gets cut. They should also take classes to learn how to help someone who is choking or has stopped breathing. Learning the abdominal thrust and rescue breathing from a trained instructor can help a young person save a life someday.

Young people should know what to do in an emergency. They should also know that preventing accidents can keep them safe. Learning and practicing safety rules can let them avoid situations that require paramedics.

> *Learn more about the work of paramedics. Interview a paramedic or an emergency medical technician. Or write for information to the National Association for Emergency Medical Technicians, 9140 Ward Parkway, Kansas City, MO 64114.*

Main Ideas

- Knowing how and why accidents happen in or near your home can help you prevent them.
- You can prevent accidents by getting rid of dangerous conditions.
- In any disaster or emergency, stay calm. If your supplies are prepared and you can act quickly and safely, you can help yourself and others.
- An accident or emergency may leave a person injured or ill. In the few minutes before medical help arrives, you can do certain things to help the person.
- You can learn first aid to help someone who is choking, has stopped breathing, is bleeding, or is poisoned.

Key Words

Write the numbers 1 to 10 in your health notebook or on a separate sheet of paper. After each number, copy the sentence and fill in the missing term. Page numbers in ( ) tell you where to look in the chapter if you need help.

accident (312)
flammable (314)
fire extinguisher (323)
hurricane (327)
electrical storm (330)
earthquake (333)
fracture (335)
frostbite (337)
seizure (339)
shock (347)

1. A condition in which the circulatory system slows down is called ___?___ .

2. An unexpected happening that can cause someone to be hurt is an ___?___ .

3. A broken or cracked bone is also known as a ___?___ .

4. When a part of the body freezes, the person has a case of ___?___ .

5. Material that burns easily is ___?___ .

6. An ___?___ is a strong shaking of the ground caused by underground volcano action or shifting rock layers.

7. A violent storm with high winds and heavy rain is a ___?___ .

8. A sudden uncontrollable attack caused by unusual nerve activity in the brain is a ___?___ .

9. A metal tank filled with water or chemicals for putting out a fire is a ___?___ .

10. An ___?___ is a storm that has strong winds and rain with lightning.

Write the numbers 11 to 22 on your paper. After each number, write a sentence that defines the term. Page numbers in ( ) tell you where to look in the chapter if you need help.

11. electric shock (313)
12. poison (316)
13. emergency (320)
14. disaster (327)
15. tornado (329)
16. blizzard (332)
17. first aid (335)
18. splint (335)
19. hypothermia (338)
20. hyperthermia (338)
21. abdominal thrusts (342)
22. rescue breathing (345)

Remembering What You Learned

Page numbers in ( ) tell you where to look in the chapter if you need help.

1. How can you prevent accidents involving electrical wires? (313–314)

2. In what kinds of containers should you store flammable liquids? (315)

3. What are two ways to prevent young children from having accidents with poisons? (317)

4. Why is it important to remain calm in an emergency? (321)

5. What are four emergency telephone numbers you should keep near a telephone in your home? (321)

6. What is the best way to put out a small fire? (325)

7. Why should you keep away from windows during a hurricane? (328)

8. Why should you stay away from hills or open areas during an electrical storm? (331)

9. What should you do if you are caught outdoors during a blizzard and are unable to make your way to a building? (332)

10. What should you do first to help someone who is receiving an electric shock? (348)

11. Why should you use a pillow to support a fracture? (335)

12. How should you treat a minor burn? (337)

13. What are the signs of frostbite? (337)

14. What should you do for a person who is choking? (342–343)

15. For what four reasons might a person's breathing slow down or stop? (344–345)

16. What injuries can bring on shock? (347)

Thinking About What You Learned

1. Why is it important to know what to do in an emergency?

2. How can you receive an electric shock without touching a wire?

3. How can electricity cause a fire?

4. What would you do if you were on an upper floor in a burning building?

Writing About What You Learned

Write an outline of general safety procedures, and give a copy to each of your family members. Include in the outline a drawing of escape routes to use in a fire, a list of supplies in your household emergency kit, guidelines for natural disasters, and a list of emergency phone numbers.

Applying What You Learned

SOCIAL STUDIES

Research a natural disaster that is well known in history. What emergency plans did people set up after seeing the effects of the disaster?

Modified True or False

Write the numbers 1 to 15 in your health notebook or on a separate sheet of paper. After each number, write *true* or *false* to describe the sentence. If the sentence is false, also write a term that replaces the underlined term and makes the sentence true.

1. <u>Nylon</u> is flammable.

2. Electricity can flow through <u>rubber</u>.

3. If you have a bone sticking out through skin, you have a <u>fracture</u>.

4. In the worst burns, the skin turns <u>red</u>.

5. You could get frostbite and <u>hyperthermia</u> in a blizzard.

6. The first-aid procedure for choking is called <u>abdominal thrusts</u>.

7. Bleach can be a <u>poison</u>.

8. In an emergency, you should use a <u>pillow</u> to support a fracture.

9. A <u>tornado</u> is a tall funnel of wind whirling at high speed.

10. If the <u>respiratory system</u> slows down, a person may go into shock.

11. Wearing thick boots and long pants can protect you from <u>snakebite</u>.

12. Never put <u>water</u> on a grease fire.

13. Fire cannot burn without <u>carbon dioxide</u>.

14. A high fever may cause a <u>seizure</u>.

15. Rolling a person onto his or her side after a seizure prevents choking on <u>saliva</u>.

Short Answer

Write the numbers 16 to 23 on your paper. Write a complete sentence to answer each question.

16. What is the difference between a hurricane and a tornado?

17. What causes a seizure?

18. Why is a radio powered by batteries valuable in a disaster?

19. What should you do if you are trapped in a burning building?

20. What is the most serious kind of burn?

21. What first aid should you give a person who has mild hyperthermia?

22. What kinds of things should you have ready for a disaster?

23. What are three kinds of fire extinguishers?

Essay

Write the numbers 24 and 25 on your paper. Write paragraphs with complete sentences to answer each question.

24. Create a checklist of hazards you can look for in each room of your home. Describe how doing this survey will make you safer.

25. You are in a car accident in the middle of a blizzard. Your head is cut and it is bleeding. Describe what first aid you would give yourself and how you would keep yourself safe until help arrived.

ACTIVITIES FOR HOME OR SCHOOL

Projects to Do

1. Find at least three places in your home where poisons can be stored safely.

2. Alone or with another student, make a list of items to be included in at least one of the following:
   a. a home first-aid kit
   b. emergency supplies for a disaster
   c. an automobile first-aid kit
   d. emergency supplies for a winter trip

   Share your list with your family. Ask permission to assemble such a kit.

■ *Every home should have a basic first-aid kit.*

3. Make a poster to display in your home that shows the first-aid steps for stopped breathing, choking, or broken bones. Draw a picture to illustrate each step. With permission, hang the poster in a place in your home where everyone can see it.

Information to Find

1. Numbers to call in an emergency are listed inside the front cover of local telephone books. You can also find other emergency information in the first few pages of the book. What emergency information does your telephone book show?

2. Emergency medical technicians (EMTs) are an important part of the emergency medical system. Find out what EMTs do and where they work in your community. Explain how an EMT contributes to the safety of people in your community.

3. Find out if classes in basic first aid or CPR training are offered in your community. If classes are offered, which organizations offer them? What is the minimum age to take the classes? Call different agencies or community colleges to get this information.

Books to Read

Here are some books you can look for in your school library or the public library to find more information about safety and first aid.

American Red Cross. *Standard First Aid and Personal Safety.* American Red Cross.

Fleischer, Gary R. *First Aid for Kids.* Barron's Educational Series.

McGee, Eddie. *The Emergency Handbook.* Wanderer Books.

CHAPTER 11

HEALTH AND THE ENVIRONMENT

All the living and nonliving things around you make up your environment. Your environment has everything you need in order to live. The environment contributes to your wellness. A clean environment can help you take care of your needs and stay healthy. A damaged environment, however, may threaten your wellness.

The quality of your environment depends on decisions you and others make about it. Wise decisions and actions can help everyone enjoy a healthful environment now and in the future.

GETTING READY TO LEARN

Key Questions

- Why is it important to know how you and your family could harm your environment?
- How can you learn about healthful choices that will protect your environment?
- How can you take responsibility for protecting your home and community environments?

Main Chapter Sections

1 Using Resources Wisely
2 When People Use Resources Unwisely
3 Environmental Health Services
4 Decisions for Now and the Future

357

1 Using Resources Wisely

People use many parts of their environment every day. Air, food, water, and shelter all come from the environment. People take metal, oil, and other materials from their surroundings to make and run machines. Paper, plastic, and glass are made from things found in the environment, too. Materials that people use from the environment are called **resources.**

KEY WORDS

resources
conserve
car pool
recycling
deposit

resources (REE sawrs uhz), materials that people use from the environment.

■ *The environment provides the necessary resources to build modern cities.*

conserve (kuhn SURV), to save.

Scientists estimate that each person in the United States uses an average of 42,000 pounds (19,000 kilograms) of resources each year. Half of these resources end up as waste materials. Some of these resources could be saved. People must do more to prevent the resources they need from disappearing. They must **conserve,** or save, these resources by using them wisely and carefully.

358

How Can You and Your Family Conserve Water?

Two summers ago, Linda's community did not receive enough rain. Without rain, the town's water supply became too low to meet all the needs of the town and the farms nearby. During that summer, Linda and her family learned many ways to conserve water.

■ Trees are a renewable resource.

■ Water is one of the most important resources.

■ *Every member of a family can help conserve water.*

Linda's family made this list of guidelines for conserving water. They wrote the guidelines on signs and posted the signs near all the water faucets inside their home.

■ Take a shower in 3 minutes or less!
■ Do not let the water run at other times, such as when you wash your hair, or brush your teeth. Turn the water off until you are ready to rinse.
■ Do not use the washing machine or the dishwasher unless it is full.
■ Save leftover water when you wash dishes, take a bath, or cook. Use this water for plants.

Linda's family members also conserved water outside their home. They repaired leaky faucets. They swept the driveway and the sidewalk instead of hosing them down. They made sure the hose had a rubber washer, which helps stop leaks. They also made sure that the hose was screwed tightly to the faucet.

Linda and her family still follow these guidelines, even though their town has enough water again. They conserve water now so the supply will not run low again in the future.

How Can You and Your Family Conserve Energy?

Different kinds of energy are used in homes every day. Some of the environment's resources are used to provide this energy.

Van's family tries to conserve resources by using less energy. In the area where they live, the winter is cold. Van and his father prepare for the cold weather by sealing windows and doors. Sealed windows and doors help keep warm air inside and cold air outside. Then less energy is needed to keep the home warm. People in Van's home wear sweaters instead of turning up the heat when they feel cold. All of these actions help save energy and conserve resources.

■ Energy can be conserved by sealing windows and doors to keep heat from escaping during the winter.

Van's home is heated by the burning of natural gas. The lights and appliances run on electrical energy. The electricity comes from a nearby energy plant that burns oil. By using less heat and electricity, Van's family conserves gas, oil, and other resources that make the energy they need.

How Can You and Your Family Conserve Oil?

Oil from the ground is a resource that is used to make heating fuel. Oil is also used to make gasoline. Diego's family uses gasoline wisely in order to conserve oil. They try not to use the family car very often. Diego rides his bicycle to school and to band practice. His mother takes the bus to work. Diego and his family shop for food only once a week. If they only need one or two items, they do not drive the car to the store. Instead they keep a list of the items they need and buy everything at one time.

car pool, a group of people who ride together regularly in one car.

Diego's father and three other people drive to work in a car pool. A **car pool** is a group of people who ride together regularly in one car. The members of the car pool take turns driving the group to work. A car pool conserves gasoline because the members do not use separate cars.

Oil is used to make more than just gasoline. Plastics, for example, are made from oil. Diego's family saves plastic containers and uses them again when possible. By using plastic goods more than once, they conserve oil.

How Can You and Your Family Help Conserve Other Resources?

Emma knows that the supply of metals is limited. She has decided to conserve one such metal, aluminum, by saving used cans for recycling. **Recycling** involves reusing something or making it into a useful new item. Emma and her friends pick up cans they see in parks and on streets. At home Emma and her family save all empty cans. They also save newspapers and bottles. Every month Emma takes all their cans, papers, and bottles to the recycling center in her community. The recycling center is a place where people in the community can bring these materials to be recycled.

■ Car pools are a good way of conserving gasoline.

recycling (ree SY klihng), reusing something or making it into a useful new item.

■ Recycling aluminum cans conserves not only deposits of aluminum ore but also the energy needed to turn the ore into metal.

■ Recycling centers collect cans, glass, and paper and then send them out to be made into new products.

Recycling conserves resources and energy in several ways. Recycled cans are melted down and made into new cans. This conserves aluminum. Bottles are crushed and melted to make glass for new bottles. Old newspapers are shredded and used to make more paper. Recycling paper goods conserves the trees from which the paper is made.

The supply of trees is not as limited as the supply of some resources, such as oil. People can grow more trees to replace the ones used to make paper and other wood products. People cannot replace the supply of oil. But it takes time to grow trees, so it is still important to conserve them.

Thinking About Your Health

What Are Your Attitudes About Conserving Energy?

Conserving energy is a challenging responsibility. It takes careful planning and work. Your attitude about conserving energy is very important. Think about who is responsible for taking the following actions:

■ conserving water
■ saving energy
■ recycling
■ car pooling

What do you think about sharing the responsibility for conserving energy resources? How are your attitudes important for keeping your community's environment healthful?

Some states have laws that encourage people to conserve certain materials. These laws require stores to charge a **deposit** for soft-drink containers made of glass or aluminum. The deposit is money customers must pay for each can or bottle that is bought. The deposit is returned to customers when they bring empty cans or bottles back to the store. Then the store sends all the empty cans and bottles to be recycled.

deposit (dih PAHZ uht), money paid for a reusable item that can be returned for a refund.

■ *Some states have laws that require a deposit on certain kinds of beverage containers. The deposit is returned when the containers are returned for recycling.*

STOP REVIEW SECTION 1

REMEMBER?

1. Name four resources that people can conserve in their homes.
2. Name five ways to conserve water.
3. What is a recycling center?

THINK!

4. What problems might result if no one tried to conserve resources?
5. How can you conserve resources at school?

2 When People Use Resources Unwisely

polluted (puh LOOT uhd), filled with materials that can harm the health of living things.

pollution (puh LOO shuhn), harmful matter in the environment.

Abusing resources, or using them unwisely, may cause the environment to become **polluted,** or filled with materials that can harm your health. Harmful matter in the environment is called **pollution.** It can change your environment in ways that are harmful to your health and the health of other living things.

■ There are many different sources of pollution. Some are more noticeable than others.

What Is Acid Rain?

acid rain (AS uhd · RAYN), a kind of pollution that is formed when soft coal or oil is burned, causing certain chemicals to mix with water in the air.

You may have heard the remark, "You never get something for nothing." Everything has a price, though the price is not always just money. One price of using some kinds of energy is pollution. For example, when some kinds of fuel are burned for energy, their wastes pollute the environment. One such form of pollution is called **acid rain.**

■ *Acid rain can kill entire forests and damage certain materials, such as stone and metal.*

Acid rain is formed when soft coal or oil is burned. This burning makes certain chemicals rise and mix with the water in the air. When the chemicals and the water mix, acids are formed. These acids then fall to Earth in rain, snow, sleet, or hail.

Acid rain can cause much damage to the environment. When it falls on lakes, rivers, and streams, it can kill fish and plants. When it falls on land, it can harm trees and crops. Over time acid rain can damage the stone in buildings and statues and corrode the metal in bridges.

Acid rain can cause damage in places far from where it formed. Winds can carry the clouds that hold acid rain to other areas. For example, acid rain that is formed in the Great Lakes region of the United States can fall in eastern Canada.

Many people believe that acid rain is too great a price to pay for using soft coal and oil as fuel. But there are not many other practical sources of energy, so fuels that cause the problem are still used. Solutions to the problem have been offered. One solution is to place special devices over chimneys. These devices help to trap some of the chemicals. Another solution to the problem of acid rain might be to find new sources of energy other than soft coal or oil. But such methods are very costly.

What Are Toxic Wastes?

Toxic wastes are one of the most serious forms of pollution. **Toxic wastes** are leftovers from making goods such as plastics, insecticides, and even some medicines. These wastes can injure or kill people, animals, and plants.

toxic wastes (TAHK sihk • WAYSTS), poisonous wastes left over from making goods such as plastics, insecticides, and some medicines.

■ *The improper disposal of toxic wastes can cause water pollution and the death of water plants and fish.*

368

Manufacturers once put these wastes into steel drums and buried the drums in dumps. They thought the wastes could not harm anyone if they were disposed of in this way. Over time, however, the drums rusted in the damp ground. The toxic wastes leaked out and got into the soil, air, and water. There are over 10,000 toxic-waste dumps in the United States. They are now releasing, or may soon release, poisons into the environment.

■ *Toxic wastes can be harmful to people. Cleaning up toxic wastes requires special precautions to protect the workers.*

Before people knew about the risks, many neighborhoods were built near these dumps. When the leaks began, the poisonous chemicals caused cancer, liver disease, reproductive problems in people and animals, and other diseases. Physicians are finding more and more diseases in people who grew up in neighborhoods located near toxic-waste dumps. Scientists fear that the diseases they are now seeing are just the first of perhaps millions of cases.

Government officials have directed manufacturers to clean up toxic-waste dumps. Workers remove the wastes, filter the water, and replace the soil. But the work is slow. Only a few dumps have been cleaned up. Scientists are also working to find ways to make the environment safe from toxic wastes. They are trying to find better ways to store new wastes and to treat the wastes to make them safe.

369

What Diseases Can Air Pollution Cause?

Air pollution results when many kinds of harmful chemicals and tiny bits of matter get into the air. Some factories allow smoke and chemicals to escape into the air. Cars, trucks, buses, and airplanes release smoke and gases from the fuels they use. All of this activity in everyday life pollutes the air.

■ Cars, buses, trucks, and airplanes are all sources of harmful air pollution.

Air pollution is breathed in by people and enters their lungs. The lungs act as a filter and trap harmful particles inside the body. Since many of the substances in polluted air can cause disease, air pollution is a major health hazard.

The lungs are severely affected by air pollution from tobacco smoke, coal smoke, and car exhausts. This pollution causes changes in lung tissue. Over time the chemicals in air pollution can cause a long-term lung disease called *chronic bronchitis*. The chemicals irritate the lining of the lung's bronchial tubes. The lining gives off extra mucus that clogs the tubes. This makes the person short of breath. The person needs to cough a lot to get rid of the mucus.

WHAT MAKES THE AIR DIRTY?

- Coal and oil furnaces
- Refineries
- Motor vehicles
- Smelters
- Wood stoves

HOW THE BODY IS HARMED

- Liver: Lead from the burning of leaded gasoline can cause liver disease.
- Heart: Carbon monoxide from motor vehicle fumes can keep the heart muscle from getting the proper amount of oxygen.
- Eyes: Fumes from wood stoves and refineries can irritate the eyes.
- Respiratory system: Chemicals from furnaces and motor vehicles damage cilia in passageways that lead to the lungs. Breathing becomes very difficult.
- Skin: Chemicals from coal and oil furnaces can cause skin cancer.
- Nervous system: Fumes from leaded gasoline damage nerves in the body.

Emphysema is another lung disease that can be caused by air pollution. The chemicals in the pollution make the alveoli in the lungs swell and rupture. This keeps oxygen from passing into the blood. People with severe emphysema have to gasp for breath. They may have to carry a tank of oxygen with them all the time.

Air pollution affects other body systems, too. Long exposure to air pollution can produce cancer cells. People may get rashes and skin cancer if they live in high-pollution areas. The eyes and the linings of the mouth, nose, and throat can be damaged by polluted air. Air pollution can also cause headaches, lack of concentration, and allergic reactions.

REVIEW
SECTION 2

REMEMBER?

1. How is acid rain formed?
2. Toxic wastes are left over when many products are made. Name two of these products.
3. What are two lung diseases caused by air pollution?

THINK!

4. What might happen if communities do not clean up toxic-waste dumps?
5. How can you and your family help control air pollution in your community?

Health Close-up

Benefits and Limits of Technology

The environment is changing all the time. Many of the changes are caused by technology. Technology is the use of scientific knowledge to meet people's needs and wants. It has led to the development of trains, cars, computers, and many other machines and devices.

Technology has brought changes that have improved people's health. It has led to the invention of refrigerators and freezers. These devices help keep stored foods free of harmful microbes. Modern technology has also produced vaccines and medicines.

Not all of the changes brought by technology have been healthful. Some products of technology have caused pollution. They have added harmful substances to air and water. Some kinds of machinery and other devices create loud noise, another form of pollution. All these forms of pollution harm both the environment and people's health.

While technology has contributed to many kinds of pollution, it also is helping prevent pollution and clean up the environment. Technology is providing new methods to clean up factory smoke and to reduce exhaust from motor vehicles. Water-treatment plants use new ways of removing dirt, chemicals, and microbes from polluted water. New ways to dispose of solid wastes include plants that burn the wastes to produce energy.

Technology brings many benefits. With careful use, people can prevent it

■ In some communities, wastes are converted into energy.

from harming the environment. People need to consider all the ways new discoveries and inventions affect their health and their surroundings. Then people can make careful decisions about using technology in ways that keep them and their environment healthy.

Thinking Beyond

1. How does technology affect the way you learn about pollution?
2. Imagine a world in which all health problems have been solved by technology. What, do you think, would be the benefits and limits of this situation?

373

3 Environmental Health Services

Almost every community, no matter what its size, has a local health department. The department may be run by the city, the county, or a group of counties. The health department is responsible for helping to protect the health of the people in the community. Part of this task is making sure the environment is clean and safe. The health department checks food and water supplies. It also makes sure that wastes are treated so they will not spread disease.

How Does a Community Control Food Safety?

sanitarians (san uh TAIR ee uhnz), health workers who check the safety of food supplies.

All places where food is made, eaten, or sold must meet certain health standards. Inspectors called **sanitarians** visit food businesses to see that health laws are being obeyed. They check restaurants, bakeries, and grocery stores for dirt, insects, and other pests. Sanitarians check the equipment used to prepare food to see if it has been properly cleaned. They make sure food is stored properly and kept cold or frozen if necessary. They may test samples of the food for harmful microbes. Sanitarians also make sure that people

■ A sanitarian checks to see that eggs are processed under clean conditions.

who work with food do not have communicable diseases. Such diseases can be spread to others by way of the food. Sometimes sanitarians find that a food business has broken some health law. Then the health department may make the business close until changes are made to correct the problem.

Sanitarians also visit dairies to make sure that milk receives proper treatment, such as being pasteurized. The dairy cows are checked to see if they are clean and healthy.

■ *Health workers check community water supplies, swimming pools, and lakes to be sure they are safe to use.*

How Does a Community Control Water Quality?

When you drink a glass of water from the tap, you are relying on your health department. Communities often get their water from rivers and lakes, which can become polluted. Health workers test drinking water in different parts of the community. They find out whether it has harmful substances in it. If they find anything, they can warn the community to boil the water or buy water. Health workers also test ice cubes and bottled water sold by private companies. They test the water in lakes, public swimming pools, and other places where people swim. All of this testing helps ensure that the water you use is clean and safe.

■ Open garbage dumps are breeding grounds for flies, rats, and disease microbes.

How Does a Community Dispose of Solid Wastes?

Communities have large amounts of solid wastes. Solid wastes include garbage and trash. They also include bottles, cans, and paper wrappings. Improper disposal of these wastes can cause the microbes in them to spread. Solid wastes also attract insects and other harmful pests. For these reasons, the local health department watches over the disposal of solid wastes. Workers check the places where communities put their wastes. They make sure that the places are safe and the disposal methods will not spread disease. Sometimes solid wastes are burned. In some communities, the wastes are buried in landfills.

In some cases, landfills can cause water pollution. Rainwater can be polluted by the wastes and then seep into the water supply. To stop water pollution, health workers check landfill sites. They make sure that landfills are located a safe distance from water supplies.

■ In sanitary landfills, garbage is covered each day with a layer of soil to help stop the spread of disease.

Your health department works to make your community and environment safe from disease. It helps to guard your health and the health of your family and friends. By finding out about your health department, you can see how taxes and service fees are used to protect the health of people in your community.

STOP REVIEW SECTION 3

REMEMBER?

1. In what three ways does your health department work to protect you and your environment?
2. How can landfills cause water pollution?

THINK!

3. How would the absence of a local health department in your community affect you?
4. What might happen in a community that does not protect its water supply?

Making Wellness Choices

Stacy and her family live near a lake. Until recently they often enjoyed using it. They swam and fished there. Then more houses were built along the lake. Some of the new neighbors polluted the lake by dumping their wastewater into it. Stacy and her family cannot use the lake anymore. The water may make them ill if they swim in it. Some of the fish are dying.

? What might Stacy's family have done to prevent the harm that came to the lake? What might the people who built the new houses have done to protect the lake? What might be done now? Explain your wellness choices.

SECTION 4 Decisions for Now and the Future

People's lives a hundred years ago were very different from people's lives today. In some ways, the environment then was more healthful than it is now. In most communities, people had a lot of room. The air and water were free from chemicals.

■ *In the past, unhealthful living conditions were the cause of many serious illnesses.*

But in other ways, today's environment is better. In the past, pollution from human and animal wastes often entered the water supplies. Many people died from diseases because they drank polluted water. A hundred years ago, people threw trash and garbage from their homes into streets and rivers.

What Decisions Have to Be Made?

People of the future may look back on today as "the bad old days," the time before people learned to keep their environment clean. Or they may think of today as "the good old days." You can help affect their judgment.

378

A water purifier, such as the one on this faucet, can help to clean drinking water.

Some decisions will have to be made about how people use resources to make energy. Today, most of the energy comes from the burning of oil, coal, and natural gas. Some energy comes from flowing water, and some comes from the sun. Still other energy comes from nuclear energy plants. We need to decide what resources to use to provide energy.

Other decisions will concern how people help others meet basic needs. As a community, people need to decide, for example, how to provide shelter for those who are poor or who have no jobs. How to provide health care for all citizens is another important issue.

The energy of the sun can be used to heat water or to produce electricity.

■ *Members of a community can work together to clean up the local environment.*

How Can You Help Make Decisions That Will Affect Your Environment?

Young people make decisions about the environment all the time. They choose to take care of it in these ways: They pick up litter. They take care of plants. They keep solid wastes out of waterways. They might even report polluters to parents, teachers, or other authorities. These actions can affect your environment now and in the future.

If officials in your community are making a decision that will change the environment, you can help them make a good decision by doing the following:

1. Find out when the decision is to be made. Know how changes could influence your environment. As part of a community, you have a say in decisions about your environment.

2. Find out what the choices are. Write or talk to people who will make the decision. Find out all you can about the subject.
3. Think about the consequences of all the possible choices. Learn how different choices would affect the environment. Will a change in the environment result in pollution or wasted resources? Or will it make the environment cleaner and healthier?
4. Tell your opinion to the people who will make the decision. Tell them why you are for or against one of the choices.
5. Stand by your informed opinion, even if it does not match the final decision.
6. After the decision has been made, look back and see what has happened to the environment.

By helping other people make decisions about the environment now, you are working for a clean and healthful environment for the future. By doing this, you are becoming more responsible for your health and well-being.

REVIEW SECTION 4

REMEMBER?

1. What are two ways in which the environment is more healthful today than in the past?
2. What steps can you follow in making an informed decision?

THINK!

3. What kinds of decisions can your family make now that might help your community's environment ten years from now?
4. How might people join together to protect the members of a community or its resources?

People in Health

An Interview with an Environmental Engineer

Bill Pearson understands how important a clean environment is to health. He is an environmental engineer with the Indian Health Service in Rockville, Maryland.

What do environmental engineers do for the environment?

Those who work for the Indian Health Service try to improve the health of American Indians by making the Indians' environment a healthful place to live in. We provide disposal systems for solid waste. We build safe water systems. We also work to control air pollution, toxic wastes, and hazardous radiation in Indian communities.

■ *Mr. Pearson is an officer in the United States Public Health Service.*

What is the Indian Health Service?

The Indian Health Service is the newest of the seven agencies of the United States Public Health Service. Its purpose is to provide public health services, including environmental engineering services, to more than 1 million American Indians. These people live in communities across the United States, from Florida to Alaska. Our services include medical services, such as those available in hospitals or clinics. We also teach people about good health habits to prevent some problems from happening.

What are some problems that environmental engineers try to solve?

Our chief concerns are providing waste disposal and safe water. We work with community leaders, Indian tribal representatives, and other community members. As a result of our programs, almost three-fourths of the Indian communities now have safe water to drink. They also have ways to safely get rid of wastes.

How do environmental engineers help control disease?

Epidemics have been a problem for the American Indians living on some reservations in Arizona and New Mexico. So we formed a disease-control program. We found out that fleas carried by prairie dogs were spreading disease. We try to control disease first by making sure that the people are aware of the cause of the problem. They know now to stay away from the prairie dogs. Sometimes, however, the fleas get out of control. We have to go into an area and spray the prairie-dog holes. We use a chemical that kills fleas but does not injure the prairie dogs or poison the environment.

How much do the people you work with care about the environment?

I think the history of Indian people shows that they have a great deal of love and respect for the environment. They are always ready to make an effort to protect the environment. In many cases, the tribes have refused chances for economic development because they believed those chances would create a threat to the environment or to other people and their rights.

What is the hardest part of being an environmental engineer?

Sometimes I have to convince people that they must be extra careful to protect the environment. This extra care may cost money. But my feeling is that protecting the environment does not cost; it pays. It pays because it preserves the environment. It helps protect the health of people now and for years to come.

■ *Environmental engineers provide sanitary waste disposal and safe drinking water.*

What training does a person need in order to become an environmental engineer?

A young person needs to study science and mathematics. But I think communication skills are just as important. Environmental engineers need to be able to listen, speak, and write effectively to succeed in making people understand how important a clean environment is to good health.

Learn more about environmental engineers. Interview an environmental engineer. Or write for information to the American Academy of Environmental Engineers, 130 Holiday Court, #100, Annapolis, MD 21401.

Main Ideas

- A clean environment can help you meet your needs and keep you healthy.
- Resources are wasted when they are used unwisely.
- The environment's resources are the source of all the energy people use.
- The lungs are most affected by air pollution from tobacco smoke, coal smoke, and car exhausts.
- Local health departments help people keep community environments safe and healthful.
- The environment is always changing and will continue to do so. Future changes in the environment and their healthfulness depend on decisions people make today.

Key Words

Write the numbers 1 to 10 in your health notebook or on a separate sheet of paper. After each number, copy the sentence and fill in the missing term. Page numbers in ( ) tell you where to look in the chapter if you need help.

resources (358)	polluted (366)
conserve (358)	pollution (366)
car pool (362)	acid rain (366)
recycling (363)	toxic wastes (368)
deposit (365)	sanitarians (374)

1. If the air is ___?___, it is filled with materials that could harm your health.

2. Materials that people use from the environment are ___?___.

3. Hazardous wastes called ___?___ are left over when certain kinds of goods are made.

4. When you are reusing something or making it into a useful new item, you are ___?___ it.

5. Harmful matter in the environment is generally called ___?___.

6. A group of people who ride together regularly in one car belong to a ___?___.

7. As a customer, sometimes you pay a ___?___ for bottles of soft drinks.

8. ___?___ is formed when soft coal or oil is burned and the chemicals that are given off mix with water in the air.

9. When you save energy, you are able to ___?___ it.

10. Health workers called ___?___ help keep food safe to eat.

Remembering What You Learned

Page numbers in ( ) tell you where to look in the chapter if you need help.

1. What happens to resources that are used in a community? (358)

2. What can we do to prevent our resources from disappearing completely? (358–365)

3. How does a car pool help reduce air pollution? (362)

4. Give two examples of how conserving energy can conserve resources. (361–362)

5. How do toxic wastes make people ill? (369)

6. How does air pollution affect the lungs? (370–372)

7. What do sanitarians look for when they visit food businesses? (374–375)

8. How do health workers know if water is polluted? (375)

9. What are the dangers that can develop when wastes are not disposed of properly? (376)

10. How is today's environment more healthful than it was a hundred years ago? (378)

11. Name two things you can decide to do to take care of your environment. (380–381)

Thinking About What You Learned

1. What might happen to your health if your environment is not clean?

2. What are some resources that you can try to conserve?

3. How can your family conserve energy at home?

4. Why is recycling an important way to conserve resources?

5. How can a community protect its environment?

Writing About What You Learned

1. Everyone likes to learn in a clean environment. Write a paragraph that describes how you would feel if your school building was not very clean. Write a second paragraph that describes the things you can do to help keep your school building free from litter and other pollution.

2. Write a speech about how conserving resources benefits your community. Include certain examples of what is being done in your community to conserve resources.

Applying What You Learned

SOCIAL STUDIES

Make a bulletin board display that shows ways of keeping the environment a clean and safe place in which to live, work, and play. Use pictures and newspaper or magazine articles that show how important it is to keep your community pollution-free.

LANGUAGE ARTS

Present a speech to your class about toxic wastes and the dangers they can cause in your community. Include what is being done to clean up the pollution from these harmful substances.

Modified True or False

Write the numbers 1 to 15 in your health notebook or on a separate sheet of paper. After each number, write *true* or *false* to describe the sentence. If the sentence is false, also write a term that replaces the underlined term and makes the sentence true.

1. Health workers who check the safety of food supplies are <u>sanitarians</u>.

2. <u>Acid rain</u> must be disposed of after making certain products.

3. Returning aluminum cans is a form of <u>recycling</u>.

4. Carpooling helps <u>conserve</u> fuel.

5. Emphysema is a lung disease that can be caused by <u>toxic wastes</u>.

6. Coal and oil are <u>resources</u>.

7. Garbage is a <u>solid waste</u>.

8. Most energy today comes from the burning of <u>wastes</u>, coal, and gas.

9. If you pay money for a reusable item, part of the money is a <u>deposit</u>.

10. When soft coal or oil is burned, chemicals mix with water in the air to form <u>acid rain</u>.

11. Fish will die in <u>polluted</u> water.

12. People with <u>cancer</u> have excess mucus in their lungs.

13. Air pollution can cause <u>allergic reactions</u>.

14. Sanitarians make sure that people who work with food do not have <u>noncommunicable</u> diseases.

15. Health workers check landfill sites to stop <u>air</u> pollution.

Short Answer

Write the numbers 16 to 23 on your paper. Write a complete sentence to answer each question.

16. Why do you have to pay a deposit when you buy soft drinks in glass bottles?

17. Why must landfills be located a safe distance from water supplies?

18. How do most communities dispose of solid wastes?

19. How are acid rain and toxic waste formed?

20. How does carpooling conserve resources?

21. What are three ways you could conserve water?

22. How does a community control the quality of its water?

23. Name three natural resources.

Essay

Write the numbers 24 and 25 on your paper. Write paragraphs with complete sentences to answer each question.

24. What decisions can you make today to help produce a more healthful environment for the future?

25. How is our environment better today than it was 200 years ago? How is it worse?

ACTIVITIES FOR HOME OR SCHOOL

Projects to Do

1. Look at a map of your community. Draw a circle around each green space that the map shows. A *green space* is a place, such as a park, for grass, trees, or other plants. Which parts of your community may need more green space? List ways people can add green space.

2. Ask an older adult, such as a grandparent, how the environment has changed since he or she was your age. What kinds of pollution were present then? Has pollution affected your wellness?

■ *Many communities protect special features of the environment.*

Information to Find

1. Find out about health problems, such as emphysema, that can be caused or made worse by pollution. Ask your school nurse or someone at the American Lung Association for information.

2. Find out about new developments in using unlimited energy resources, such as the sun or wind. What problems still need to be solved before many people can benefit from these resources?

3. Find out how families with little money can have safe, clean housing. Call your local government office to learn if there is a housing program. Does your community have a shelter for people without homes?

Books to Read

Here are some books you can look for in your school library or the public library to find more information about pollution and the environment.

Lambert, David. *Pollution and Conservation.* Franklin Watts.

Miller, Christina G., and Louise A. Berry. *Acid Rain: A Source Book for Young People.* Messner.

Pringle, Laurence. *Throwing Things Away.* T. Y. Crowell.

Santrey, Laurence. *Conservation and Pollution.* Troll Associates.

Woods, Geraldine, and Harold Woods. *Pollution.* Franklin Watts.

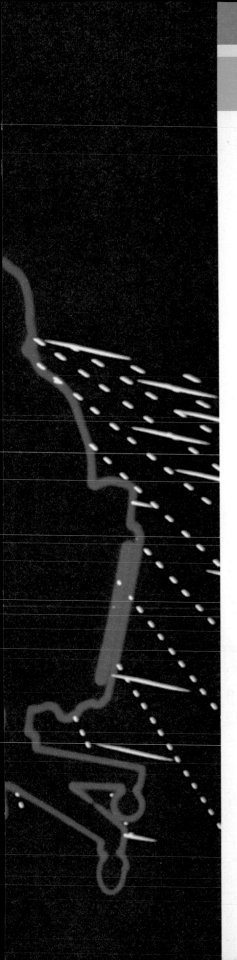

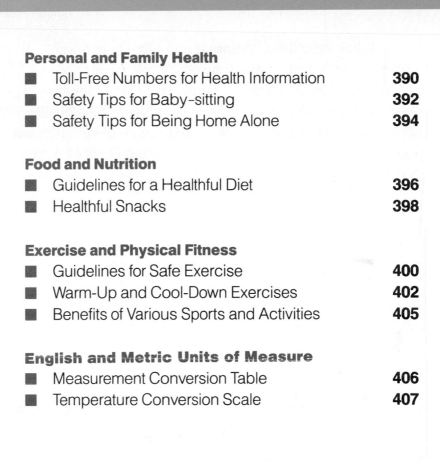

REFERENCE

Personal and Family Health

Food and Nutrition

Exercise and Physical Fitness

English and Metric Units of Measure

Toll-Free Numbers for Health Information

The following toll-free numbers can provide you with immediate information about health problems or concerns. To call any of these numbers, simply dial 1 and then the number that is listed. Your call will be received by a qualified person who may be able to provide you with the information you need or refer you to someone who can. Do not hesitate to call if you have a question or concern.

General Health	(800) 336-4797	**Headache**	(800) 843-2256
In Maryland	(301) 565-4167		
		Hearing	(800) 222-EARS
AIDS and HIV Infection	(800) 342-AIDS		
In Washington, D.C.	(202) 332-2437	**Learning Disabilities (Dyslexia)**	(800) ABCD-123
Information in Spanish	(800) 344-SIDA		
Auto Safety	(800) 424-9393	**Missing Children**	(800) 843-5678
In Washington, D.C.	(202) 366-0123	English and Spanish	
Cancer	(800) 525-3777		
English and Spanish	(800) 4-CANCER	**Pregnancy**	(800) 238-4269
In Alaska	(800) 638-6070		
		Runaway Hotline	(800) 231-6946
Child Abuse	(800) 422-4453		
	(800) 421-0353	**Runaway Switchboard**	(800) 621-4000
Cocaine	(800) COCAINE	**Sexually Transmitted Diseases**	(800) 227-8922
Consumer Product Safety	(800) 638-CPSC		
Diabetes	(800) 223-1138	**Sports and Fitness**	(800) 227-3988
	(800) ADA-DISC		
		Teen Crisis (Suicide)	(800) 621-4000
Drug Abuse	(800) 662-HELP		
		Vision Problems	(800) 232-5463
Eating Disorders	(800) 334-8415	In New York	(212) 620-2147

Telephone Etiquette

The following tips will help you communicate effectively when calling any of the numbers listed or when making any other important telephone calls:

■ Before placing a call, spend a few minutes thinking about what you want to say and what you are interested in finding out. You may want to write down your questions on a notepad for ready reference. It is also a good idea to have a notepad and pencil or pen handy for taking notes during the conversation.

■ Select a telephone in a quiet location where you are sure you will not be disturbed.

■ When the party you are calling answers the telephone, give your name immediately: "Hello, my name is Alicia."

■ State the reason you are calling: "I am calling because I would like more information about...."

■ Ask your question or questions. If necessary, refer to your notepad. After asking a question, be sure to give the person time to answer. Give him or her your undivided attention. If necessary, take notes so you will remember the answer.

■ Upon completing the conversation, thank the person for his or her time and say good-bye in a polite manner.

■ While the information is still fresh in your mind, add to your notes as necessary.

Safety Tips for Baby-sitting

Baby-sitting can be a very rewarding and enjoyable activity. When accepting a job as a baby-sitter, discuss with the parents

- ■ when they expect you to arrive.
- ■ how long they will be away.
- ■ what your responsibilities will be.
- ■ the amount of pay you will receive.
- ■ what arrangements will be made for your transportation to and from the home.

When baby-sitting, your primary concern is for the safety of the children. You are responsible for them, and they depend on you to make safe decisions. The following tips will help you be a successful and safe baby-sitter:

- ■ Arrive for baby-sitting several minutes early so there will be time for the parents to give you important information about the care of their children.
- ■ Write down where the parents can be reached.

- Know where emergency telephone numbers, such as those for the fire and police departments and for the children's physician, are located.
- Ask where first-aid supplies and any special medications the children must take are located. Note: You should not give any medications, even children's aspirin or cough syrup, unless specifically directed to do so by either the parents or a physician.
- Ask what and when the children should eat and how the food should be prepared.
- Ask what activities are allowed and preferred before bedtime.
- Ask when the children should go to bed and what the normal routine is for preparing for bed.

Additional Safety Tips

- Never leave an infant alone on a changing table, sofa, or bed.
- Never leave a child at home alone, even for a short time.
- Check children often while they are playing and while they are sleeping.
- Never leave a young child alone in a bathtub.
- Never leave children alone near or in a swimming pool.
- Never let a child play with a plastic bag.
- Keep breakable and dangerous items out of reach of children.
- Know where all the outside doors are, and keep them locked.
- Unless the parents have personally given you other instructions, do not unlock the doors for anyone except the parents.
- If the phone rings, take a message in a brief and businesslike manner. Do not tell the caller that you are the baby-sitter or that the parents are out. Simply say that the person asked for is busy now and that you will give him or her the message.
- In case of an accident or illness, depend on parents, neighbors, or emergency personnel instead of trying to handle the situation yourself.

- Keep the outside doors and windows of your home locked.

- If someone you do not expect comes to the door, keep the door closed and locked. Ask, "Who is it?" through the closed door. Do not tell the person you are alone. The most you should do is offer to give your parents a message. If the person is selling something, you can simply say, "We're not interested," and nothing more.

- If someone calls on the telephone, be polite but do not offer any information. Do not tell the person that you are alone. Say that your parents are busy but you would be glad to take a message.

- If someone calls who is nasty or mean, hang up immediately. Tell your parents about the call when they get home.

■ If you suddenly see or smell smoke that has an unknown source, leave the house or apartment immediately. If you live in an apartment, do not take the elevator. Go to a neighbor's house, and call the fire department right away.

■ If you have a medical emergency, call 911 or 0 (zero) for the operator. Describe the problem, and give your full name, address, and telephone number. Wait for instructions. Hang up only when told to do so.

■ Avoid being bored when you are home alone. Work on a hobby, read books or magazines, do your homework, or clean your room.

■ Avoid spending your time alone watching television, unless there is a specific program you and your parents agree you should watch. Do not waste time watching just any program that happens to be on.

Guidelines for a Healthful Diet

- Eat a variety of healthful foods from the following food groups:
  - Bread, Cereal, Rice, and Pasta Group
  - Vegetable Group
  - Fruit Group
  - Milk, Yogurt, and Cheese Group
  - Meat, Poultry, Fish, Dry Beans, Eggs, and Nuts Group
- Eat few foods that are high in fat content, such as deep-fried foods, butter and other fat-rich products, and red meat.

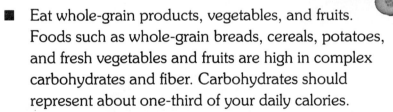

- Eat whole-grain products, vegetables, and fruits. Foods such as whole-grain breads, cereals, potatoes, and fresh vegetables and fruits are high in complex carbohydrates and fiber. Carbohydrates should represent about one-third of your daily calories.
- Achieve and maintain your ideal body weight. You may become overweight by eating more calories than your body uses. You can reduce your weight by eating fewer calories and less fat and by exercising more.
- Limit the amount of sweets that you eat. These foods are high in calories but provide very few nutrients.
- Avoid using additional salt, or sodium, in your diet. Limit your use of the saltshaker, and reduce your intake of foods such as pretzels, salted crackers, dill pickles, and cured or smoked meats.
- Drink plenty of water. Your body needs a ready supply of water to help transport nutrients, eliminate wastes, and regulate body temperature.

Food Needs of Young People 9 to 12 Years of Age

Food Group	Recommended Daily Amounts	Average Serving
Bread, Cereal, Rice, and Pasta	6– 11 servings	1 slice bread 1 ounce dry cereal 1/2 cup cooked cereal, rice or pasta
Vegetable	3– 5 servings	1 cup raw, leafy vegetables 1/2 cup cooked or chopped raw vegetables 3/4 cup vegetable juice
Fruit	2– 4 servings	1 medium-sized apple, banana, or orange 1/2 cup chopped, cooked, or canned fruit 3/4 cup fruit juice
Milk, Yogurt, and Cheese	2– 3 servings	1 cup milk or yogurt 1 1/2 ounce natural cheese 2 ounces processed cheese
Meat, Poultry, Fish, Dry Beans, Eggs, and Nuts	2– 3 servings	2–3 ounces cooked lean meat, poultry, or fish 1/2 cup cooked dry beans, 1 egg, or 2 tablespoons peanut butter count as 1 ounce lean meat

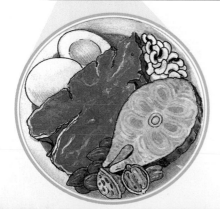

Healthful Snacks

Your health and growth depend greatly on the foods you eat. Therefore, you should try to eat the most nutritious and healthful foods that you can. This applies whether you are eating a formal meal or just having a snack. Unfortunately, many of the foods that are often eaten as snacks are not very healthful. They contain many calories and few or no nutrients. The foods listed here will help you to "snack smart." These foods are easy to find, nutritious, and taste great!

Crunchies
Apples and pears
Broccoli spears
Carrot and celery sticks
Cauliflower chunks
Green-pepper sticks
Radishes
Unsalted rice cakes
Zucchini slices

Hot Stuff
Soups: clear soups, homemade vegetable or tomato soups
Cocoa made with nonfat milk
Tortillas topped with green chilies and a little
   grated mozzarella

Munchies

Almonds and walnuts
Bagels
Bread sticks
Popcorn (prepared without butter, margarine, oil, or salt)
Mixture of 2 cups soy nuts, 2 cups raw peanuts roasted in oven, and 1 cup raisins or other dried fruit
Mozzarella (made from part-skim milk)
Unsalted sunflower seeds
Whole-grain breads

Thirst Quenchers

Nonfat milk or buttermilk
Unsweetened juices
Unsweetened fruit juice concentrate mixed with club soda

Sweet Stuff

Baked apple (plain—without sugar or pastry)
Dried fruit
Fresh fruit
Raisins
Thin slice of angel food cake
Unsweetened canned fruit

Adapted from *Nutritious Nibbles: A Guide to Healthy Snacking* (Retitled: "Healthful Snacks"). Copyright © 1984 by American Heart Association. Reprinted by permission of American Heart Association.

REFERENCE

Guidelines for Safe Exercise

Exercise is a necessary part of a healthful life-style. Exercise can help you tone your muscles and improve your cardiovascular system. Exercise can also help you look and feel your best.

- Start each workout by doing warm-up exercises. First, spend a few minutes stretching your muscles as shown on pages 402 to 404. These exercises will improve your flexibility. Then spend a few minutes gradually working into the main activity of your workout. By taking it slowly, you will gradually increase your heart rate and prepare yourself for vigorous exercise. An adequate warm-up will reduce your chances of injury during the workout and will make the workout less of a strain and more enjoyable.
- Set realistic goals for the workout. Do not try to do too much too fast.
- Stop exercising if pain occurs. Continuing to exercise while in pain may lead to serious injuries.
- Avoid exercising in high-heat situations. If you are not used to the heat, exercise less than your normal amount.
- Drink plenty of fluids, particularly water.

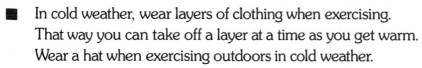

- In cold weather, wear layers of clothing when exercising. That way you can take off a layer at a time as you get warm. Wear a hat when exercising outdoors in cold weather.
- Do not do vigorous exercises immediately before or after a meal. It is best to exercise at least one hour before or two hours after eating.
- Avoid exercising on extremely hard surfaces, such as concrete. Surfaces with more "give," such as grass, dirt, and wooden floors, are easier on the joints of your body. Also avoid exercising on an uneven surface, which may cause you to fall and injure yourself.
- Wear shoes that are comfortable and suited to the type of exercise you are doing. The shoes should provide necessary cushioning and support.

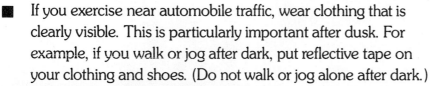

- If you exercise near automobile traffic, wear clothing that is clearly visible. This is particularly important after dusk. For example, if you walk or jog after dark, put reflective tape on your clothing and shoes. (Do not walk or jog alone after dark.)
- At the end of your exercise routine, spend a few minutes doing cool-down exercises. Your cool-down should be the opposite of your warm-up. Gradually decrease the vigor of your workout to slowly decrease your heart rate. Then finish with at least two minutes of flexibility exercises.
- Get plenty of rest and sleep between workouts.

Warm-Up and Cool-Down Exercises

Every workout should begin with warm-up exercises and end with cool-down exercises. Start your warm-up by doing the flexibility exercises shown here. Spend at least two minutes doing these nine exercises. Then spend another few minutes easing into the main activity of your workout. This portion of your workout increases your heart rate gradually. At the end of your warm-up, you will be ready to begin the vigorous portion of your workout. Your muscles will be flexible, and your heart rate will be at a safe level.

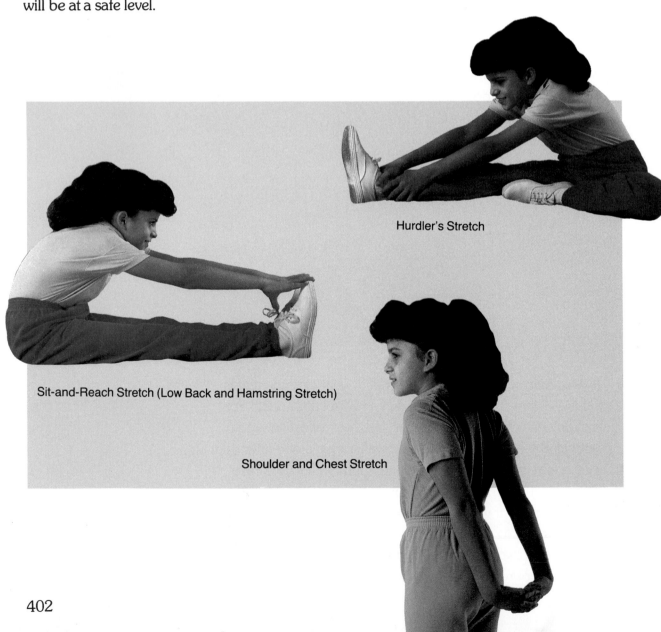

Hurdler's Stretch

Sit-and-Reach Stretch (Low Back and Hamstring Stretch)

Shoulder and Chest Stretch

Upper Back and Shoulder Stretch

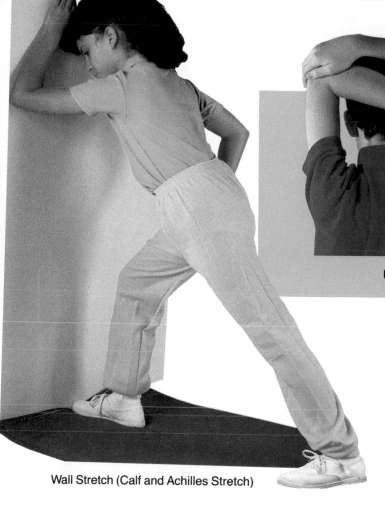

Wall Stretch (Calf and Achilles Stretch)

Toe-Touch Stretch

403

Thigh Stretch

Butterfly Stretch (Inner Thigh Stretch)

Trunk Twister

At the end of your workout, spend at least five minutes doing cool-down exercises. Do this by simply reversing the sequence of your warm-up. Gradually slow the pace of your activity to slowly decrease your heart rate. Then do a few minutes of flexibility exercises as shown here.

Tips for Safe Stretching

- Avoid bouncing.
- Hold each stretch for 15 to 20 seconds.
- Breathe normally.
- Stretch to the point at which you feel a slight pull. Do not stretch so hard that you feel pain.

Benefits of Various Sports and Activities

Activity	Health and Fitness Rating			Calories Used per Hour by a Person Weighing:		
	Endurance	Strength	Flexibility	77 lbs. (35 kg)	99 lbs. (45 kg)	110 lbs. (50 kg)
Aerobic dancing	High	Low	High	405	480	515
Archery	Low	Low	Low	195	230	245
Badminton	Medium	Low	Low	215	255	277
Backpacking	Medium	High	Low	375	435	470
Baseball*	Low	Low	Low	175	205	220
Basketball*	High	Medium	Medium	345	405	435
Bicycling						
(moderate)	High	Medium	Low	150	175	190
(vigorous)	High	High	Low	410	480	515
Billiards	Low	Low	Low	105	120	130
Bowling	Low	Low	Low	165	195	210
Canoeing	Low	Medium	Low	390	460	490
Fencing	Medium	Low	Medium	185	220	235
Football*	High	High	Medium	520	610	660
Golf	Low	Low	Low	235	275	295
Gymnastics*	Medium	High	High	165	195	210
Handball	High	Medium	Medium	485	565	610
Hockey	High	Medium	Medium	385	455	485
Jogging (5.5 mph)	High	High	Low	405	480	515
Judo/Karate	Low	Medium	Medium	490	575	620
Jumping rope	High	Medium	Low	865	1015	1090
Racquetball	High	Medium	Medium	340	410	450
Skating						
(ice and roller)	Medium	Medium	Low	215	255	275
Skateboarding	Low	Low	Low	150	175	190
Skiing						
(downhill)	Low	Medium	Low	370	435	465
(cross-country)	High	High	Low	435	510	550
Soccer	High	Medium	Medium	375	435	470
Swimming	High	Medium	High	185	220	235
Table tennis	Low	Low	Low	185	220	235
Tennis	Medium	Medium	Low	265	310	335
Volleyball	Medium	Low	Low	215	255	275
Walking (briskly)	High	Low	Low	165	205	225
Watching TV	Low	Low	Low	50	55	60
Waterskiing	Low	Medium	Low	255	305	335
Weight training	Low	High	Low	235	280	300
Wrestling*	Medium	High	High	490	575	620

*Preparing for these and a few other sports often includes special training that increases cardiovascular fitness, strength, and flexibility. The ratings in this chart are based only on the activity identified. The ratings do not account for any specialized training.

Measurement Conversion Table

Metric Units	Converting Metric to English	Converting English to Metric
Length		
kilometer (km) = 1,000 meters	1 kilometer = 0.62 mile	1 mile = 1.609 kilometers
meter (m) = 100 centimeters	1 meter = 1.09 yards	1 yard = 0.914 meter
	1 meter = 3.28 feet	1 foot = 0.305 meter
centimeter (cm) = 0.01 meter	1 centimeter = 0.394 inch	1 foot = 30.5 centimeters
millimeter (mm) = 0.001 meter	1 millimeter = 0.039 inch	1 inch = 2.54 centimeters
Mass		
kilogram (kg) = 1,000 grams	1 kilogram = 2.205 pounds	1 pound = 0.454 kilogram
gram (g) = 0.001 kilogram	1 gram = 0.0353 ounce	1 ounce = 28.35 grams
Volume		
kiloliter (kl) = 1,000 liters	1 kiloliter = 264.17 gallons	1 gallon = 3.785 liters
liter (l) = 1,000 milliliters	1 liter = 1.06 quarts	1 quart = 0.946 liter
milliliter (ml) = 0.001 liter	1 milliliter = 0.034 fluidounce	1 pint = 0.47 liter
		1 fluidounce = 29.57 milliliters

Temperature Conversion Scale

The left side of the thermometer is marked off in degrees Fahrenheit (F). To read the corresponding temperature in degrees Celsius (C), look at the right side of the thermometer. For example, 50 degrees Fahrenheit is the same temperature as 10 degrees Celsius. You may also use the formulas below to make conversions.

Conversion of Fahrenheit to Celsius:

degrees Celsius =
5/9 (degrees Fahrenheit − 32)

Conversion of Celsius to Fahrenheit:

degrees Fahrenheit =
9/5 degrees Celsius + 32

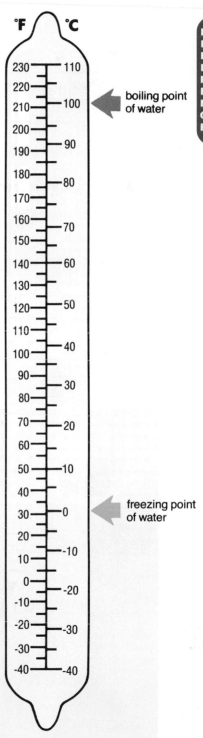

°F   °C

230 — 110
220 —
210 — 100   ◀ boiling point of water
200 —
190 — 90
180 —
      — 80
170 —
160 —
      — 70
150 —
140 — 60
130 —
120 — 50
110 —
100 — 40
90 —
      — 30
80 —
70 — 20
60 —
50 — 10
40 —
30 — 0   ◀ freezing point of water
20 —
10 — −10
0 —
      — −20
−10 —
−20 — −30
−30 —
−40 — −40

Glossary

PRONUNCIATION KEY

Sound	As In	Phonetic Respelling	Sound	As In	Phonetic Respelling
a	bat	(BAT)	oy	foil	(FOYL)
ah	lock	(LAHK)	s	cell	(SEHL)
	argue	(AHR gyoo)		sit	(SIHT)
ai	rare	(RAIR)	sh	sheep	(SHEEP)
aw	law	(LAW)	th	that	(THAT)
awr	horn	(HAWRN)	th	thin	(THIHN)
ay	face	(FAYS)	u	pull	(PUL)
ch	chapel	(CHAP uhl)	uh	medal	(MEHD uhl)
ee	eat	(EET)		talent	(TAL uhnt)
	feet	(FEET)		pencil	(PEHN suhl)
	ski	(SKEE)		onion	(UHN yuhn)
eh	test	(TEHST)		playful	(PLAY fuhl)
eye	idea	(eye DEE uh)		dull	(DUHL)
ih	bit	(BIHT)	uhr	paper	(PAY puhr)
ihng	going	(GOH ihng)	ur	fern	(FURN)
k	card	(KAHRD)	y	ripe	(RYP)
	kite	(KYT)	y	yes	(YEHS)
oh	over	(OH vuhr)	z	bags	(BAGZ)
oo	pool	(POOL)	zh	treasure	(TREHZH uhr)
ow	out	(OWT)			

A

abdominal thrusts (ab DAHM uhn uhl • THRUHSTS), first-aid technique for helping someone who is choking. (**342**)

abstain (ab STAYN), to choose to do without. (**302**)

accident (AK suh duhnt), unexpected event that may cause someone harm. (**312**)

acid rain (AS uhd • RAYN), harmful rain that is formed when certain types of air pollution combine with water vapor in the air. (**366**)

acquired immunodeficiency syndrome (uh KWYRD • ihm yuh noh dih FIHSH uhn see • SIHN drohm), *See* AIDS.

additive (AD uht ihv), preservative, dye, or other substance added to food. (**159**)

adrenal gland (uh DREEN uhl • GLAND), gland that makes many different kinds of hormones. (**79**)

advertising (AD vuhr tyz ihng), process of giving consumers information that encourages them to buy goods or services. (**124**)

aerobic exercise (air OH bihk • EHK suhr syz), intense exercise that lasts for at least 20 minutes and is done regularly; second part of a workout, after a warm-up and before a cool-down. (**187**)

AIDS (AYDZ), acquired immunodeficiency syndrome; incurable disease caused by HIV, a virus that enters the body and kills certain white blood cells; weakens the body's immunity to other diseases. (**225**)

alcoholic (al kuh HAWL ihk), person with a physical and emotional dependence on alcohol. (**292**)

alcoholism (AL kuh haw lihz uhm), condition in which a person is dependent on alcohol; is considered a disease. (**292**)

alveoli (al VEE uh ly), small, hollow air sacs inside the lungs; where oxygen and carbon dioxide are exchanged. (**41**)

antibiotic (ant ih by AHT ihk), medicine that kills or controls the growth of certain kinds of bacteria. (**212**)

antibodies (ANT ih bahd eez), substances in the blood that help white blood cells destroy disease-causing microbes. (**33, 210**)

aptitude (AP tuh tood), natural ability or skill. (**4**)

artery (AHRT uh ree), blood vessel that carries blood away from the heart. (**36**)

astigmatism (uh STIHG muh tihz uhm), condition in which either the cornea or the lens of the eye is curved unevenly; causes vision to be blurred. (**113**)

atrium (AY tree uhm), one of the two upper chambers of the heart. (**35**)

attitude (AT uh tood), how a person thinks and feels about something. (**5**)

B

bacteria (bak TIHR ee uh), very small, single-cell microbes; each microbe of this type is called a bacterium. (**207**)

balanced diet (BAL uhnst • DY uht), food choices that contain a variety of foods from each of the five basic food groups; gives the body the nutrients needed to stay healthy. (**150**)

bile (BYL), fluid made by the liver and used in the small intestine to help digest fats. (**46**)

blackout (BLAK owt), loss of memory for a certain time. (**294**)

blizzard (BLIHZ uhrd), dangerous, violent snowstorm with strong winds, heavy snowfall, and very cold temperatures. (**332**)

blood pressure (BLUHD • PREHSH uhr), force of blood against the walls of the arteries. (**177**)

body system (BAHD ee • SIHS tuhm), group of organs that work together to do a certain job in the body. (**30**)

booster (BOO stuhr), additional vaccine given to extend the effects of an earlier dose of the same vaccine; sometimes needed to maintain immunity to a disease. (**213**)

bronchial tube (BRAHNG kee uhl • TOOB), one of the two tubes through which air passes from the bottom of the trachea into the lungs. (**39**)

bubonic plague (byoo BAHN ihk • PLAYG), communicable disease caused by a microbe carried by rats and fleas. (**216**)

calculus (KAL kyuh luhs), hard, yellow material that can build up on teeth; also called tartar. (**107**)

calorie (KAL uh ree), unit of measure for the energy the body obtains from food. (**154**)

cancer (KAN suhr), noncommunicable disease in which harmful cells grow in an uncontrolled way and take the place of healthy cells. (**231**)

capillary (KAP uh lehr ee), tiny blood vessel that connects an artery to a vein; nutrients and wastes are exchanged through its walls. (**36**)

car pool (KAHR • POOL), group of people who travel together regularly in one car; conserves gasoline. (**362**)

carbohydrate (kahr boh HY drayt), nutrient in foods such as fruits, vegetables, and grains; should be the body's main source of energy. (**146**)

carbon dioxide (KAHR buhn • dy AHK syd), gas that is one of the wastes given off by the cells of the body. (**33**)

carbon monoxide (KAHR buhn • muh NAHK syd), poisonous gas in cigarette smoke. (**278**)

carcinogen (kahr SIHN uh juhn), substance that can cause cancer. (**231**)

cardiorespiratory fitness (KAHRD ee oh RES puh ruh tohr ee • FIHT nuhs), condition of the heart and lungs. (**184**)

cartilage (KAHRT uhl ihj), stiff, smooth tissue between the bones in movable joints; keeps the bones from grinding against each other. (**54**)

cataracts (KAT uh rakts), milky spots on the lens of the eye; may cause blindness. (**139**)

cavity (KAV uht ee), hole in a tooth caused by tooth decay. (**105**)

cell (SEHL), smallest working part of the human body and other living things. (**28**)

cell membrane (SEHL • MEHM brayn), thin outer covering of a cell; holds the cell together. (**28**)

cerebellum (sehr uh BEHL uhm), the part of the brain that makes the body's muscles work together; controls most body movements. (**60**)

cerebrum (suh REE bruhm), largest part of the brain; where most thinking takes place. (**60**)

cholesterol (kuh LEHS tuh rohl), waxy substance that is found naturally in a person's blood; too much can lead to heart and blood vessel problems. (**155**)

chromosomes (KROH muh sohmz), long strands of matter in the nucleus of each body cell; contain the codes for a person's inherited traits. (**84**)

chronic (KRAHN ihk), lasting for a long time. **(228)**

communicable disease (kuh MYOO nih kuh buhl • dihz EEZ), illness that can spread from one person to another; caused by microbes. **(206)**

compete (kuhm PEET), to test one's abilities against those of other people. **(15)**

conjunctivitis (kuhn juhngk tih VYT uhs), infection of the lining of the eyelid and the tissues under the eyelid; also called pinkeye. **(115)**

consequence (KAHN suh kwehns), what happens as a result of a behavior. **(12)**

conserve (kuhn SURV), to save resources by using them wisely and carefully. **(358)**

consumer (kuhn SOO muhr), person who buys or uses goods and services. **(122)**

convenience food (kuhn VEEN yuhns • FOOD), food that is partly or completely prepared when purchased. **(158)**

cool-down (KOOL down), exercise in which body movements are gradually reduced in order to slow heartbeat and breathing rates to normal; should last at least five minutes at the end of a workout. **(189)**

cooperate (koh AHP uh rayt), to work together for a common purpose. **(17)**

corrective lenses (kuh REHK tihv • LEHNZ uhz), eyeglasses or contact lenses for reducing vision problems. **(113)**

cytoplasm (SYT uh plaz uhm), the portion of a cell between the nucleus and cell membrane; made up of many parts that help the cell work. **(29)**

D

decibel (DEHS uh behl), unit of measure for the loudness of sound. **(117)**

deposit (dih PAHZ uht), additional money that a consumer pays for a product that comes in a reusable container; returned to the consumer when the empty container is brought back to the store. **(365)**

depressant (dih PREHS uhnt), drug that slows down the body's systems. **(257)**

dermis (DUR muhs), layer of skin under the epidermis. **(108)**

diabetes mellitus (dy uh BEET eez • MEHL uht uhs), noncommunicable disease in which a person's body is unable to make enough insulin. **(233)**

disaster (dih ZAS tuhr), emergency situation sometimes caused by forces in nature. **(327)**

disease (dihz EEZ), any condition that damages or weakens a part of the body; breakdown in the way the body works. **(206)**

dominant (DAHM uh nuhnt), describes the stronger member of a pair of genes; codes in the stronger gene keep the codes in the other gene from being carried out. **(87)**

REFERENCE

dosage　(DOH sihj), correct amount of medicine to be taken at one time.　(**246**)

drug abuse　(DRUHG • uh BYOOS), repeated use of any drug for the wrong reasons; can harm the body and cause other problems.　(**250**)

drug dependence　(DRUHG • dih PEHN duhns), harmful condition in which a person has a physical or emotional need to take one or more drugs.　(**250**)

E

earthquake　(URTH kwayk), strong shaking or sliding of the ground caused by underground volcanic action or by the shifting of rock layers.　(**333**)

efficient　(ih FIHSH uhnt), able to do more with less effort, as the body can when it is physically fit.　(**176**)

electric shock　(ih LEHK trihk • SHAHK), painful jolt caused by direct contact with electricity.　(**313**)

electrical storm　(ih LEHK trih kuhl • STAWRM), storm with strong winds, rain, and lightning.　(**330**)

emergency　(ih MUR juhn see), unexpected situation that calls for quick action, as in a serious accident.　(**320**)

endocrine glands　(EHN duh kruhn • GLANDZ), organs of the endocrine system that help control the way the body works and changes.　(**77**)

endocrine system　(EHN duh kruhn • SIHS tuhm), body system made up of glands that direct growth, development, and the way the body works.　(**77**)

endurance　(ihn DUR uhns), ability to be active for a long time without becoming too tired to continue.　(**180**)

epidemic　(ehp uh DEHM ihk), rapid spread of a disease to large numbers of people.　(**216**)

epidermis　(ehp uh DUR muhs), outer layer of skin; the body's outer defense against infection.　(**108**)

ethanol　(EHTH uh nawl), chemical name for the alcohol found in beer, wine, and whiskey.　(**289**)

exercise　(EHK suhr syz), any activity that strengthens or develops the body or parts of the body.　(**174**)

exercise program　(EHK suhr syz • PROH gram), plan for doing exercise for a certain amount of time several days a week.　(**183**)

F

farsightedness　(FAHR SYT uhd nuhs), condition in which the distance between the front of the eye and the retina is less than normal; makes nearby objects appear blurred.　(**113**)

fat　(FAT), nutrient that gives the body energy.　(**144**)

fatigue　(fuh TEEG), tiredness.　(**191**)

fertilized cell (FUR tuhl yzd • SEHL), cell formed by the combination of two reproductive cells, one from a male and one from a female. **(72)**

fiber (FY buhr), part of food from some plants; helps keep the body's digestive system working as it should. **(149)**

fire extinguisher (FYR • ihk STIHNG gwihsh uhr), metal tank containing water or chemicals that is used to put out a fire. **(323)**

first aid (FURST • AYD), immediate care given to someone who is injured or suddenly ill. **(335)**

flammable (FLAM uh buhl), capable of burning. **(314)**

flashback (FLASH bak), repeating effect of some hallucinogens; occurs again and again after the person has stopped taking the drug. **(259)**

flexibility (flehk suh BIHL uht ee), body's ability to bend, turn, and stretch easily. **(180)**

fluoride (FLUR yd), substance often put in toothpaste and drinking water to keep tooth enamel strong and help prevent tooth decay. **(106)**

fracture (FRAK chuhr), broken or cracked bone. **(335)**

frequency (FREE kwuhn see), number of times something occurs. **(187)**

frostbite (FRAWST byt), condition in which certain tissues of the body freeze. **(337)**

fumes (FYOOMZ), gases given off by solvents; may cause illness if breathed in. **(263)**

fungi (FUHN jy), one of the four main types of microbes, which can grow on or inside the body and cause disease; each microbe of this type is called a fungus. **(208)**

G

gallbladder (GAWL blad uhr), digestive organ that stores bile for use in the small intestine. **(46)**

genes (JEENZ), tiny bits of information that influence heredity; found on chromosomes. **(84)**

goal (GOHL), something a person wants to achieve. **(8)**

gonad (GOH nad), organ that makes reproductive cells and hormones. **(80)**

growth hormone (GROHTH • HAWR mohn), hormone that is produced by the pituitary gland and makes the body grow. **(78)**

growth spurt (GROHTH • SPURT), time of rapid growth. **(74)**

H

hallucinogen (huh LOOS uhn uh juhn), drug that changes the way a person senses the world. **(259)**

413

hangover (HANG oh vuhr), illness a person gets after drinking too much alcohol. (**290**)

hemisphere (HEHM uh sfihr), half of a sphere, or ball-shaped object, such as the brain. (**61**)

hemoglobin (HEE muh gloh buhn), substance in red blood cells that picks up and carries oxygen in the body; gives blood its red color. (**33**)

hepatitis (hehp uh TYT uhs), communicable liver disease caused by a virus; spreads from person to person usually on unwashed hands or by sharing food. (**223**)

heredity (huh REHD uht ee), passing of certain characteristics from parents to their children. (**83**)

hormone (HAWR mohn), chemical messenger that helps control a body activity by changing the way the cells work. (**77**)

hurricane (HUR uh kayn), violent storm with high winds and heavy rains. (**327**)

hygiene habits (HY jeen • HAB uhts), ways in which people routinely keep themselves clean and reduce the chance of spreading disease. (**213**)

hyperthermia (hy puhr THUR mee uh), dangerous condition in which the body temperature becomes too high and the person is unable to sweat; can cause death if untreated; also called heatstroke. (**338**)

hypothermia (hy poh THUR mee uh), dangerous condition in which the body temperature becomes too low; can cause death if untreated. (**338**)

I

immune system (ihm YOON • SIHS tuhm), system that fights microbes that have entered the body; includes the circulatory system. (**33**)

immunity (ihm YOO nuht ee), condition in which the body has resistance against the microbes that cause a certain disease. (**210**)

infection (ihn FEHK shuhn), condition in which microbes multiply inside the body. (**209**)

ingredients (ihn GREED ee uhnts), things from which food and other products are made. (**123**)

inhalant (ihn HAY luhnt), chemical that has a druglike effect on a person when it is breathed into the body. (**261**)

inherited trait (ihn HEHR uh tehd • TRAYT), characteristic a person receives from one or both parents. (**83**)

injection (ihn JEHK shuhn), method of giving a vaccine or other medicine by putting it into the body through a needle; also called a shot. (**213**)

insulin (IHN suh luhn), hormone that helps the body use sugar; carries glucose from blood into cells. (**45, 96, 233**)

intensity (ihn TEHN suht ee), amount of force with which something is done. (**187**)

interest (IHN truhst), activity a person enjoys doing. (**3**)

intoxicated (ihn TAHK suh kayt uhd), condition in which a person is strongly affected by alcohol after drinking it. (**290**)

K

kidney (KIHD nee), one of the two bean-shaped organs in the body that remove most of the cell wastes and extra water from the blood. (**48**)

L

leukoplakia (loo koh PLAY kee uh), disease in which leathery, white patches form in the mouth; often caused by tobacco use. (**283**)

lymph (LIHMF), mixture of plasma and tissue fluid that surrounds body cells; carries wastes and other materials. (**38**)

M

malnutrition (mal noo TRIHSH uhn), health problem that results from the body not receiving the nutrients it needs. (**294**)

medicine (MEHD uh suhn), drug that people use to cure or treat certain health problems. (**244**)

medicine abuse (MEHD uh suhn • uh BYOOS), use of a medicine without following the directions and safety guidelines. (**248**)

microbe (MY krohb), tiny living creature; some microbes cause communicable diseases. (**207**)

mineral (MIHN uh ruhl), nutrient that is used by the body to help build body parts and control nerve and muscle activity. (**146**)

mucus (MYOO kuhs), sticky substance on the inside of the body's nasal passages, trachea, and bronchial tubes. (**41**)

N

narcotic (nahr KAHT ihk), strong drug that slows down the heart, the brain, and the rest of the nervous system; also stops the brain from sensing pain. (**258**)

nearsightedness (NIHR syt uhd nuhs), condition in which the distance between the front of the eye and the retina is greater than normal; makes faraway objects appear blurred. (**113**)

neurons (NOO rahnz), nerve cells, which make up the body's nervous system. (**59**)

415

nicotine (NIHK uh teen), stimulant drug present in tobacco products. (**251, 255, 277**)

noncommunicable disease (nahn kuh MYOO nih kuh buhl • dihz EEZ), disease that comes from inside a person's body; not caused by microbes and not passed from one person to another. (**227**)

nucleus (NOO klee uhs), small central core of almost all cells; stores information and directs all activities of the cell. (**28**)

nutrients (NOO tree uhnts), the parts of food that the body needs for energy, growth, and good health. (**30**)

nutritional deficiency (noo TRIHSH uhn uhl • dih FIHSH uhn see), lack of a certain nutrient in the diet. (**152**)

O

organ (AWR guhn), body part made up of groups of tissues working together to do a certain job. (**29**)

OTC medicine (OH TEE SEE • MEHD uh suhn), over-the-counter medicine; medicine that can be bought by adults without a prescription. (**245**)

overdose (OH vuhr dohs), drug dose large enough to cause serious harm to the body. (**251**)

ovum (OH vuhm), female reproductive cell; also called an egg cell. (**73**)

oxygen (AHK sih juhn), gas in the air; needed by the cells of the body. (**30**)

P

pancreas (PANG kree uhs), digestive organ that makes pancreatic juices, which help break down starches, proteins, and fats in food. (**45**)

penicillin (pehn uh SIHL uhn), substance that kills bacteria in the body; world's first antibiotic. (**215**)

peristalsis (pehr uh STAWL suhs), wavelike squeezing action that moves food through the digestive system. (**45**)

physically fit (FIHZ ih klee • FIHT), condition in which the body is able to work at its best. (**174**)

pituitary gland (puh TOO uh tair ee • GLAND), endocrine organ that makes several hormones, one of which affects how much the body grows. (**78**)

plaque (PLAK), sticky substance that builds up on teeth and can dissolve tooth enamel. (**105**)

plasma (PLAZ muh), clear, light-yellow liquid that makes up most of the blood. (**32**)

platelets (PLAYT luhts), tiny cell parts in the blood that help it thicken, or clot, when a person gets a cut or wound. (**34**)

REFERENCE

poison (POYZ uhn), any substance that makes a person sick when it gets inside the body. (**316**)

polluted (puh LOOT uhd), containing materials that could harm people's health. (**366**)

pollution (puh LOO shuhn), harmful matter in the environment. (**366**)

posture (PAHS chuhr), how a person holds his or her body. (**178**)

prescription (prih SKRIHP shuhn), order given by a physician or other qualified doctor for a medicine. (**245**)

preservative (prih ZUR vuht ihv), chemical added to some foods to keep them from spoiling. (**159**)

protein (PROH teen), nutrient that helps body cells grow and repair themselves. (**144**)

protozoa (proht uh ZOH uh), large single-cell microbes that can move from place to place on their own; each of these microbes is called a protozoan. (**208**)

puberty (PYOO buhrt ee), time of life when the gonads start to make their own hormones; from the Latin word for adult. (**80**)

R

recessive (rih SEHS ihv), describes the weaker member of a pair of genes; the codes in this gene are not carried out but are "hidden" by the codes in the dominant gene. (**87**)

recipe (REHS uh pee), directions for making a certain food. (**142**)

recycling (ree SY klihng), reusing something or making it into something useful again. (**363**)

rescue breathing (REHS kyoo • BREETH ihng), first-aid technique for helping someone whose breathing has stopped. (**345**)

resistance (rih ZIHS tuhns), ability of the body to fight microbes that cause disease. (**211**)

resource (REE sawrs), material people use from the environment. (**358**)

S

saliva (suh LY vuh), liquid in the mouth that starts to break down food for digestion. (**43**)

sanitarian (san uh TAIR ee uhn), health worker who checks food businesses to make sure health laws are being obeyed. (**374**)

sanitation (san uh TAY shuhn), process of keeping an area clean and free of disease microbes. (**212**)

scoliosis (skoh lee OH suhs), S-shaped curve of a person's spine. (**69**)

seizure (SEE zhuhr), condition in which parts of the body suddenly move without control; caused by unusual nerve cell activity in the brain. (**339**)

self-concept (sehlf KAHN sehpt), how a person thinks about himself or herself. (**2**)

417

self-esteem (sehlf uh STEEM), person's feeling that he or she likes and respects himself or herself. (**6**)

sewage (SOO ihj), liquid and solid wastes from drains and toilets in homes and other buildings. (**218**)

sexually transmitted disease (SEHKSH uh wuh lee • trans MIHT uhd • dihz EEZ), disease spread by intimate body contact; also called STD. (**225**)

shock (SHAHK), dangerous condition in which the circulatory system slows down; often occurs when a person suffers a serious injury. (**347**)

side effect (SYD • ih FEHKT), unwanted or unneeded reaction that a person may have to a medicine. (**245**)

sidestream smoke (SYD streem • SMOHK), smoke that leaves the lighted end of a cigarette; not inhaled by the smoker. (**284**)

skeleton (SKEHL uht uhn), framework of bones inside the body. (**52**)

specialist (SPEHSH uhl luhst), physician who has extented his or her training for two or more years to study certain problems of the body. (**126**)

sperm cell (SPURM • SEHL), male reproductive cell. (**73**)

splint (SPLIHNT), something straight used to hold a broken bone still. (**335**)

stimulant (STIHM yuh luhnt), drug that speeds up the body's circulatory and nervous systems. (**255**)

stress (STREHS), tension caused by worry or by strong feelings. (**193**)

sty (STY), infection of the oil or sweat glands in the eyelid. (**115**)

symptom (SIHMP tuhm), sign of disease, or feeling caused by a disease. (**222**)

T

tar (TAHR), sticky, brown substance that comes from cigarette smoke; contains most of the cancer-causing chemicals in cigarette smoke. (**277**)

target heart rate (TAHR guht • HAHRT • RAYT), rate at which the heart needs to beat to ensure that the cardiorespiratory system is working hard enough to make itself stronger. (**188**)

thyroid gland (THY royd • GLAND), gland that controls how fast the body cells use nutrients for energy, repair, and growth. (**79**)

tissue (TIHSH oo), group of cells that are alike and work together to do a certain job. (**29**)

tolerance (TAHL uh ruhns), adjustment of the body to certain amounts of a drug. (**251**)

tornado (tawr NAY doh), tall funnel of wind that whirls at very high speed. (**329**)

toxic waste (TAHK sihk • WAYST), poisonous substances left over from making products such as plastics, insecticides, and some medicines. (**368**)

toxin (TAHK suhn), harmful waste that is made by microbes; can cause disease by interfering with the way the body works. (**209**)

trachea (TRAY kee uh), windpipe, or the air passage between the throat and lungs. (**39**)

transmitted (trans MIHT uhd), passed on; spread from person to person. (**224**)

tumor (TOO muhr), lump of cells that forms in the body. (**231**)

U

ulcer (UHL suhr), painful sore in the stomach or other organ of the digestive system. (**294**)

urine (YUR uhn), liquid body waste that has been filtered from the blood by the kidneys. (**48**)

V

vaccine (vak SEEN), substance that protects people from getting a certain disease; makes a person immune to a disease without having to be ill. (**212**)

vein (VAYN), blood vessel that carries blood toward the heart. (**36**)

ventricle (VEHN trih kuhl), one of the two lower chambers of the heart. (**35**)

vigorous (VIHG uh ruhs), carried out with force and strength. (**174**)

virus (VY ruhs), smallest kind of microbe; consists of a tiny piece of living matter that can reproduce in cells. (**207**)

vitamin (VYT uh muhn), nutrient that helps a specific reaction occur in the body. (**146**)

W

warm-up (WAWRM uhp), first part of a workout; prepares the body for harder exercise by gently increasing heartbeat and breathing rates and by stretching muscles. (**187**)

wellness (WEHL nuhs), high level of health. (**6**)

withdrawal (wihth DRAW uhl), stopping the use of a drug that has produced a physical dependence; usually causes painful physical symptoms. (**250**)

workout (WUR kowt), exercise routine. (**187**)

Index

M

REFERENCE

CREDITS

Harcourt Brace & Company Photographs

KEY: (t) top, (b) bottom, (l) left, (r) right, (c) center.

ii–iii(inset), Terry Sinclair; vi(t), Earl Kogler; (b), Earl Kogler; vii(b), Rob Downey; viii(t), Charlie Burton; ix(t), Annette Stahl; (b), Julie Fletcher; x(b), Richard Haynes; xii(t), Charlie Burton; (b), Maria Paraskevas; xiii(c) Philip Gould; (bl), Tom Stromme; (br), Ken Lax; xiv(t), Richard Haynes; (c), Jerry White; xv(l), Jeff Blanton; (r), Jeff Blanton; (bl), Maria Paraskevas; (br), Richard Haynes; xvi–1(background), Maria Paraskevas; 2(l), Earl Kogler; (r), Eric Camden; 3, Earl Kogler; 4(r), Earl Kogler; (b), Eric Camden; 6(l), Earl Kogler; (r), Earl Kogler; 8(t), Earl Kogler; (l), Earl Kogler; (r), Earl Kogler; 9(l), Earl Kogler; (c), Earl Kogler; (r), Earl Kogler; 10, Earl Kogler; 11, Earl Kogler; 12, Richard Haynes; 15(b), Eric Camden; 16, Earl Kogler; (r), Earl Kogler; 17, Richard Haynes; 19, Earl Kogler; 20, Jerry White; 21, Jerry White; 28(l), Earl Kogler; (r), Eric Camden; 43, Earl Kogler; 50(l), Earl Kogler; (r), Earl Kogler; 52, Earl Kogler; 54, Earl Kogler; 56(l), Earl Kogler; (b), Earl Kogler; 64, Jerry White; 65, Jerry White; 70–71(background), Terry Sinclair; (l), Jeff Blanton; 72, Jeff Blanton; 74–75, Eric Camden; 92, Jeff Blanton; 93, Greg Leary; 94(t), Rob Downey; (b), Rob Downey; 96, Ken Biggs; 97, Ken Biggs; 101, Rob Downey; 102–103(background), Terry Sinclair; (bl), Charlie Burton; 104, Jeff Blanton; 105(tl), David Phillips; 106(l), Rob Downey; (b), Jeff Blanton; 108, Jerry White; 109, Rob Downey; 110(l), David Phillips; (r), Rob Downey; 111(l), Greg Leary; (r), David Phillips; 114(t), Rob Downey; (b), Rob Downey; 116(b), Rob Downey; 118, Rob Downey; 121, David Phillips; 122, Charlie Burton; 123(l), Charlie Burton; (r), Maria Paraskevas; 128(l), Charlie Burton; (r), Charlie Burton; 129, Charlie Burton; 134, Ken Lax; 135, Ken Lax; 139, Charlie Burton; 140–141(background), Annette Stahl; (r) Maria Paraskevas; 142, Charlie Burton; 144, Maria Paraskevas; 145, Annette Stahl; 146, Richard Haynes; 147(l), Charlie Burton; (c), Charlie Burton; (r), Charlie Burton; 149, Bob Garas; 151, Charlie Burton; 153(t), Charlie Burton; (l), Charlie Burton; (r), Charlie Burton; 155, Maria Paraskevas; 159(t) Maria Paraskevas; (b), Charlie Burton; 160, Earl Kogler; (inset), Earl Kogler; 162, Charlie Burton; 163(t), Charlie Burton; (b), Charlie Burton; 166, Philip Gould; 167, Philip Gould; 171, Charlie Burton; 172–173(background), Terry Sinclair; 174(l), Charlie Burton; (cl), Charlie Burton; (cr), Charlie Burton; (r), Charlie Burton; 178(bl), Maria Paraskevas; (br), Richard Haynes; 179(l), Charlie Burton; (r), Richard Haynes; 181, Maria Paraskevas; 183(l), Richard Haynes; (c), Richard Haynes; (r), Richard Haynes; 184, Greg Leary; 185(b), Greg Leary; 186(t), Julie Fletcher; (b), Julie Fletcher; 187(l), Beverly Brosius; (c), Beverly Brosius; (r), Beverly Brosius; 188(l), Jerry White; 191, Bob Garas; 193(l), Maria Paraskevas; (b), Beverly Brosius; 196(l), Maria Paraskevas; (r), Maria Paraskevas; (b), Maria Paraskevas; 198, Patricia Fisher; 199, Wayne Fisher; 203, Joy Glenn; 204–205(background), Terry Sinclair; 211(r), Beverly Brosius; 212(r), Maria Paraskevas; 213(l), Richard Haynes; (r), Richard Haynes; 217(r), Julie Fletcher; 219, Beverly Brosius; 223, Julie Fletcher; 224(l), Annette Stahl; (c), Annette Stahl; (r), Annette Stahl; 225(l), Annette Stahl; (r), Annette Stahl; 236, Edwin Lombardo; 237, Edwin Lombardo; 241, Richard Haynes; 244(l), Jerry White; 245(l), Eric Camden; (r), Jerry White; 246(l), Annette Stahl; (r), Annette Stahl; 252(l), Beverly Brosius; (r), Beverly Brosius; 253(t), David Phillips; 255, Maria Paraskevas; 256(l), Greg Leary; 258(l), Maria Paraskevas; 265(l), Annette Stahl; (r), Julie Fletcher; 268, Brent Jones; 269, Brent Jones; 273, Richard Haynes; 284, Jerry White; 285, Jerry White; 286(t), Earl Kogler; (r), Joy Glenn; 288, Richard Haynes; 292, Jerry White; 293, Richard Haynes; 294, Annette Stahl; 298, Richard Haynes; 299, Richard Haynes; 300(l), Julie Fletcher; (r), Jerry White; 301, Joy Glenn; 304, Tom Stromme; 305, Tom Stromme; 309, Beverly Brosius; 310–311(background), Jerry White; 310(bl), Richard Haynes; 311(b), Joy Glenn; 312(l), Earl Kogler; (r), Earl Kogler; (b), Earl Kogler; 313, Beverly Brosius; 314(t), Annette Stahl; (b), Earl Kogler; 315, Julie Fletcher; 316, Richard Haynes; 317(l), Earl Kogler; (r), Annette Stahl; 321, Joy Glenn; 323(l), Jerry White; 324, Richard Haynes; 325(l), Earl Kogler; (r), Earl Kogler; (b), Earl Kogler; 326(l), Earl Kogler; (r), Earl Kogler; 327, Annette Stahl; 329(l), Richard Haynes; 332(l), Eric Camden; 336(t), Eric Camden; (b), Richard Haynes; 338, Richard Haynes; 340, Maria Paraskevas; 350, Dave Davis; 351, Dave Davis; 355, Richard Haynes; 356–357(background), Terry Sinclair; 359(b), Richard Haynes; 360(l), Eric Camden; (r), Eric Camden; 361(l), Julie Fletcher; 363(tl), Earl Kogler; (bl), Joy Glenn; (br), Joy Glenn; 379(l), Greg Leary; 382, Greg Pease; 383, Greg Pease; 387, Annette Stahl; 391–399, Terry Sinclair; 400, Maria Paraskevas; 401–405, Terry Sinclair.

All Other Photographs

ii–iii(background), Ken Lax; vii(t), Jeffrey Reed/The Stock Shop; viii(b), Tony Freeman/PhotoEdit; x(t), Chris Hackett/The Image Bank; (c), Don Riepe/Peter Arnold, Inc.; xi(t), Tim McCabe/Taurus Photos; (b), Peter A. Simon/Phototake; xiii(t), Wallet/Jerrican/Photo Researchers; xiv(b), Art Tilley/After Image; xvi–1(tl), Felicia Martinez/PhotoEdit; (tr), Robert J. Capece/Monkmeyer Press; (bl), Audrey Gottlieb/Monkmeyer Press; (br), Barbara Kirk/The Stock Market; 4(l), Edward Lettau/Photo Researchers; 5, Charles E. Mohr/Photo Researchers; 14, Catherine Ursillo/Photo Researchers; 15(t), J. Williamson/Photo Researchers; 18, Bob Daemmrich/Stock, Boston; 25, Tony Freeman/PhotoEdit; 26–27(background), Martin M. Rotker/Taurus Photo; (t), Thompson/Stammers/SPL/Photo Researchers; (l), Manfred Kage/Peter Arnold, Inc.; (r), Howard Sochurek/The Stock Market; (b), Martin M. Rotker/SPL/Taurus Photos; 32, David York/Medichrome; 33(l), CNRI/SPL/Photo Researchers; (r), CNRI/SPL/Photo Researchers; 34(t), Biology Media/Photo Researchers; (b), Lennart Nilsson/Boehringer Ingelheim International GMBH; 36, Biophoto Associates/Photo Researchers; 39, David Madison/Bruce Coleman, Inc.; 47, A. Glauberman/Photo Researchers; 48, Coco McCoy/Rainbow; 57, Tony Freeman/PhotoEdit; 59, CNRI/SPL/Photo Researchers; 60, R. Laird/FPG; 61(l), Martin M. Rotker/Taurus Photos; (r), Martin M. Rotker/Taurus Photos; 69, Blair Seitz/Photo Researchers; 70–71(t), Tony Freeman/PhotoEdit; (r), Larry Manning/Woodfin Camp & Assoc.; (b), Andree Abecassis/The Stock Market; 76, William Hubbell/Woodfin Camp & Assoc.; 78, Lenore Weber/Taurus Photos; 79, T. Zimmerman/FPG; 83(t), Jeffrey Reed/The Stock Shop; (b), Joan Menschenfreund/Taurus Photos; 84, Biophoto Associates/Photo Researchers; 86(t), Omikron/Photo Researchers; (b), Photo Researchers; (r), Tom Grill/Comstock; 88(l), Linda K. Moore/Rainbow; (r), D. Davidson/Tom Stack & Assoc.; 89, Richard Hutchings/Photo Researchers; 91(l), Michael Nichols/Magnum Photos; (r), Michael Nichols/Magnum Photos; 102–103(tl), Robert Frerck/After Image; (tr), Michal Heron/Monkmeyer Press; (br), Gabe Palmer/After Image; 105(b), Biophoto Associates/Photo Researchers; 107, D. C. Lowe/Medichrome; 113(l), Victoria Beller-Smith/The Stock Market; (r), Dan McCoy/Rainbow; 115(l), SPL/Photo Researchers; (r), Martin M. Rotker/Taurus Photos; 116(l), Ted Horowitz/The Stock Market; 119(l), Bob Daemmrich/Stock, Boston; (r), Coco McCoy/Rainbow; (b), Blair Seitz/Photo Researchers; 125(l), Robert Brenner/PhotoEdit; (r), Chris Jones/The Stock Market; 126(t), Julie Houck/Uniphoto; (l), Weinberg-Clark/The Image Bank; (r), Jay Freis/The Image Bank; 127, Len Lause/Uniphoto; 130(l), Wil & Deni McIntyre/Photo Researchers; (r), National Institute of Health; 131, Weinberg-Clark/The Image Bank; 132(l), American Diabetes Association; (r), American Diabetes Association; 140–141(t), Peter Menzel/Stock, Boston; (l), Dick Luria/After Image; (c), Peter Menzel/Stock, Boston; 143, Katrina Thomas/Photo Researchers; 152, Leonard Lee Rue III/Photo Researchers; 154, Tom Tucker/Monkmeyer Press; 156, Bob Daemmrich/Stock, Boston; 158(l), Dick Hanley/Photo Researchers; (c), David Falconer/After Image; (r), Peter Menzel/After Image; 164, William L. Hamilton/Shostal Assoc.; 172–173(tl), Roger Allyn Lee/Four by Five; (tr), Bruce Curtis/Peter Arnold, Inc.; (bl), Spencer Grant/Stock, Boston; (br), Dave Black/Black Shoots Sports; 176, Tony Freeman/PhotoEdit; 180(l), Lorraine Rorke/After Image; (r), Dan McCoy/Rainbow; 182, Hank Morgan/Rainbow; 185(t), Bruce M. Wellman/Stock, Boston; 188(l), Lorraine Rorke/After Image; (c), Bruce Curtis/Peter Arnold, Inc.; (r), Brian Parker/Tom Stack & Assoc.; 189(t), David R. Stoecklein/The Stock Market; (b), Richard Wood/Taurus Photos; 192, Barbara Kirk/The Stock Market; 194, Tom Stack; 195(l), Dan McCoy/Rainbow; (r), Dan McCoy/Rainbow; 204–205(tl), Ted Horowitz/The Stock Market; (tr), Blair Seitz/Photo Researchers; (bl), Don Fawcett/Photo Researchers; (br), Pam Hasegawa/Taurus Photos; 206, Lewis Portnoy/The Stock Market; 207(t), CNRI/SPL/Photo Researchers; (l), CNRI/SPL/Photo Researchers; (c), CNRI/SPL/Photo Researchers; (r), CNRI/SPL/Photo Researchers; 208(t), Joaquin Carrillo/Photo Researchers; (c), M.I. Walker/Photo Researchers; (r), Philip Harris-Biological Ltd./Photo Researchers; 209, Tom Grill/Comstock; 210(l), Marcel Besis/SPL/Photo Researchers; (r), Andrejs Liepins/SPL/Photo Researchers; 211(l), Brian Parker/Tom Stack & Assoc.; (c), Pam Hasegawa/Taurus Photos; 212(l), Alvis Upitis/The Image Bank; 214(l), Sheila Terry/SPL/Photo Researchers; (r), CNRI/SPL/Photo Researchers; 215(l), Dr. J. Burgess/SPL/Photo Researchers; (c), Dr. J. Burgess/SPL/Photo Researchers; (r), The Granger Collection; 216, The Granger Collection; 217(l), Lenore Weber/Taurus Photos; 218(l), Ed Wheeler/The Stock Market; (r), Larry Lefever/Grant Heilman Photography; 221, Photo courtesy of Parke-Davis, Division of Warner-Lambert Company; 222, Gabe Palmer/The Stock Market;